Robert Schwandl

URBAN RAIL in CANADA

Kalaallit Nunaat
Grønland
(DK)

U. S. A.
Alaska

Yukon

Northwest
Territories

Nunavut

Newfoundland and
Labrador

British
Columbia

Alberta

CANADA

Manitoba

Québec

Edmonton
110

Calgary
122

Vancouver
136

Saskat-
chewan

Ontario

Québec
4

PE

NB   *NS*

Ottawa
38

Montréal
6

Pacific Ocean

Waterloo Region
104

Toronto
50

U. S. A.

Atlantic Ocean

MÉXICO

U-Bahn, Stadtbahn, Straßenbahn & S-Bahn

Berlin 2024

Robert Schwandl

URBAN RAIL in CANADA

U-Bahn · Stadtbahn · Straßenbahn · S-Bahn
Metro · Subway · Light Rail · Tram · Streetcar · Commuter Rail

Calgary, Edmonton, Hamilton, Mississauga, Montreal, Ottawa, Quebec City, Toronto, Vancouver & Waterloo Region

Mein Dank für ihre Hilfe geht an | My sincere thanks are due to:

Bernhard Kußmagk, Brigitte Braucek, Felix Thoma and especially to Matt McLauchlin!

... und natürlich an alle, die Fotos beigetragen haben!
... and, of course, to all those who have contributed some of their photographs!

Robert Schwandl Verlag
Hektorstraße 3
D-10711 Berlin

Tel. 030 - 3759 1284 (0049 - 30 - 3759 1284)
Fax 030 - 3759 1285 (0049 - 30 - 3759 1285)

www.robert-schwandl.de
books@robert-schwandl.de

1. Auflage, 2024

English Text by Robert Schwandl & Mark Davies

Druck: PIEREG Druckcenter Berlin GmbH

ISBN 978-3-936573-73-2

Alle Preisangaben in kanadischen Dollars (CAD) und ohne Gewähr!
All prices shown in Canadian dollars (CAD) and subject to change!

01-01-2024: 1.00 CAD = 0.68 EUR, 0.75 USD, 0.59 GBP

Inhalt | *Contents*

kursiv: Straßenbahn im Bau oder geplant
in italics: tram system under construction or planned

Montréal - REM

Waterloo Region

Ottawa

VORWORT

Nach den drei Bänden, die ich zwischen 2010 und 2014 über den städtischen Schienennahverkehr in den USA gemacht hatte (Reihe „Subways & Light Rail in den USA"), wollte ich unmittelbar einen Band über Kanada anschließen, doch ähnlich wie bei so manchem Bauprojekt verzögerte sich das Ganze um 10 Jahre! Der Hauptgrund dafür war vor allem der Umstand, dass es in Kanada zu viele laufende Projekte gab und gibt, so dass nie der richtige Zeitpunkt zu sein schien, denn so ein Buch soll ja nicht sofort nach Erscheinen seine Aktualität verlieren. Nun habe ich mich doch entschlossen, nicht länger zu warten, denn während sich manche Projekte (wie die Eglinton Crosstown Line in Toronto) aus verschiedenen Gründen immer weiter verzögern, werden neue in Angriff genommen. Was den städtischen Schienennahverkehr in Kanada angeht, bleibt es also auch in den nächsten Jahren spannend. Alle Bauvorhaben, die bis Ende des Jahrzehnts umgesetzt werden sollen, sind so weit wie möglich in diesem Buch enthalten, natürlich mit Vorbehalt, denn auch in Kanada sind Verkehrsprojekte abhängig von politischen Entscheidungen (so ist z.B. das bereits in trockenen Tüchern geglaubte Straßenbahnprojekt in Quebec City bei Redaktionsschluss wieder ungewiss). Vergleicht man die Zahl der aktuellen Projekte jedoch mit denen in anderen westlichen Ländern, stehen die Zeichen der Zeit in Kanada momentan gut für mehr Straßenbahnen, Stadtbahnen, U-Bahnen und sogar S-Bahnen.

Wir starten unsere Reise im Osten des Landes in Quebec City, wo eine Straßenbahn gebaut werden soll, und legen bis Vancouver fast 4000 km zurück. Wir sehen dabei aber nur einen schmalen Streifen im Süden des riesigen Landes (mit rund 10 Mio. km² das zweitgrößte Land der Erde nach Russland, etwa gleich groß wie die Volksrepublik China und 28-mal so groß wie Deutschland!). In diesem schmalen Streifen leben aber rund 80% der knapp 40 Mio. Kanadier. Durch die zahlreichen Farbfotos, die größtenteils während einer längeren Reise im Sommer 2023 entstanden sind, sowie die detaillierten Netzpläne bekommen auch Sie sicher Lust, diese Gegend selbst zu erkunden. Oder Sie waren schon dort, dann wird das Buch bestimmt die eine oder andere Erinnerung wecken und Sie auf den neuesten Stand bringen.

Berlin, im Januar 2024

Robert Schwandl

FOREWORD

After the three volumes that I had written between 2010 and 2014 on urban rail transport in the USA ('Subways & Light Rail in the USA' series), I wanted to continue immediately with a volume on Canada, but similar to many construction projects, this book has seen a delay of 10 years! The main reason for this was the fact that there were and are so many ongoing projects in Canada that it never seemed to be the right moment, because a book like this shouldn't become outdated right after it is published. However, I have now decided not to wait any longer, because while some projects (like the Eglinton Crosstown Line in Toronto) continue to be delayed for various reasons, new ones are being started. So when it comes to urban rail transport in Canada, things will remain exciting in the coming years. All the construction projects that are to be implemented by the end of the decade are included in this book as best as possible, but with caution, as also in Canada transport projects depend on political decisions (e.g. at the time of going to press, the tram project in Quebec City, which was already believed to be in the clear, is again uncertain). However, if you compare the number of current projects with those in other western countries, the signs of the times are currently good for more Canadian tram, light rail, metro and even suburban rail lines.

We start our journey in the east of the country in Quebec City, where a tram system is to be built, and travel almost 4000 km west to Vancouver. However, we only see a narrow strip in the south of the huge country (at almost 10 million km² the second largest country in the world after Russia, about the same size as the People's Republic of China and 40 times the size of the U.K.!), but in which roughly 80% of a total of just 40 million Canadians live. With numerous colour photos taken during a long trip in the summer of 2023, as well as detailed network maps, you may just want to start planning your own visit to this country. If, on the other hand, you have already been there, then hopefully the book will bring back some pleasant memories and give you an updated overview of all the systems.

Berlin, January 2024

Robert Schwandl

Rue de la Couronne/Rue St-Joseph · (Image © Alstom/Ville de Québec)

QUÉBEC, QC

Die *Ville de Québec* (Quebec-Stadt) ist die Hauptstadt der französischsprachigen Provinz Québec mit einer Bevölkerung von 550.000 in der Stadt selbst und etwa 800.000 in der Metropolregion, die als „Capitale-Nationale" bezeichnet wird. Die Stadt liegt 235 km nordöstlich von Montréal, und den Bahnhof Québec Gare du Palais erreicht man mit dem Zug von Montréal aus fünfmal täglich in 3¼ Stunden.

Der Bau einer modernen Straßenbahn sollte im Jahr 2024 beginnen und bis 2029 dauern, doch bis Ende 2023 waren keine akzeptablen Angebote eingegangen. Die Linie würde vom Südwesten (Pôle Le Gendre) nach Nordosten (Pôle D'Estimauville) verlaufen und verschiedene „Pôles d'échanges" (Umsteigeanlagen zwischen Straßenbahn und Bus) sowie die Universität erschließen. Sie bekäme durchgehend einen eigenen Gleiskörper, größtenteils mit Rasengleis. Auf der 19,3 km langen Strecke würde es auch einen 2 km langen Tunnel mit zwei unterirdischen Stationen geben: Colline Parlementaire (Parlamentshügel) im Regierungsviertel von Québec und D'Youville in der Nähe des gleichnamigen Platzes, dem Zugang zum historischen Stadtzentrum. Zwischen 1897 und 1948 verkehrte in Québec bereits eine elektrische Straßenbahn.

Im Jahr 2023 bestellte Québec bei Alstom Transport Canada 34 Fahrzeuge (plus einer Option auf 5 weitere) vom Typ Citadis Spirit. Die 100% niederflurigen vierteiligen Fahrzeuge sollen 46,7 m lang und 2,65 m breit sein. Sie sollen in Saint-Bruno-de-Montarville in der Nähe von Montréal entworfen und in La Pocatière, etwa 110 km nordöstlich von Québec, hergestellt werden.

The Ville de Québec (Quebec City) is the capital of the French-speaking province of Quebec, with a population of 550,000 in the city proper, and some 800,000 in the metropolitan area known as the 'Capitale-Nationale' region. The city is located 235 km northeast of Montreal, and Québec Gare du Palais can be reached by train from Montreal five times a day in 3¼ hours.

The construction of a modern tram line was planned to start in 2024 for a scheduled opening in 2029, but by late 2023 no acceptable offers had been received. The line would run roughly from the southwest (Pôle Le Gendre) to the northeast (Pôle D'Estimauville), serving various 'pôles d'échanges' (hubs) between tram and buses as well as Laval University. It would have its dedicated right-of-way throughout, mostly with grassed track. The 19.3 km route would also feature a 2 km tunnel with two underground stations, Colline Parlementaire (Parliament Hill) in Quebec City's government district and D'Youville near the square of that name, the gateway to the city's historic centre. Between 1897 and 1948, Quebec City had a first-generation electric tram network.

In 2023, Quebec City selected Alstom Transport Canada to supply 34 (plus an option for 5 additional) Citadis Spirit trams. The 100% low-floor 4-section vehicles would be 46.7 m long and 2.65 m wide. Designed in Saint-Bruno-de-Montarville near Montreal, they would be manufactured at La Pocatière, about 110 km northeast of Quebec City.

(Image © Alstom/Ville de Québec)

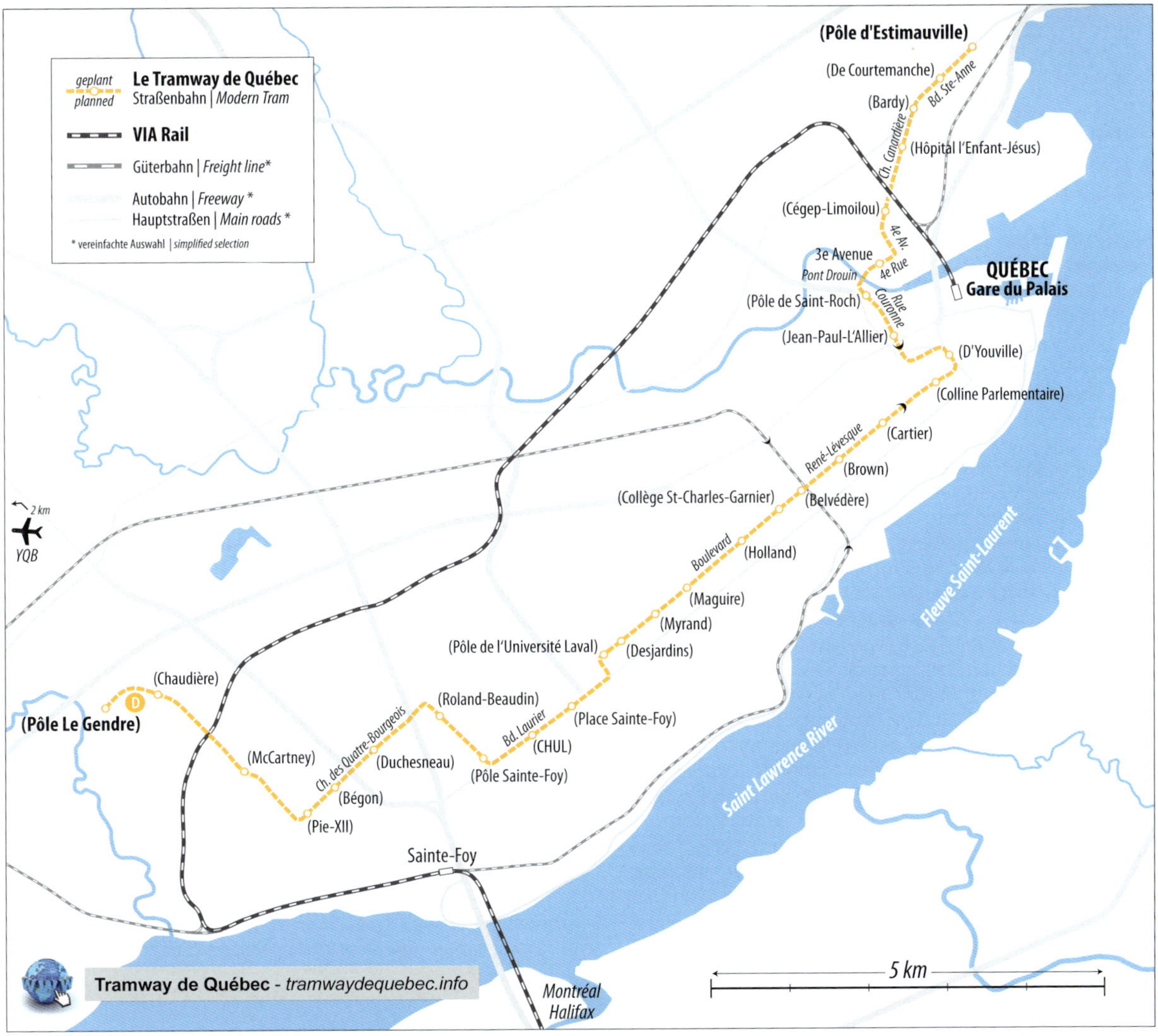

Le Tramway de Québec
Straßenbahn | *Modern Tram*

geplant / planned

VIA Rail

Güterbahn | *Freight line**

Autobahn | *Freeway **
Hauptstraßen | *Main roads **

* vereinfachte Auswahl | *simplified selection*

↑ 2 km
✈ YQB

(Pôle d'Estimauville)

(De Courtemanche)

(Bardy) — Bd. Ste-Anne

Ch. Canadienne

(Hôpital l'Enfant-Jésus)

(Cégep-Limoilou)

4e Av.

3e Avenue
Pont Drouin
4e Rue

Rue Couronne

QUÉBEC
Gare du Palais

(Pôle de Saint-Roch)

(Jean-Paul-L'Allier)

(D'Youville)

(Colline Parlementaire)

René-Lévesque

(Cartier)

(Brown)

(Collège St-Charles-Garnier)

(Belvédère)

Boulevard

(Holland)

(Maguire)

(Myrand)

(Pôle de l'Université Laval)

(Desjardins)

(Chaudière)

(Roland-Beaudin)

Ch. des Quatre-Bourgeois

(Place Sainte-Foy)

(Pôle Le Gendre) Ⓓ

Bd. Laurier

(McCartney)

(Duchesneau)

(CHUL)

(Bégon)

(Pôle Sainte-Foy)

(Pie-XII)

Sainte-Foy

Fleuve Saint-Laurent

Saint Lawrence River

Montréal
Halifax

⊢————— 5 km —————⊣

Tramway de Québec - *tramwaydequebec.info*

5

Blick vom Hausberg Mont Royal nach Süden | *View south from Mount Royal*

MONTRÉAL, QC

Mit rund 1,8 Mio. Einwohnern auf einer Fläche von 365 km² ist Montréal die bevölkerungsreichste Stadt in der Provinz Québec und die zweitgrößte in Kanada. Sie liegt nur 55 km nördlich der Grenze zu den USA. Das Stadtgebiet umfasst den größten Teil der Île de Montréal (Insel von Montréal), zu der auch mehrere kleinere Gemeinden gehören, insbesondere die überwiegend englischsprachigen Orte am westlichen Seeufer, während die Stadt Montréal selbst überwiegend französischsprachig ist; Straßenschilder, Bahnhofsnamen usw. sind nur auf Französisch, englischsprachige Auskünfte sind jedoch meist auch erhältlich. Die Metropolregion umfasst eine Fläche von etwa 4.740 km² (4.260 km² Landfläche beiderseits des Sankt-Lorenz-Stroms) und eine Bevölkerung von fast 4,3 Millionen.

Montréal liegt an Kanadas wichtigster Eisenbahnstrecke, die von Windsor im Westen (auf der gegenüberliegenden Flussseite von Detroit) nach Québec City im Osten führt. Züge der staatlichen Bahngesellschaft *VIA Rail* fahren vom Kopfbahnhof Montréal Gare Centrale ab: 6x pro Tag nach Toronto (ca. 5 Stunden), 5x nach Ottawa (2h15) und 5x nach Québec (3h30). Nicht täglich, aber mehrmals pro Woche verkehren Fernzüge nach Jonquière und Senneterre im Norden der Provinz Québec sowie nach Halifax in Nova Scotia. Der „Adirondack" von Amtrak verbindet Montréal täglich mit New York (613 km) in ca. 11½ Stunden.

Anders als Toronto verfügt die Metropolregion Montréal über einen echten Verkehrsverbund, der alle Verkehrsmittel („Tous modes") unabhängig vom Betreiber umfasst und für den die „Autorité régionale de transport metropolitain"

With some 1.8 million inhabitants in a land area of 365 km², Montreal is the most populous city in the province of Quebec and the second-largest in Canada, located only 55 km north of the U.S. border. The city territory covers most of the Island of Montreal, which also includes several smaller municipalities, notably those predominantly English-speaking towns along the West Island's Lakeshore, while the city of Montreal itself is predominantly French-speaking and road signs, station names etc. are in French only, although English information is also widely available. Montreal's metropolitan area covers an area of approximately 4,740 km² (4,260 km² land area on either side of the Saint-Lawrence River) with a population of nearly 4.3 million.

Montreal lies along Canada's main rail corridor, which extends from Windsor in the west (just across the river from Detroit) to Quebec City in the east, with national rail operator VIA Rail offering frequent trains from Montreal Central Station: six daily to Toronto (~5h), five to Ottawa (2h15m) and five to Quebec City (3h30m). Though not daily, but several times a week, long-distance trains operate to Jonquière and Senneterre in the north of the province of Quebec as well as to Halifax in Nova Scotia. The daily international "Adirondack", operated by Amtrak, links Montreal to New York City (613 km) in approximately 11½ hours.

Unlike Toronto, the Montreal metropolitan area boasts a fully integrated fare system which covers all modes, independent of the operator, and is managed

ARTM - *www.artm.quebec*   STM - *www.stm.info*   REM - *rem.info*   EXO - *exo.quebec*   VIA Rail - *www.viarail.ca*

(ARTM) verantwortlich ist. Die Region ist in einfache Tarifbereiche unterteilt: die Zone A entspricht der Insel von Montréal, die Zone B umfasst die Agglomeration Longueuil am Südufer des Flusses sowie die Stadt Laval im Norden, und die Zone C deckt den Rest des Verbundgebiets ab; für Fahrten außerhalb des Gesamtgebiets wird der Tarif der Zone D angewandt. Der größte Teil des U-Bahn-Netzes liegt in der Zone A, lediglich für die U-Bahn-Stationen in Laval und Longueuil sowie für die REM-Stationen südlich des Flusses ist ein Ticket für die Zone B erforderlich; der zukünftige REM-Ast nach Deux-Montagnes liegt teilweise in der Zone C, in der sich auch viele der Vorortbahnhöfe des exo-Netzes befinden. Die aktuellen Fahrpreise für die Zonen A, AB und ABC sind:
- Einzelfahrt 3,75/4,50/6,75 $
- 24-Stunden-Ticket 11,00/12,75/16,75 $
- 3-Tage-Karte 21,25/27,00/39,00 $
Die meisten Fahrpreise werden mit der „Carte OPUS" bezahlt (6 $ für die Karte), aber für Besucher gibt es auch die „Occasionnelle" zur einmaligen Nutzung.

Der Schienennahverkehr von Montréal bestand lange Zeit lediglich aus einem homogenen U-Bahn-Netz mit vier Linien, betrieben von der *Société de transport de Montréal* (STM), und einer typischen nordamerikanischen Vorortbahn mit wenigen Zügen, die meist nur in der Hauptverkehrsrichtung verkehren. Jahrelang wurden keine größeren Projekte umgesetzt, bis kürzlich REM als neuartige Bahn eröffnet wurde – eine fahrerlose regionale Metro, die durch Umbau einer bestehenden Vorortlinie und den Neubau mehrerer Äste entstand, von denen einer ab etwa 2027 den internationalen Flughafen anbinden soll. Die seit den 1980er Jahren geplante Nordverlängerung der „Ligne bleue" ist nun endlich auch im Bau.

Montréal hatte einst ein ausgedehntes Straßenbahnnetz, das bereits 1861 mit Pferdebahnen in der Rue Notre-Dame begann. Ab 1892 betrieb die *Montreal Street Railway Company* (MSRC) elektrische Straßenbahnen in der Stadt. Dieses Unternehmen schloss sich 1911 mit zwei Überlandbahnen zur *Montreal Tramways Company* (MTC) zusammen. Die Straßenbahn erlebte ihre Blütezeit in den 1920er und frühen 1930er Jahren. Nach dem Zweiten Weltkrieg geriet das private Unternehmen jedoch in Schwierigkeiten und wurde schließlich 1951 von der städtischen *Commission de Transport de Montréal* (CTM), einem Vorgänger der heutigen STM, übernommen. Die CTM folgte jedoch dem Trend in den USA und ersetzte bis 1959 sämtliche Straßenbahnen durch Busse. Im neuen Jahrtausend gab es, inspiriert durch die Wiederbelebung der Straßenbahn in Frankreich, mehrere Vorschläge, in Montréal eine moderne Straßenbahn zu bauen, aber bislang wurde nichts davon verwirklicht. Zwischen 1937 und 1966 verkehrten in Montréal auch Obusse, unter anderem entlang der Rue Beaubien.

by the 'Autorité régionale de transport metropolitain' (ARTM). The region is divided into simple fare zones, with zone A representing the Island of Montreal, zone B the Agglomeration of Longueuil on the South Shore as well as the City of Laval to the north, and zone C the rest of the North and South Shores. Zone D fares may apply to areas outside the combined territory. Most of the Montreal Metro network lies within zone A, but a zone B ticket is required for metro stations in Laval and Longueuil as well as the REM stations on the South Shore; the future REM Deux-Montagnes branch will enter zone C, where many of the EXO commuter rail stations can also be found. Current fares for zones A, AB and ABC are:
- single journey $3.75/4.50/6.75
- 24 hours $11.00/12.75/16.75
- 3 days $21.25/27.00/39.00
Most fares are paid with the OPUS Card ($6 for the card), but for visitors the 'occasional smart card' (L'Occasionnelle) is on offer too.

Unlike Toronto's diversity, Montreal's urban rail system until recently only consisted of a rather homogeneous metro network with four lines, operated by the Société de transport de Montréal (STM), and a typical North American commuter railway with a limited number of trains and mainly operating in the peak direction only. For many years, no major projects had been carried out until the recently inaugurated REM was added as a novel rail line in Greater Montreal – a driverless regional metro created by upgrading an existing commuter line and constructing various branches, one of them planned to serve the city's international airport from around 2027. Planned since the 1980s, a northern extension of the Blue Line is now finally also under construction.

Montreal once had an extensive streetcar network, starting with horse trams in as early as 1861 on Rue Notre-Dame. From 1892, the Montreal Street Railway Company (MSRC) operated electric streetcars in the city. This company together with two suburban tram operators were merged in 1911 to become the Montreal Tramways Company (MTC), and the system enjoyed its heyday in the 1920s and early 1930s. After World War II, the private company struggled and was eventually taken over in 1951 by the municipal Commission de transport de Montréal (CTM), a predecessor of today's STM. The CTM, however, followed the trend in the U.S.A., and by 1959 all the tram routes had been replaced by buses. In the new millennium, inspired by the tramway revival in France, there have been several proposals to bring trams back onto Montreal's streets, but none have come to fruition. Between 1937 and 1966, trolleybuses also operated in Montreal, among other streets along Rue Beaubien.

● Square Victoria-OACI

MONTRÉAL

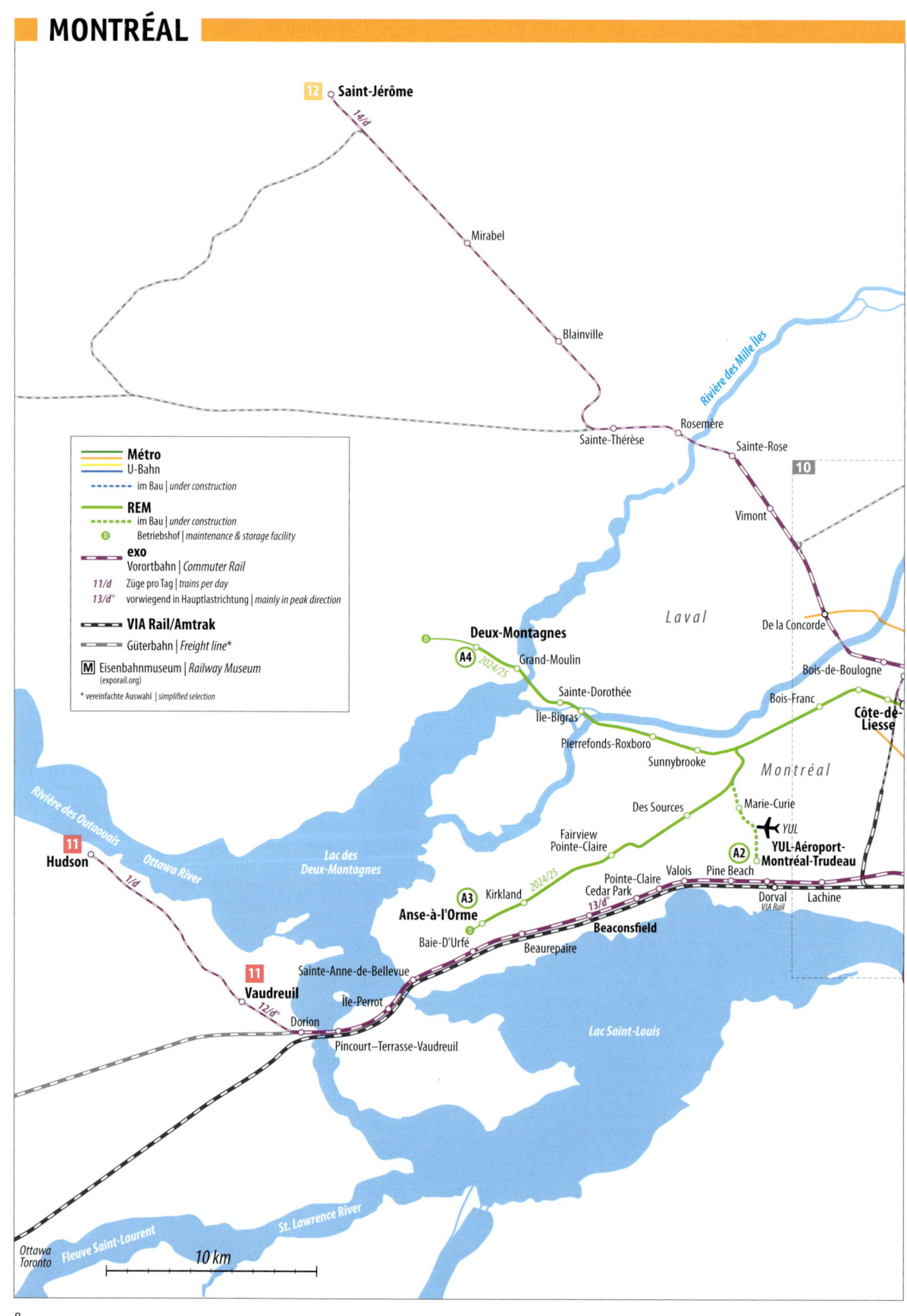

12 Saint-Jérôme

14/d

Mirabel

Blainville

Rivière des Mille Îles

Sainte-Thérèse

Rosemère

Sainte-Rose

10

Vimont

De la Concorde

Laval

Bois-de-Boulogne

Métro
U-Bahn

im Bau | *under construction*

REM

im Bau | *under construction*

Ⓑ Betriebshof | *maintenance & storage facility*

exo
Vorortbahn | *Commuter Rail*

11/d Züge pro Tag | *trains per day*

13/d° vorwiegend in Hauptlastrichtung | *mainly in peak direction*

VIA Rail/Amtrak

Güterbahn | *Freight line**

M Eisenbahnmuseum | *Railway Museum*
(exporail.org)

* vereinfachte Auswahl | *simplified selection*

Deux-Montagnes

Ⓑ (A4) 2024/25 Grand-Moulin

Sainte-Dorothée

Bois-Franc

Côte-de-Liesse

Île-Bigras

Pierrefonds-Roxboro

Sunnybrooke

Montréal

Des Sources

Marie-Curie

Rivière des Outaouais

Fairview
Pointe-Claire

YUL

(A2) YUL-Aéroport-Montréal-Trudeau

11
Hudson

1/d

Ottawa River

Lac des Deux-Montagnes

(A3) Kirkland

2024/25

Pointe-Claire Valois Pine Beach

Cedar Park

Anse-à-l'Orme

Pointe-Claire

13/d°

Dorval
VIA Rail

Lachine

Baie-D'Urfé

Beaconsfield

Beaurepaire

11
Vaudreuil

12/d°

Sainte-Anne-de-Bellevue

Île-Perrot

Lac Saint-Louis

Dorion

Pincourt–Terrasse-Vaudreuil

Ottawa
Toronto

Fleuve Saint-Laurent

St. Lawrence River

10 km

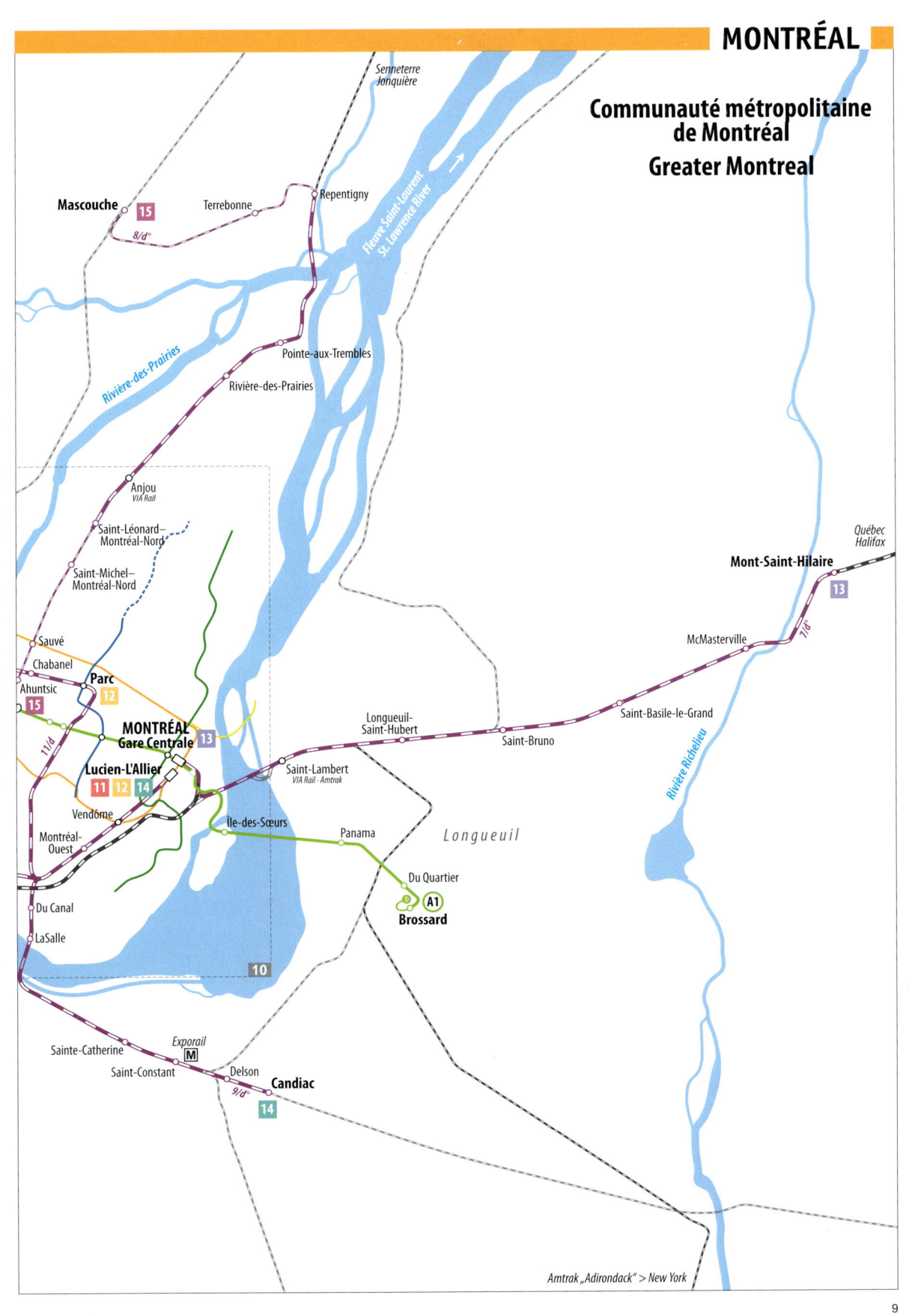

Communauté métropolitaine
de Montréal
Greater Montreal

Senneterre
Jonquière

Mascouche `15`
Terrebonne
Repentigny
8/d°

Fleuve Saint-Laurent
St. Lawrence River

Pointe-aux-Trembles
Rivière-des-Prairies

Rivière-des-Prairies

Anjou
VIA Rail

Saint-Léonard–
Montréal-Nord

Saint-Michel–
Montréal-Nord

Québec
Halifax

Mont-Saint-Hilaire `13`
7/d°

Sauvé
Chabanel
Parc `12`
Ahuntsic
`15`
11/d°

McMasterville

MONTRÉAL
Gare Centrale `13`

Longueuil-
Saint-Hubert
Saint-Basile-le-Grand

Lucien-L'Allier
`11` `12` `14`

Saint-Lambert
VIA Rail · Amtrak

Saint-Bruno

Rivière Richelieu

Vendôme

Montréal-
Ouest

Île-des-Sœurs
Panama

Longueuil

Du Quartier

Du Canal

`A1`
Brossard

LaSalle

`10`

Sainte-Catherine
Exporail
`M`
Saint-Constant
Delson
Candiac
9/d°
`14`

Amtrak „Adirondack" > New York

9

MONTRÉAL

Métro
U-Bahn

im Bau | under construction
Ⓓ Betriebshof/Abstellanlage
Depot / Maintenance Facility

REM

exo
Vorortbahn | Commuter Rail

VIA Rail/Amtrak

Güterbahn | Freight line*

Autobahn | Freeway *
Hauptstraßen | Main roads *

* vereinfachte Auswahl | simplified selection

Mascouche

Anjou
VIA Rail

Saint-Léonard–
Montréal-Nord

Saint-Michel–
Montréal-Nord

(Anjou)

(Langelier)

(Lacordaire)

(Viau)

(Pie-IX)

Ligne bleue
Saint-Michel

D'Iberville

Fabre

Jean-Talon

De Castelnau

Rosemont

Beaubien

Laurier

Mont-Royal

Ligne verte
Honoré-Beaugrand

Radisson

Langelier

Cadillac

Assomption

Ⓓ Viau

Pie-IX

Joliette

Préfontaine

Frontenac

Papineau

Ligne orange
Montmorency
Ⓓ
De la Concorde
Cartier Ⓓ
Henri-Bourassa
Sauvé
VIA Rail
Crémazie
Jarry
Atelier D'Youville Ⓓ
Chabanel
Ahuntsic

Bois-de-Boulogne

Du Ruisseau

15
Côte-de-Liesse

Montpellier

Ligne orange
Côte-Vertu
Ⓓ

Ville-de-Mont-Royal

Canora

12 **Parc**

Acadie

Outremont

Édouard-Montpetit

Ligne jaune
Longueuil
Université-de-Sherbrooke

Beaudry

Berri-UQAM

Sherbrooke

Ligne jaune

Saint-Laurent

Place-des-Arts

McGill

Champ-de-Mars

Place-d'Armes

Square-Victoria-OACI

Bonaventure
(Griffintown–Bernard-Landry)

Jean-Drapeau

Expo Express
1967-1972

REM
2024/25

Bois-Franc

Du Collège

De la Savane

Université-de-Montréal

Côte-des-Neiges

Namur

Plamondon

Côte-Sainte-Catherine

Ligne bleue
Snowdon

Villa-Maria

Vendôme

MONTRÉAL
Gare Centrale

13

Peel

Guy-Concordia

Atwater

Lucien-L'Allier

11 **12** **14**

Georges-Vanier

Lionel-Groulx

Charlevoix

Place
Saint-Henri

LaSalle

De l'Église

Verdun

Jolicoeur

Monk

Ⓓ
Angrignon
Ligne verte

Île-des-Sœurs

REM

Mont-Saint-Hilaire

Gare de triage
Marshalling yard
Rangierbahnhof

Montréal-Ouest

Vaudreuil
Hudson
Lachine

Du Canal

LaSalle

Candiac

St-Jérôme

St. Laurent River
Fleuve Saint-Laurent

5 km

❶ Honoré-Beaugrand – Angrignon
❷ Montmorency – Côte-Vertu
❹ Berri-UQAM – Longueuil
❺ Saint-Michel – Snowdon
Ⓡ Deux-Montagnes
Anse-à-l'Orme > Brossard

Laurier

Ligne orange

Mont-Royal

Ligne verte

Papineau

Rue Berri

Boulevard De Maisonneuve Est

Sherbrooke

Beaudry

Berri-UQAM

Rue St-Denis

Saint-Laurent

Champ-de-Mars

Ligne jaune

Place-des-Arts

REM

Place-d'Armes

Avenue Viger Est

McGill

MONTRÉAL
Gare Centrale

13

Vieux
Montréal

Square-Victoria-OACI

Peel

Gare Centrale

Bonaventure

(Griffintown–Bernard-Landry)
(proj.)

Guy-Concordia

Boulevard De Maisonneuve Ouest

Lucien-L'Allier

Lucien-L'Allier

11 12 14

Place d'Accueil

13

Atwater

Georges-Vanier

REM

11·12·14

Lionel-Groulx

Ligne verte

Ligne orange

Expo Express

500 m

Kartenhintergrund | Map background © OpenStreetMap

Mont-Royal

LaSalle

MÉTRO

Das U-Bahn-Netz von Montréal besteht aus vier Linien, die alle dieselben technischen Merkmale aufweisen – die „Métro" wurde Anfang der 1960er Jahre entworfen und war stark von der Pariser Métro inspiriert, u.a. fahren die Züge auf Gummireifen, da man damals davon ausging, dass dies eine schnellere Beschleunigung und Steigungen von bis zu 6,5% erlauben würde. Aufgrund der strengen Winter wurde die U-Bahn von Montréal gänzlich unterirdisch errichtet, wobei die meisten Strecken durch Felsgestein gebohrt wurden, während für die Bahnhofsrohbauten teilweise die offene Bauweise angewandt wurde. Von Anfang an sollte jede Station gestalterisch einzigartig werden, was sich an zahlreichen Kunstwerken widerspiegelt, die auf allen Ebenen verteilt zu sehen sind. Die vier Linien, deren Gesamtlänge 66 km beträgt, werden meist nach ihrer Kennfarbe benannt, während ihre jeweiligen Linien-nummern nur zeitweise auf Netzplänen und Schildern zu sehen waren – in letzter Zeit wieder häufiger, nicht zuletzt, um farbenblinde Fahrgäste bei der Orientierung zu unterstützen. Die Linienfarben sind jedoch nicht Teil der Bahnhofsgestaltung wie etwa in Boston, Mailand oder Wien. Die Bahnhofszugänge sind an einem eindeutigen Logo, einem weißen Kreis mit einem weißen Abwärtspfeil auf blauem Hintergrund und dem Wort „MÉTRO" darunter, zu erkennen. Lässt man die Gelbe Linie und ihre langen Unterwassertunnel außer Acht, beträgt der durchschnitt-liche Stationsabstand auf den anderen drei Linien 920 m. Bis 2023 waren lediglich 28 von insgesamt 72 U-Bahn-höfen, die größtenteils über Seitenbahnsteige verfügen, mit Aufzügen zugänglich.

Wie in Toronto fing alles mit einem U-Strab-Projekt für das bestehende Straßenbahnnetz an. Im Jahr 1944

Montreal's metro system consists of four lines which all have the same technical features — designed in the early 1960s and inspired by the Paris Métro, the trains run on rubber tyres, at the time said to allow faster acceleration and steeper grades of up to 6.5%. Prompted by the harsh winters, the Montreal metro was built 100% underground, with most routes drilled through rock, while cut-and-cover was used for some station boxes. From the very beginning, a unique design was chosen for each station, including numerous works of art exhibited throughout the stations. The four lines, which add up to a total network length of 66 km, are mostly identified by their colours, whereas their respective numbers have only intermittently appeared on maps and signage, more frequently again in recent times, not least to help colour-blind passengers. The line colours, however, are not systematically used in the station design like in Boston, Milan or Vienna. Station accesses can be identified by a clear logo, a white circle with a white down arrow on a blue background and the word 'MÉTRO' below. Leaving the Yellow Line and its long underwater tunnels aside, the average distance between stations is 920 m on the other three lines. By 2023, only 28 of the 72 stations, which mostly have side platforms, had been made fully accessible with elevators.

Like in Toronto, the first proposals for an underground railway involved constructing downtown tunnels for the existing streetcars. In 1944, the Montreal Tramways Company even presented a project for a real metro, but it was not until the Commission de transport de Montréal (CTM) took over that a more realistic project was put forward in 1953, with an initial 12.5 km line along Rue

präsentierte die *Montreal Tramways Company* sogar ein Projekt für eine echte U-Bahn, doch erst nach Übernahme durch die *Commission de Transport de Montréal* (CTM) wurde 1953 ein realistischeres Projekt mit einer ersten 12,5 km langen Strecke entlang der Rue Saint-Denis, Rue Saint-Jacques und Rue Sainte-Catherine vorgeschlagen. Nicht zuletzt angetrieben durch Torontos erste U-Bahn-Linie, die 1954 eröffnet wurde, verabschiedete Montréal schließlich 1961 ein Projekt mit drei Linien – einer Ost-West-Linie von Atwater bis Frontenac (grün), einer Nord-Süd-Linie von Henri-Bourassa bis Bonaventure (orange) sowie einer Linie unter dem Mount Royal (rot), die aus einer bestehenden Vorortbahn (siehe S. 35) entstehen sollte, und zwar mit einem Ast nach Cartierville und einem nach Montréal Nord auf der Trasse der heutigen Mascouche-Linie. Die Rote Linie (oder Linie 3) wurde jedoch bald zugunsten der Linie 4 (Gelbe Linie) auf Eis gelegt, mit der eine Verbindung zum Expo 67-Gelände auf der Île Sainte-Hélène geschaffen werden sollte. Die Linie 3, deren Nummer auf dem Métro-Netzplan weiterhin fehlt, wurde schließlich fast 60 Jahre später in Form des neuen REM-Netzes realisiert.

Nachdem das Grundnetz im Frühjahr 1967 pünktlich zur Expo 67 fertiggestellt war, ging der Ausbau in den 1970er und 1980er Jahren weiter, einschließlich der 1988 vollendeten Tangentiallinie 5 (blau). Danach dauerte es fast 20 Jahre, bis 2007 drei neue Stationen in der Nachbarstadt Laval dazukamen. Es werden wieder über 20 Jahre vergangen sein, wenn die lang geplante Verlängerung der Blauen Linie von Saint-Michel nach Anjou endlich eröffnet wird.

Derzeit ist der Bau einer völlig neuen Linie, der „Ligne Rose" oder „Pink Line", im Gespräch. Diese würde in etwa von Montréal Nord (Léger/Langelier) über das Stadtzentrum nach Westen bis Lachine führen und die Blaue Linie an dem im Bau befindlichen Bahnhof Pie-IX, die Orange Linie an den Stationen Mont-Royal und Vendôme und die Grüne Linie am Place-des-Arts kreuzen; durch die Innenstadt soll sie entlang des Boulevard René-Lévesque verlaufen, mit einer Station am Gare Centrale mit Übergang zur REM. Während der östliche und mittlere Abschnitt unterirdisch gebaut würden, werden für den westlichen Teil einige oberirdische Abschnitte in Betracht gezogen.

Immer wieder kursiert auch die Idee einer Verlängerung der Gelben Linie von ihrem derzeitigen Endpunkt Berri-UQAM bis McGill im Herzen der Stadt, um die Grüne Linie zu entlasten.

Saint-Denis, Saint-Jacques and Sainte-Catherine. Spurred by Toronto's first Subway line opened in 1954, Montreal eventually went ahead with a 3-line network approved in 1961 — an east-west line from Atwater to Frontenac (green), a north-south line from Henri-Bourassa to Bonaventure (orange), and a line through Mount Royal (red) to be developed out of the existing suburban line (see p. 35), with one branch going to Cartierville and one to Montréal-Nord on what is now the Mascouche line. The Red Line (or Line 3), however, was soon put on hold in favour of Line 4 (Yellow Line), which was considered a priority to create a link to the Expo 67 site on Île Sainte-Hélène. Though its number never appeared on the metro map, line 3 was finally realised in the form of the new REM system almost 60 years later.

With the initial network completed in the spring of 1967 in time for Expo 67, expansion continued through the 1970s and 1980s, including the tangential line 5 (blue), which was finished in 1988. After that, it took almost 20 years for three new stations to be added in 2007 in the neighbouring city of Laval. Again, more than 20 years will have passed by the time the long-planned extension of the Blue Line from Saint-Michel to Anjou finally opens.

The construction of a completely new line, the Ligne rose or Pink Line, is currently on the table, but no definitive decisions have been made. The line would run roughly from Montréal-Nord (Léger/Langelier) via the city centre west to Lachine, intersecting with the Blue Line at the station under construction at Pie-IX, with the Orange Line at Mont-Royal and Vendôme and with the Green Line at Place-des-Arts; running through the city centre along Boulevard René-Lévesque, there would also be a station at Gare Centrale with interchange to the REM. While the eastern and central sections would be underground, some surface stretches are considered for the western part.

Time and again, an extension of the Yellow Line from its current terminus at Berri-UQAM to McGill in the heart of the city has been proposed to reduce overcrowding on the Green Line.

● **Côte-Vertu**

MR-73 @ ● Université de Montréal

● U-Bahn-Fahrzeuge

Da alle Strecken nach den gleichen Parametern gebaut sind, kann theoretisch jeder Zug auf jeder Strecke fahren. Der Betrieb begann 1966 mit **MR-63**-Wagen, die auf dem gummibereiften Pariser Typ MP-59 basierten und vor Ort von Canadian Vickers produziert wurden. Montréal entschied sich für nur 2,5 m breite Wagen im Gegensatz zu den 3,1 m breiten Zügen in Toronto, damit zwei Züge problemlos in einen zweigleisigen 7,1 m breiten Tunnel passen. Es handelte sich um fest gekoppelte 3-Wagen-Einheiten mit 16,9 m langen motorisierten Endwagen und dazwischen einem nicht angetriebenen 16,2 m langen Wagen, jeweils mit vier Türen pro Seite. Sie konnten einzeln oder in Doppelbzw. Dreifachtraktion eingesetzt werden, ein 9-Wagen-Zug war somit 152,4 m lang. Zwischen 1963 und 1967 wurden insgesamt 369 Wagen gebaut und einige blieben bis 2018 im Einsatz. Ihre hellblaue Lackierung wurde von den Nationalfarben Québecs inspiriert.

Für das wachsende Netz folgte zwischen 1974 und 1980 die Baureihe **MR-73**. Davon wurden insgesamt 423 Wagen von Bombardier in La Pocatière, 110 km nordöstlich von Québec City, hergestellt. Diese Wagen hatten die gleichen Maße wie der Vorgängertyp und ließen sich von den später äußerlich angepassten MR-63-Wagen durch ihre aufrechten

● *Metro Rolling Stock*

With all the lines built to the same specifications, theoretically any train can run on any line. Service started in 1966 with **MR-63** *rolling stock, based on the rubber-tyred Paris MP-59 model and produced locally by Canadian Vickers. Montreal opted for cars only 2.5 m wide as opposed to the 3.1 m wide trains in Toronto in order to make two trains fit easily into a double-track 7.1 m wide tunnel. The cars formed permanently coupled 3-car sets, with two motor cars (16.9 m) and a trailer in the middle (16.2 m), each car having four sets of doors per side. They could operate as single, double or triple sets, with a full-length train thus consisting of 9 cars (152.4 m). A total of 369 cars were built between 1963 and 1967 and some remained in service until 2018. Their light blue livery was inspired by the national colours of Quebec.*

For the expanding network, the **MR-73** *cars followed between 1974 and 1980. A total of 423 cars were manufactured by Bombardier at La Pocatière, 110 km northeast of Quebec City. The new cars had the same dimensions as the MR-63 and can be distinguished from the refurbished MR-63 cars by their upright rectangular headlights. Their maximum speed is 72 km/h. They were all refurbished in 2005-2008, and although over 60 cars*

MR-73

MR-73 – Fahrwerk mit Gummirädern | *bogie with rubber tyres*

MPM-10 „Azur" @ ● Pie-IX

rechteckigen Scheinwerfer unterscheiden. Ihre Höchstgeschwindigkeit beträgt 72 km/h. Sie wurden alle in den Jahren 2005-2008 modernisiert, und auch wenn bereits über 60 Wagen ausgemustert wurden, werden einige bis Mitte der 2030er Jahre im Einsatz bleiben.

Die neueste Fahrzeuggeneration ist die Baureihe **MPM-10** „Azur", die zwischen 2013 und 2021 gemeinsam von Bombardier und Alstom in Québec hergestellt wurde, wobei der erste Zug erst 2016 in den Fahrgasteinsatz kam. Insgesamt wurden 71 Neun-Wagen-Züge ausgeliefert, bei denen alle Wagen durchgehend begehbar sind. Ihre Höchstgeschwindigkeit beträgt 100 km/h. Sie ersetzten alle MR-63-Wagen und einige der MR-73. Wie die älteren Typen haben sie keine Klimaanlage, aber ein Belüftungssystem.

Seit 1976 ist die Métro von Montréal mit einem ATO-System für den automatischen Betrieb ausgestattet, allerdings mit einem Fahrer an Bord. Die Stromzufuhr (750 V Gleichstrom) erfolgt über eine seitliche Schiene, die in das Spurführungssystem integriert ist. Zwischen den Gummireifen, die auf Metallträgern oder Betonbahnen rollen, laufen die Züge mit herkömmlichen Stahlrädern auf Normalspurgleisen. Wie die Métro-Linien sind auch alle Betriebshöfe vollständig unterirdisch (lediglich Angrignon liegt oberirdisch, ist aber eingehaust).

have already been retired, some will remain in service until the mid-2030s.

*The newest generation is the **MPM-10** "Azur", which was manufactured in Quebec jointly by Bombardier and Alstom between 2013 and 2021, although the first train did not enter service until 2016. A total of 71 nine-car trains have been delivered, with all cars interconnected by gangways. Their maximum speed is 100 km/h. They have replaced all of the MR-63s and some of the MR-73s. Like the older types they are not equipped with air-conditioning, but have a ventilation system.*

Since 1976, the Montreal Metro has been equipped with an ATO system for automatic operation, though with a driver on board. The traction power of 750 V DC is supplied via a third rail incorporated into the guiding rail system. Between the rubber tyres, which roll on metal beams or concrete runways, the trains have conventional steel wheels running on standard-gauge tracks. Like the metro lines, all the maintenance and storage facilities are fully underground (except Angrignon, which is on the surface but fully encased).

MR-73 & MR-63
(Foto © Mousseau/MUCTC)

MPM-10 „Azur"

McGill

Ligne ① - Verte

Die Grüne Linie verläuft in etwa parallel zum Sankt-Lorenz-Strom von Nordosten nach Südwesten. Im Stadtzentrum erschließt sie die wichtigsten Einkaufsgegenden und Kultureinrichtungen (U-Bahnhof Place-des-Arts); sie wurde jedoch nicht unter der Hauptverkehrsader Rue Sainte-Catherine ausgerichtet, sondern einen Block weiter oben unter dem heutigen Boulevard De Maisonneuve. Über ein ausgedehntes Netz unterirdischer Gänge sind die zentralen Métro-Stationen jedoch direkt von vielen Einkaufszentren und Bürotürmen aus zugänglich. Mit 440 m ist der kürzeste Stationsabstand zwischen Peel und McGill zu finden.

The Green Line runs roughly parallel to the Saint Lawrence River from the northeast to the southwest. In the city centre it serves the main shopping areas and cultural institutions (Place-des-Arts station), although it was not aligned under the main artery which is Rue Sainte-Catherine, but one block up under what would become Boulevard De Maisonneuve. Via an extensive network of underground walkways, however, the central Métro stations are directly connected to many shopping malls and office towers. At 440 m, the shortest distance between two stations can be found between Peel and McGill.

In 1976, the Green Line was extended northeast in time for the 1976 Olympic Games, with the Olympic Stadium being located right between Pie-IX and Viau stations.

The western extension from Atwater, completed in 1978, features a long S-curve chosen to create a convenient cross-platform interchange with the Orange Line at the bi-level Lionel-Groulx, where inbound trains stop on the upper level and outbound trains on the lower. Stacked platforms were also built at Charlevoix (lower platform at a depth of 29.6 m) and De l'Église. Compared

Saint-Laurent

Ligne ① - Verte
- 22.1 km, 27 Stations (Ⓤ)

14-10-1966: Atwater – Papineau
19-12-1966: Papineau – Frontenac
21-12-1966: + Beaudry
06-06-1976: Frontenac – Honoré-Beaugrand
03-09-1978: Atwater – Angrignon

Lionel-Groulx – Umsteigen am selben Bahnsteig | *Cross-platform interchange*

1976 wurde die Grüne Linie pünktlich zu den Olympischen Spielen 1976 nach Nordosten verlängert; das Olympiastadion liegt direkt zwischen den Bahnhöfen Pie-IX und Viau.

Die 1978 fertiggestellte Westverlängerung ab Atwater führt über eine lange Kurve zur Station Lionel-Groulx, wo man bequem am selben Bahnsteig zur Orangen Linie umsteigen kann, auf der oberen Ebene Richtung Stadtzentrum, unten stadtauswärts. In den Bahnhöfen Charlevoix (der untere Bahnsteig befindet sich in einer Tiefe von 29,6 m) und De l'Église liegen die Bahnsteige übereinander. Im Vergleich zum Rest des Netzes verläuft der südliche Abschnitt eher flach unter der Erde, wobei die Bahnsteige an der Endstation Angrignon nur 4,3 m tief liegen und durch Fenster auf beiden Seiten Tageslicht eindringt.

Auf der Grünen Linie verkehren vorwiegend Azur-Züge, wochentags sind aber auch einige MR-73 zu sehen.

Langelier

to the rest of the network, the southernmost section has a rather shallow alignment, with the platforms at the terminus Angrignon only 4.3 m below the surface and illuminated by daylight through windows on either side.

The Green Line is operated with Azur trains, but on weekdays some MR-73s can also be seen.

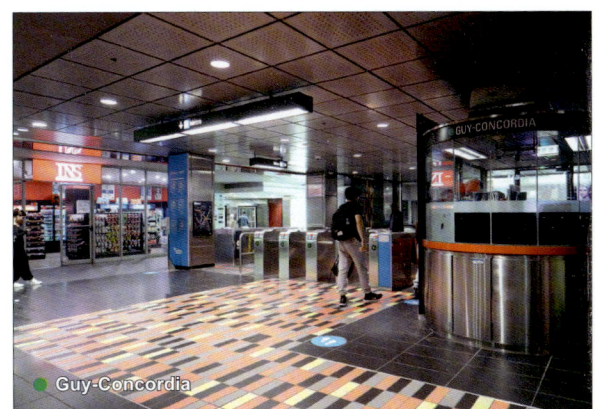

Guy-Concordia

Beaudry

MONTRÉAL

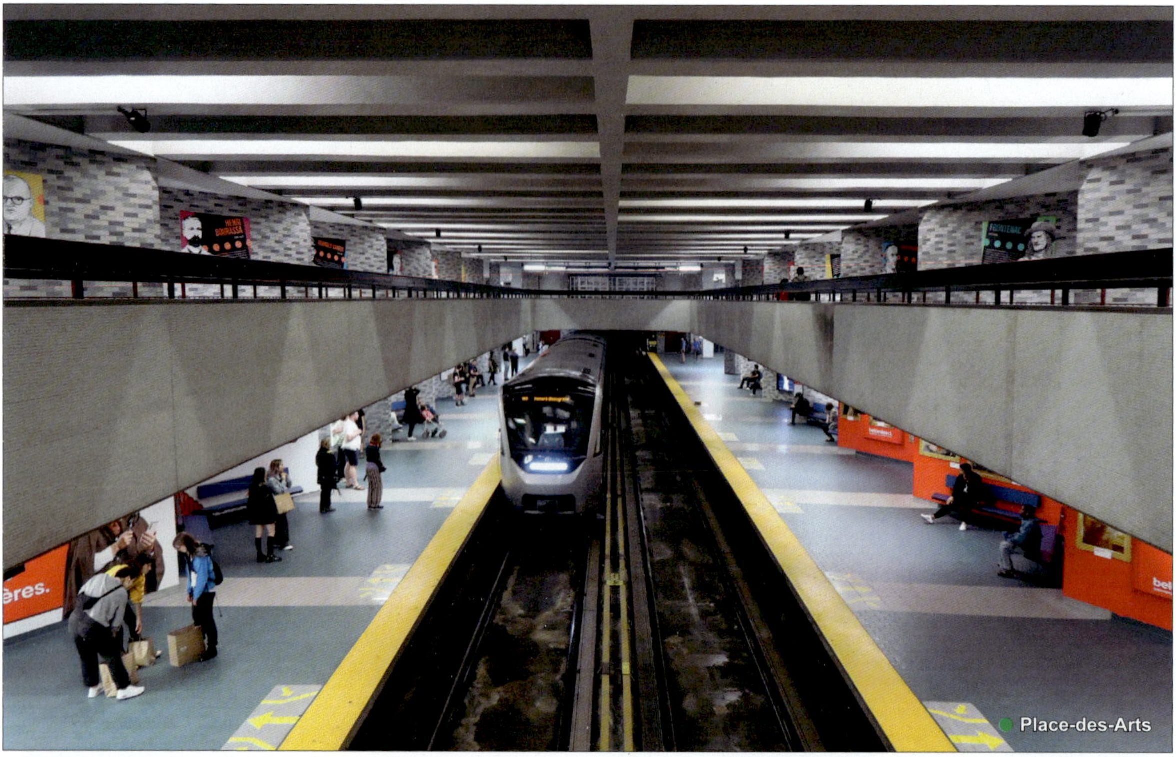

Place-des-Arts

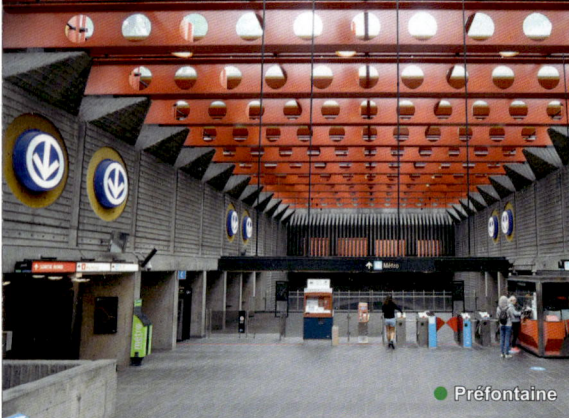

Préfontaine

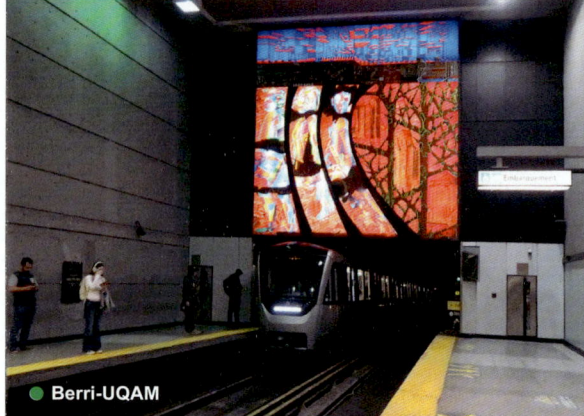

Berri-UQAM

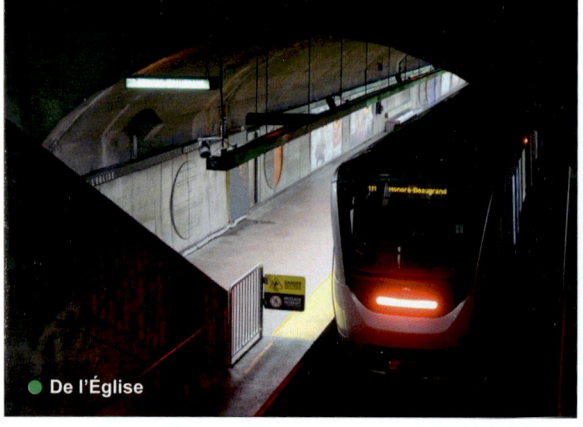

De l'Église

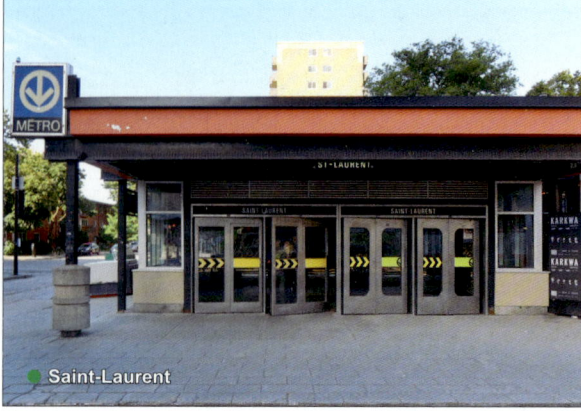

Saint-Laurent

Radisson

Verdun

Jolicoeur

Angrignon

Angrignon

Place-Saint-Henri

Ligne ② - Orange

Die Orange Linie besteht aus zwei Nordwest-Südost-Strecken, die über eine Innenstadtstrecke verbunden sind, die in einer Entfernung von nur 600-700 m parallel zur Grünen Linie verläuft. Die Orange Line erschließt das Geschäftsviertel rund um Square Victoria, Vieux Montréal (Altstadt) und das Rathaus rund um Place d'Armes und Champ-de-Mars sowie zwei Bahnhöfe – die U-Bahn-Station Bonaventure wurde zwischen Gare Centrale und Gare Windsor angesiedelt, doch letzterer wurde 1996 geschlossen und die Vorortbahnsteige wurden etwa 200 m weiter nach Westen verschoben, wo ein Übergang zur U-Bahn-Station Lucien-L'Allier (benannt nach einem der Väter der Métro von Montréal) geschaffen wurde. Am Knoten Berri-UQAM nutzt die Orange Linie die obere Ebene, während die Grüne Linie senkrecht darunter und die Gelbe Linie parallel, aber unterhalb der Grünen Linie liegt. Im U-Bahnhof Lionel-Groulx kann zur Grünen Linie und im U-Bahnhof Snowdon zur Blauen Linie bequem am selben Bahnsteig umgestiegen werden, während im U-Bahnhof Jean-Talon einige Fahrtreppen erforderlich sind.

Innerhalb von Montréal verläuft der östliche Ast fast durchgehend unter der Rue Berri, d.h. 1-2 Blocks östlich

The Orange Line has two northwest-southeast legs connected via a city centre route which runs parallel to the Green Line at a distance of just 600-700 m. The Orange Line serves the business district around Square Victoria, Vieux Montréal (Old Montreal) and the City Hall around Place d'Armes and Champ-de-Mars, as well as two railway stations — Bonaventure metro station was placed between Gare Centrale and Gare Windsor, but the latter was closed in 1996 and the suburban platforms relocated some 200 m further west, where a link was created to Lucien-L'Allier metro station (named after one of the fathers of the Montreal Metro). At Berri-UQAM, the Orange Line uses the upper level, with the Green Line lying perpendicularly beneath it and the Yellow Line parallel to it but beneath the Green Line. Cross-platform interchange is provided with the Green Line at Lionel-Groulx and the Blue Line at Snowdon, while some flights of escalators are required at Jean-Talon.

Ligne ② - Orange
- 30.0 km, 31 Stations (Ⓤ)

14-10-1966: Place-d'Armes – Henri-Bourassa
06-02-1967: Place-d'Armes – Square-Victoria
13-02-1967: Square-Victoria – Bonaventure
28-04-1980: Bonaventure – Place-Saint-Henri
07-09-1981: Place-Saint-Henri – Snowdon
04-01-1982: Snowdon – Côte-Sainte-Catherine
29-06-1982: Côte-Sainte-Catherine – Plamondon
09-01-1984: Plamondon – Du Collège
27-10-1986: Du Collège – Côte-Vertu
28-04-2007: Henri-Bourassa – Montmorency

Du Collège

Namur

der verkehrsreicheren Rue Saint-Denis. Die letzten drei im Jahr 2007 eröffneten Stationen befinden sich in der Stadt Laval (445.000 Einw.); von der langjährigen Endstation Henri-Bourassa aus unterquert die Linie den Rivière des Prairies und erreicht in einem tiefen Tunnel die Endstation. Im Zusammenhang mit dieser Verlängerung wurde die Station Henri-Bourassa umgebaut und ein dritter (stadtauswärtiger) Bahnsteig in einer neuen Bahnsteighalle hinzugefügt, während der ursprüngliche stadtauswärtige Bahnsteig jetzt von hier endenden Zügen genutzt wird.

Der kurvenreichere Westast erreichte in den 1980er Jahren in mehreren Etappen seinen heutigen Endpunkt Côte-Vertu, eine weitere Verlängerung stand immer wieder zur Debatte, entweder nur bis zur REM-Station Bois-Franc oder weiter durch Laval, möglicherweise um einen Ring mit dem Ostast zu schaffen.

Die Orange Line wird heute ausschließlich mit Azur-Zügen betrieben.

Within Montreal, the eastern leg runs almost entirely beneath Rue Berri, 1-2 blocks east of the busier Rue Saint-Denis. The three most recent stations, opened in 2007, are in the city of Laval (pop. 445,000); leaving the former long-time terminus at Henri-Bourassa, the line dives under the Rivière des Prairies to reach the terminus in a deep-level tube. In conjunction with this extension, Henri-Bourassa was rebuilt, adding a third (outbound) platform in a new cavern, while the old outbound platform is now used by terminating trains.

The more curvaceous western leg reached its present terminus Côte-Vertu in stages during the 1980s. A further extension has been proposed time and again, with a short extension to create an interchange with the REM at Bois-Franc or a longer route into Laval, possibly creating a loop with the eastern leg.

The Orange Line is now exclusively operated with Azur trains.

De la Savane

Jarry

Cartier

Villa-Maria

Plamondon

Snowdon

Villa-Maria

Bonaventure

Sherbrooke

Crémazie

Henri-Bourassa

Montmorency

Longueuil–Université-de-Sherbrooke

Ligne ④ - Jaune

Die Gelbe Linie wurde in das ursprüngliche U-Bahn-Projekt aufgenommen, nachdem die Stadt als Austragungsort der „Expo 67" ausgewählt worden war, die auf der Île Sainte-Hélène stattfinden sollte (die entsprechende Métro-Station wurde 2001 nach Jean Drapeau, einem ehemaligen Bürgermeister und Initiator des U-Bahn-Baus, umbenannt). Die Linie 4 wird normalerweise von MR-73-Zügen mit sechs Wagen betrieben, im Sommer sind jedoch auch Züge mit neun Wagen im Einsatz.

Von ihrem 28 m tiefen Endpunkt Berri-UQAM (bis 1988 Berri-De Montigny) verläuft die Linie 4 mit einem Gefälle von 6% bergab (eine zusätzliche Station in der Altstadt würde etwa 55 m tief liegen) und unterquert den Sankt-Lorenz-Strom in einem durch Felsgestein gebohrten Tunnel; Aushubmaterial wurde verwendet, um die Île Sainte-Hélène zu vergrößern und die benachbarte Île Notre-Dame aufzuschütten.

Der südliche Endpunkt, ein wichtiger Verkehrsknotenpunkt am Südufer, liegt in der Stadt Longueuil (255.000 Einw.), weshalb ein Zone-B-Ticket erforderlich ist. Wie eine Nordverlängerung bis McGill ist auch eine östliche Verlängerung weiter nach Longueuil hinein wiederholt vorgeschlagen worden, aber bislang ist die Linie 4 seit fast 60 Jahren unverändert geblieben.

The Yellow Line was added to the original metro project after the city had been chosen to host Expo 67, which was to take place on Île Sainte-Hélène (its namesake station was renamed in 2001 after Jean Drapeau, a former mayor and initiator of the metro system). Line 4 is normally served by 6-car MR-73 trains, but 9-car trains are in service in the summer.

From its 28 m deep terminus at Berri-UQAM (until 1988 Berri-De Montigny) the line runs down on a 6% slope (an occasionally proposed infill station in the old town would lie some 55 m deep) to cross the St. Lawrence River in a tunnel drilled through bedrock; the excavated material was used to enlarge Île Sainte-Hélène and create the neighbouring Île Notre-Dame.

The southern terminus, a major transportation hub on the South Shore, lies in the municipality of Longueuil (pop. 255,000) and requires a zone B ticket. Like a northern extension to McGill, an eastern extension into Longueuil has often been proposed, but for now Line 4 has remained unaltered for almost 60 years.

Ligne ④ - Jaune
- 4.3 km, 3 Stations (Ⓤ)

31-03-1967: Berri-UQAM – Longueuil–Université-de-Sherbrooke
28-04-1967: + Jean-Drapeau

Jean-Drapeau (1967-2001 Île-Sainte-Hélène)

Expo Express auf einer zeitgenössischen Postkarte vor dem deutschen, von Frei Otto entworfenen Pavillon auf der Île Notre-Dame
Expo Express on a contemporary postcard in front of the German pavilion, designed by Frei Otto, on Île Notre-Dame

Während bereits die Linie 4 hauptsächlich für die Expo 67 gebaut wurde, investierte Montréal auch in eine temporäre Schnellbahn, den „**Expo Express**", der die Place d'Accueil (Willkommensplatz) in der Cité du Havre (Hafenstadt) mit verschiedenen Expo-Standorten auf der Île Notre-Dame und der Île Sainte-Hélène verband. Die zweigleisige, 5,5 km lange Hochbahn, die den Sankt-Lorenz-Strom auf der Pont de la Concorde überquerte, war eine vollwertige Metro, die nach dem Vorbild der Subway von Toronto errichtet wurde, d.h. die Züge waren verwandt mit der Baureihe H von Toronto und fuhren auf herkömmlichen Stahlschienen. Sie wurden, was damals recht innovativ war, im ATO-Modus, also quasi automatisch, betrieben und waren klimatisiert. Der „Expo Express" verkehrte nicht nur während der Expo 67, sondern bis 1972 auch jeden Sommer zwei Monate lang, allerdings auf einer verkürzten Strecke. Daneben gab es auch noch die „Minirail", eine automatische aufgeständerte Monorail mit mehreren Ringlinien, eine davon war sogar bis 2019 in Betrieb.

*While Line 4 was primarily built to serve Expo 67, Montreal also invested in a purpose-built temporary metro line, the **Expo Express**, which connected the Place d'Accueil (Welcome Square) in the Cité du Havre (Harbour City) with various locations on Île Notre-Dame and Île Sainte-Hélène. The 5.5 km double-track elevated line, which crossed the Saint Lawrence River on the Pont de la Concorde, was a fully-fledged metro system modelled on the Toronto Subway, i.e. with trains derived from Toronto's H series, running on conventional steel rails, and quite innovative at the time, operated in ATO mode and fully air-conditioned. The Expo Express was in service not only during the Expo 67 season, but also for two months each summer until 1972, albeit on a shortened route. Aside from that there was the 'Minirail', an automated elevated monorail with various circular routes, one of which even remained in service until 2019.*

Berri-UQAM

Berri-UQAM

● Fabre

Ligne ⑤ - Bleue

Die Blaue Linie ist eine Tangentiallinie, die eine Querverbindung zwischen den Vororten nordwestlich des Mount Royal herstellt. Auch wenn die Bahnhöfe (außer Saint-Michel) lang genug für 9-Wagen-Züge gebaut wurden, sind nur MR-73-Züge mit 6 Wagen im Einsatz, wobei der ungenutzte Teil der Bahnsteige abgesperrt ist.

Die Blaue Linie beginnt im doppelstöckigen U-Bahnhof Snowdon, der ein ähnliches Layout wie Lionel-Groulx aufweist, d.h. die Bahnsteige liegen jeweils übereinander und die Züge fahren in entgegengesetzter Richtung ein (oben endende ⑤ / ② Côte Vertu, unten ⑤ Saint-Michel / ② Montmorency), was unter anderem für eine südwestliche Verlängerung in Richtung Notre-Dame-de-Grâce und darüber hinaus konzipiert war – ein Gebiet, das nun am Rand von der künftigen „Ligne rose" erschlossen werden soll.

An der Blauen Linie liegt die Université de Montréal, die über eine Reihe unterirdischer Rolltreppen und Treppen mit dem U-Bahnhof verbunden ist. An der Station Parc wurde der U-Bahn-Eingang in das 1931 von der *Canadian Pacific Railway* errichtete Bahnhofsgebäude integriert. Zur Orangen Linie kann auch am Bahnhof Jean-Talon umgestiegen werden; hier wurden allerdings in den 1960er Jahren keine Vorleistungen erbracht, so dass umfangreiche Arbeiten erforderlich waren, um die neue Linie unter dem bestehenden U-Bahnhof unterzubringen, wobei die Bahnsteige der Blauen Linie übereinander (Richtung Snowdon auf der oberen Ebene) und mehrere Rolltreppen zum Umsteigen zwischen beiden Linien angeordnet wurden.

Die gesamte Blaue Linie wurde zwar innerhalb von nur zwei Jahren eröffnet, doch eine von Anfang an geplante

The Blue Line is a tangential line providing a cross link between the suburbs northwest of Mount Royal. Although the stations (except Saint-Michel) were built long enough for 9-car trains, only 6-car MR-73 trains are in service, with the unused part of the platforms cordoned off.

The Blue Line starts at Snowdon in a bi-level station shared with the Orange Line, with a layout similar to Lionel-Groulx, i.e. stacked tracks and trains entering in opposite directions on each level (upper level ⑤ terminating/② Côte-Vertu, lower level ⑤ Saint-Michel/ ② Montmorency); it was designed for a southwestern extension towards Notre-Dame-de-Grâce and beyond, an area now partly to be served by the future Pink Line.

The Blue Line serves the Université de Montréal, which is connected to the metro station by a series of underground escalators and stairs. At Parc, the metro entrance was integrated into the 1931 train station building erected by the Canadian Pacific Railway. The second interchange with the Orange Line, Jean-Talon, was not built future-proof in the 1960s, so extensive work was required to accommodate the new line beneath the existing station, with the Blue Line platforms stacked

Ligne ⑤ - Bleue
- 9.7 km, 12 Stations (Ⓤ)

16-06-1986: De Castelnau – Saint-Michel
15-06-1987: De Castelnau – Parc
04-01-1988: Parc – Snowdon
28-03-1988: + Acadie
   ~ 2030: Saint-Michel – Anjou

● Saint-Michel

Verlängerung nach Anjou im Nordosten wurde immer wieder verschoben, bis der Bau schließlich 2023 endlich begann; die Inbetriebnahme ist nun im Jahr 2030 geplant. Auf der 6 km langen Neubaustrecke werden fünf Stationen errichtet, deren Namen noch nicht endgültig festgelegt worden sind.

(with Snowdon-bound trains on the upper level), and several escalators to change between lines.

Although the entire Blue Line was opened within a 2-year period, its extension northeast to Anjou, planned from the beginning, had been postponed time and again. However, construction finally started in 2023 for an opening in 2030. This will add 6 km and five new stations, the names of which have not been finalised.

● Côte-des-Neiges

Jean-Talon

Outremont

Parc

Parc

De Castelnau

Snowdon

Fabre

Snowdon

Acadie

● Du Quartier

REM

Kanadas neuestes Schienennahverkehrsmittel ist Montréals REM (kurz für *Réseau Express Métropolitain*), ein fahrerloses Metro-System, das am 31. Juli 2023 nach einigen Jahren Verzögerung eröffnet wurde.

Das Projekt wurde erst 2016 vorgestellt und der erste Abschnitt sollte bereits 2020 eröffnet werden. Vorangetrieben wurde es von der Provinzregierung von Québec in Zusammenarbeit mit der „Caisse de dépôt et placement du Québec" (CDPQ), einer staatlichen Investmentbank. Die Pläne für das 67 km lange Netz umfassten vier Teile:
1) eine 16 km lange Neubaustrecke von der Innenstadt über den Sankt-Lorenz-Strom in die südlichen Vororte (Rive-Sud);
2) den Umbau der bestehenden Vorortbahnlinie nach Deux-Montagnes, einschließlich des Mount-Royal-Tunnels, zu einer Metro;
3) einen Westast nach Anse à l'Orme in Sainte-Anne-de-Bellevue an der Westspitze der Insel von Montréal;
4) einen größtenteils unterirdischen Ast zum internationalen Flughafen Montréal-Trudeau.

Die Infrastruktur ist Eigentum von *CDPQ Infra*, und der Betrieb wird von der *Groupe PMM* (*Groupe des partenaires pour la mobilité des Montréalais*) durchgeführt, zu der Alstom, Lieferant der Fahrzeuge und des Betriebssystems Urbalis 400, gehört. Auch wenn die REM betrieblich völlig unabhängig von der Métro ist, ist sie vollständig in das Zonentarifsystem der ARTM integriert. Während sich die Stationen südlich des Flusses in Zone B befinden, werden zwei Stationen am Deux-Montagnes-Ast in Zone B (Laval) und zwei in Zone C liegen, aber der größte Teil des Netzes gehört zu Zone A. Bislang ist nur der südliche Abschnitt

Canada's newest transit system is Montreal's REM (short for *Réseau Express Métropolitain* – Metropolitan Express Network), a driverless metro system opened on 31 July 2023 after several years of delay.

The project was only presented in 2016 and the first segment was then scheduled to open in 2020. It was promoted by the Quebec government in cooperation with the 'Caisse de dépôt et placement du Québec' (CDPQ), an investment bank owned by the Province of Quebec. The plans for the 67 km network included four major elements:
1) a new 16 km link from downtown Montreal to the south bank of the St. Lawrence River (Rive-Sud);
2) the rebuilding of the existing Deux-Montagnes suburban line, including the Mount Royal tunnel, for a metro-style service;
3) a western branch to Anse à l'Orme in Sainte-Anne-de-Bellevue at the western tip of the Island of Montreal;
4) a mostly underground branch to serve Montréal-Trudeau International Airport.

The infrastructure is owned by CDPQ Infra and the rail service is operated by Groupe PMM (Groupe des partenaires pour la mobilité des Montréalais), which includes Alstom, the supplier of the REM rolling stock and the operating system Urbalis 400. Though operationally completely independent of Montreal's Metro, the REM is fully integrated into the ARTM's zonal fare system. While the stations on the south shore are in zone B, two stations on the Deux-Montagnes branch will be in zone B (Laval) and two in zone C, but the major part of the system will be in zone A. With only the southern segment from

● **Gare Centrale <> Île-des-Sœurs (Canal de Lachine)**

von Gare Centrale bis Brossard in Betrieb; hier verkehrt die REM während der Hauptverkehrszeit alle 3½ Minuten und sonst alle 7½ Minuten, wobei die ersten Züge um 05:30 Uhr von Gare Centrale und Brossard abfahren, die letzten gegen 01:00 Uhr, Samstag nachts etwas später.

Trotz der Neunummerierung der EXO-Linien anlässlich der REM-Eröffnung wurde der REM selbst keine Nummer zugewiesen, wo sich doch „Linie 3" aufdrängen würde (siehe unten). Stattdessen erhielt jede der vier Endstationen einen Fahrtzielcode, A1-A4. Ebensowenig fügt sich die gewählte Linienfarbe Limonengrün in das Farbenspektrum der Métro ein, wo bereits eine Grüne Linie vorhanden ist.

Am Gare Centrale wurden vier Gleise an das REM-Projekt abgetreten, wobei die beiden mittleren abgedeckt wurden, so dass ein ziemlich breiter Mittelbahnsteig entstand. Der REM-Bahnsteig ist über die Haupthalle sowie über eine neue Treppenanlage einschließlich Fahrtreppen und Aufzügen zugänglich. Der Übergang zur Orangen Linie ist aufgrund der ungünstigen Lage der U-Bahn-Station Bonaventure etwas lang. Die REM verlässt den Gare Centrale auf dem alten Bahnviadukt durch Griffintown, wo eine Station geplant ist. Kurz vor Überquerung des Canal-de-Lachine beginnt eine rund 3 km lange S-förmige Hochbahntrasse, auf der die REM entlang und über weitläufigen Bahnanlagen verkehrt. Sie überquert dann den Arm des Sankt-Lorenz-Stroms, der die Insel von Montréal von der Île-des-Sœurs [Nonneninsel] trennt, wo sie

Gare Centrale to Brossard in operation, the REM operates every 3½ minutes during rush hour and every 7½ minutes at other times, with the first trains departing from Gare Centrale and Brossard at 05:30 and the last around 01:00, slightly later on Saturdays.

Despite the renumbering of the EXO regional rail lines on the occasion of the REM opening, the REM itself was not assigned a number in the overall Métro/EXO numbering system, when the natural choice would have been for 'Line 3' (see below). Instead, each of the four termini was given a destination code, A1-A4. Similarly, the colour chosen is lime green, when a Green Line already exists on the Métro network.

At Gare Centrale, four tracks were transferred to the REM project, and with the middle two now covered, this resulted in a rather wide island platform. The REM platform is accessible from the main concourse and via a new set of stairs, escalators and elevators. Interchange with the Orange Line is inconvenient due to the unfavourable location of the metro station Bonaventure. REM trains leave Gare Centrale on the elevated railway structure through Griffintown, where the construction of a station is planned. Just before crossing the Lachine Canal, REM trains ascend onto a new 3 km S-shaped viaduct which takes them across and alongside rail tracks and extensive yards. They cross the arm of the St. Lawrence River that separates the Island

Brossard

• Brossard

die erste Station erreicht. Von hier bis kurz vor Linienende verläuft die Strecke im Mittelstreifen einer Stadtautobahn, wobei unmittelbar nach der Station Île-des-Sœurs der fast 3 km breite Hauptarm des Sankt-Lorenz-Stroms auf der 2019 eröffneten Schrägseilbrücke „Pont Samuel-De Champlain" überquert wird, die von Anfang an als Straßen-/Eisenbahnbrücke konzipiert war. Die Station Panama ist ein wichtiger Bus-/REM-Umsteigeknoten für Longueuil und Brossard, während die Endstation Brossard mit rund 3.000 Parkplätzen als Park&Ride-Anlage gedacht ist, die von den Autobahnen 10 und 30 leicht zu erreichen ist. Die Station Du Quartier erschließt hingegen auf der Westseite ein ausgedehntes Einzelhandelsgebiet und auf der Ostseite ein neues Stadtviertel. Der REM-Betriebshof befindet sich hinter der Endstation Brossard.

Als nächstes sollen noch im Jahr 2024 der Abschnitt von Gare Centrale nach Nordwesten durch den alten Mount-Royal-Tunnel und dann oberirdisch bis Bois-Franc (12 km) sowie die beiden Westäste eröffnet werden. Auf dem unterirdischen Abschnitt werden zwei Stationen hinzugefügt, um Übergänge zur Métro zu schaffen: McGill für die Grüne Linie und in 72 m Tiefe Édouard-Montpetit für die Blaue Linie. Die fünf Bahnhöfe der ehemaligen Deux-Montagnes-Linie wurden entsprechend umgebaut, während Côte-de-Liesse als Umsteigebahnhof zur verkürzten Mascouche-EXO-Linie eingefügt wurde; dieser REM-Bahnhof verfügt über drei Gleise, um zusätzliche Züge bereitzustellen, die für den Transport der umsteigenden Fahrgäste in die Innenstadt erforderlich sein werden.

4,2 km südwestlich von Bois-Franc verzweigt sich die REM-Strecke, wobei der 13,5 km lange nördliche Ast entlang der ehemaligen Deux-Montagnes-Linie weiterführt. Auf diesem Ast wird es dieselben Bahnhöfe wie vorher

of Montreal from Nuns' Island (Île-des-Sœurs), where the first station is located. From here to shortly before the end of the line, they remain in the median of a suburban expressway, crossing the almost 3 km wide main arm of the St. Lawrence River on the new cable-stayed Samuel De Champlain Bridge, which opened in 2019 and was designed as a road/rail bridge from the start. Panama is a major bus/REM interchange for Longueuil and Brossard, while the Brossard terminus features some 3,000 parking spaces easily accessible from autoroutes 10 and 30. Du Quartier, however, serves an extensive retail area on the western side and a large transit-oriented development on the eastern. The REM's maintenance and storage facility is located beyond the line's terminus in Brossard.

The next section to open, possibly in 2024, runs northwest from Gare Centrale through the old Mount Royal tunnel and then on the surface to Bois-Franc (12 km); the two western branches may open at the same time. On the underground stretch two stations are being added to create interchanges with the Métro, McGill for the Green Line

• Brossard

Gare Centrale

geben, allerdings alle komplett umgebaut und nun größten-teils in Hochlage, da alle Bahnübergänge beseitigt wurden. Im Gegensatz zur alten Strecke, die westlich von Bois-Franc eingleisig mit Ausweichen war, ist die REM-Strecke durchgehend zweigleisig und erhält einen etwa 1,9 km langen Hochbahnabschnitt durch Pierrefonds-Roxboro. Auf diesem Ast sollen die Züge während der Hauptverkehrs-zeiten alle 5 Minuten und sonst alle 15 Minuten verkehren. Jenseits der Endstation Deux-Montagnes wurde der ehemalige EXO-Betriebshof für die REM umgebaut.

Der südliche Ast verzweigt sich erneut nach nur 1,7 km, wobei die Gabelung aufgeständert und niveaugleich ausgeführt ist. Der 13,5 km lange Westast überquert die Autoroute 40 und verläuft dann etwa 5 km in Hochlage durch ein Gewerbegebiet, wobei die Trasse einer Güterbahn genutzt werden konnte. Anschließend schwenkt er nach Norden und Westen, um nördlich parallel zur Autoroute 40 das Einkaufszentrum Fairview Pointe-Claire zu erschließen. Während Kirkland ein weiterer Hoch-bahnhof sein wird, liegt die Endstation Anse-à-l'Orme, ein wichtiger Busumsteigepunkt, ebenerdig. Hinter der End-station wird es ein kleineres Depot geben. Auf diesem Ast soll es während der Hauptverkehrszeiten einen 10-Minuten-Takt geben, sonst einen 15-Minuten-Takt.

Als letzter soll ca. 2027 der Ast zum Flughafen in Betrieb genommen werden. Dieser verläuft nur 1 km in Hochlage über die Autoroute 40 und deren Auffahrten, taucht dann aber in einen 3 km langen Tunnel mit zwei unterirdischen Stationen, Marie-Curie im Technoparc Montréal sowie YUL-Aéroport-Montréal-Trudeau, wobei letztere von der Flughafengesellschaft errichtet wird. Der Flughafen soll ebenfalls während der Hauptverkehrszeiten alle 10 Minuten und sonst alle 15 Minuten angeschlossen werden. Eine

and, at a depth of 72 m, Édouard-Montpetit for the Blue Line. The five stations on the former Deux-Montagnes line have been rebuilt accordingly, while a new station is being added at Côte-de-Liesse as an interchange to the curtailed Mascouche EXO line; this REM station features three tracks to cater for the extra trains needed to carry transferring passengers into the city centre.

4.2 km southwest of Bois-Franc, the REM route will split, with the 13.5 km northern branch continuing along the old Deux-Montagnes alignment. This branch will feature the same stations as the old commuter rail line, though all completely rebuilt and mostly raised to eliminate level crossings. Unlike the old line which was single-track with passing loops on the section west of Bois-Franc, the REM route is double-track throughout and includes a roughly 1.9 km elevated section through Pierrefonds-Roxboro. This branch is planned to be served every 5 minutes during peak hours, and every 15 minutes off-peak. Beyond the Deux-Montagnes terminus, the former EXO maintenance and storage facility has been adapted for the REM.

After just 1.7 km, the southern branch splits again in a flat elevated junction. The western 13.5 km leg crosses above Autoroute 40 and continues on a viaduct for some 5 km, taking advantage of an old freight line corridor through an industrial area. It then swings north and west to run along the north side of Autoroute 40 and serve the Fairview Pointe-Claire shopping mall. While Kirkland will be another elevated station, the terminus Anse-à-l'Orme will be at grade and a major interchange for local buses. There will also be a smaller depot beyond the terminus. This branch will have trains every 10 minutes during peak hours, and every 15 minutes off-peak.

Gare Centrale

Panama

Fahrt ins Stadtzentrum (McGill) wird 24 Minuten dauern. Eine Verlängerung vom Flughafen zum nur 1 km entfernten Bahnhof Dorval ist eine Option für die Zukunft.

Alle REM-Bahnhöfe verfügen über 80 m lange Bahnsteige, alle mit Bahnsteigtüren in voller Höhe, was in strengen Wintern oder heißen Sommern ideal ist. Vom Alstom-Werk in Indien wurden 106 Doppeltriebwagen vom Typ Metropolis geliefert, die einzeln (38,1 m) oder in Doppeltraktion eingesetzt werden. Mit 2,94 m sind sie deutlich breiter als die U-Bahn-Fahrzeuge von Montréal (2,5 m). Die normalspurigen Züge fahren mit herkömmlichen Stahlrädern auf Stahlschienen. Die Energiezufuhr erfolgt über einen Dachstromabnehmer aus einer 1500-Volt-Gleichstrom-Fahrleitung.

Im Jahr 2020 wurde der Bau der „REM de l'Est" vorgeschlagen, einer Hochbahnlinie entlang des Boulevard René-Lévesque, die den Osten der Insel von Montréal erschließen sollte, insbesondere Gebiete, die nicht von der Grünen Linie bzw. der zu verlängernden Blauen Linie abgedeckt werden. Nach Protesten vor allem gegen eine Hochbahn im Stadtzentrum gab CDPQ zwei Jahre später bekannt, dieses Projekt nicht weiterzuverfolgen. Südlich des Sankt-Lorenz-Stroms wird eine separate REM-Linie in Erwägung gezogen, um den Bahnhof Panama mit der Endstation der Gelben Linie in Longueuil zu verbinden.

The last section to open in around 2027 will be the airport branch, which is elevated for just 1 km to cross over Autoroute 40 and its access ramps, but then dives into a 3 km tunnel serving two underground stations, Marie-Curie in the Technoparc Montréal and YUL—Aéroport-Montréal-Trudeau, the latter being built by the airport authority. The airport branch is also planned to be served every 10 minutes during peak hours, and every 15 minutes off-peak. A journey to the city centre (McGill) will take 24 minutes. An extension from the airport to Dorval train station, only 1 km away, is an option for the future.

All the REM stations have 80 m platforms protected by full-height platform screen doors ideal for the harsh winters and hot summers. From their plant in India, Alstom is supplying 106 married pairs of Metropolis cars, which run as single (38.1 m) or double units. At 2.94 m, they are significantly wider than Montreal's Métro rolling stock (2.5 m). The standard-gauge trains have conventional steel wheels running on steel rails. Power is collected with a pantograph from a 1,500 V DC overhead line.

In 2020, the construction of 'REM de l'Est' was proposed, an elevated line along Blvd. René-Lévesque to serve the east of the Island of Montreal, notably areas not covered by the Green Line or the future Blue Line extension. CDPQ announced two years later that it would not be pursuing this project any longer due to opposition against an elevated line through downtown. On the South Shore, a separate REM line to connect Panama station with the Yellow Line's terminus at Longueuil is also being considered.

Du Quartier

Alstom Metropolis

Ligne Deux-Montagnes – Du Ruisseau   (2016 © Matt McLauchlin)

Die ehemalige 29,9 km lange Linie nach **Deux-Montagnes** (zwischen 2018 und 2020 „exo6") ist gänzlich im neuen REM-Netz aufgegangen. Diese Linie war die einzige Regionalbahnlinie mit einem S-Bahn-ähnlichen Betrieb, d.h. sie war elektrifiziert und wurde mit elektrischen Triebzügen ganztags im Stundentakt und während der Hauptverkehrszeit sogar alle 10-30 Minuten betrieben.

Die Geschichte der Deux-Montagnes-Linie beginnt im frühen 20. Jahrhundert, als die *Canadian Northern Railway* (CNoR) ihre transkontinentale Strecke vollendete, aber noch keine günstige Verbindung ins Zentrum von Montréal gefunden hatte, da der Korridor entlang des Flusses bereits von den Gleisen der *Canadian Pacific Railway* (CPR) und der *Grand Trunk Railway* (GTR) belegt war. CNoR entschied sich daher für einen Tunnel unter dem Mount Royal und eine Endstation in etwa dort, wo 1943 der Hauptbahnhof fertiggestellt wurde. CNoR nahm den Tunnel am 21. Oktober 1918 in Betrieb, doch das Unternehmen war bereits zahlungsunfähig und wurde kurz darauf in die neue *Canadian National Railway* eingegliedert (CNR, später CN). Der 5 km lange zweigleisige Tunnel wurde mit einer 2400-V-Gleichstrom-Oberleitung ausgerüstet; die E-Loks von *General Electric* blieben bis 1995 im Einsatz. In den 1960er Jahren, als das U-Bahn-Netz entworfen wurde, sollte die Deux-Montagnes-Linie zur „Linie 3 – Rote Linie" werden, aber am Ende wurde der Linie 4, der Gelben Linie, Vorrang eingeräumt, und die „Linie 3" kam nie zustande. CN betrieb weiter den Vorortverkehr nach Deux-Montagnes, ab 1982 allerdings im Auftrag der STCUM (*Société de Transport de la Communauté Urbaine de Montréal*). Die Strecke wurde schließlich Anfang der 1990er Jahre modernisiert, und die Elektroloks wurden durch MR-90-Triebzüge von Bombardier ersetzt, nachdem 1995 die Stromversorgung von Gleichstrom auf Wechselstrom (25 kV 60 Hz) umgestellt worden war. Hochbahnsteige gab es aber nur am Hauptbahnhof. Im Jahr 1996 ging die Strecke an die AMT (*Agence métropolitaine de transport*), die 2017 durch die RTM (*Réseau de transport métropolitain*) abgelöst wurde – drei Jahre später wurde der Betrieb auf der Deux-Montagnes-Linie eingestellt, um den Umbau für das neue REM-Netz zu ermöglichen.

Some sections of the REM network completely absorbed the former 29.9 km **Deux-Montagnes** (Two Mountains) commuter rail line (between 2018 and 2020 'exo6'). This was the only regional line with an S-Bahn-style service, i.e. electrified and operated with electric multiple units and with hourly service during off-peak hours and every 10-30 minutes during peak hours.

The history of the Deux-Montagnes line dates back to the early 20th century when the Canadian Northern Railway (CNoR) completed its transcontinental route, but had not yet established a convenient route into central Montreal, with the corridor along the river already occupied by the Canadian Pacific Railway (CPR) and the Grand Trunk Railway (GTR). CNoR therefore opted for a tunnel under Mount Royal and a terminus next to the site of Central Station, which was completed in 1943. CNoR opened the tunnel on 21 October 1918, but already insolvent by that time, the company was incorporated into the new Canadian National Railway (CNR, later CN) shortly after. The 5 km double-track tunnel had been equipped with a 2,400 V DC catenary, allowing the use of electric locos from General Electric which remained in service until 1995. In the 1960s, when the Métro network was designed, the Deux-Montagnes line was included in the plan as 'line 3 - Red Line', but in the end line 4, the Yellow Line, was given priority and 'line 3' never materialised. CN continued to operate a commuter rail service to Deux-Montagnes, though from 1982 under contract to STCUM (Société de Transport de la Communauté Urbaine de Montréal). Eventually, the line was modernised in the early 1990s, and the electric locomotives were replaced by MR-90 EMUs from Bombardier after the power supply system had been switched from DC to AC (25 kV 60 Hz) by 1995. High platforms, however, were only available at Central Station. In 1996, the line was transferred to the AMT (Agence métropolitaine de transport), which was superseded by the RTM (Réseau de transport métropolitain) in 2017. Three years later, operations on the Deux-Montagnes line ceased in order to allow for its incorporation into the new REM system.

Lucien-L'Allier

exo

In der Region von Montréal verkehren auf nicht elektrifizierten Strecken Wendezüge mit einem eher überschaubaren Fahrplan. Der Verkehrsbetrieb *Réseau de transport métropolitain* (RTM) wurde 2017 gegründet und löste damals die *Agence métropolitaine de transport* als Betreiber der Regionalbahnen und Busse in den Außenbereichen ab; seit 2018 tritt er als EXO (meist exo geschrieben) auf, ein Präfix, das „außen/außerhalb" bedeutet. Die Linien wurden anfangs als exo1 bis exo6 bezeichnet, doch Mitte 2023, zeitgleich mit Eröffnung des ersten REM-Abschnitts (dem jedoch keine Nummer zugewiesen wurde!), wurden sie in Linie 11 bis 15 umnummeriert.

Auf der Linie 11 von Lucien-L'Allier nach **Vaudreuil** verkehren täglich 13 Züge, meist zu Spitzenzeiten und in der Hauptlastrichtung, aber auch 1-2 Züge mittags. Eine Fahrt endet in Beaconsfield, während nur ein Zug pro Tag zur Hauptverkehrszeit nach Hudson weiterfährt. Samstags verkehren vier und sonntags drei Züge in jede Richtung. Zwischen Lucien-L'Allier und Vaudreuil nutzen EXO-Züge CPKC-Gleise, während VIA Rail-Züge auf den beiden parallelen Gleisen von CN verkehren. Die Linie 11 sowie die Linien 12 und 14 fuhren früher vom Bahnhof Windsor ab, dem ehemaligen westlichen Kopfbahnhof der *Canadian Pacific* in Montréal. Der Bahnhof wurde 1996 etwa 200 m nach Westen verschoben, um den Bau einer Eishockey-Arena auf dem alten Bahngelände zu ermöglichen. Der Bahnhof wird 2024/25 modernisiert, wobei auch die Bahnsteige eine Überdachung erhalten werden.

Auf der Linie 12 nach **Saint-Jérôme** verkehren über den Tag verteilt 14 Züge, die meist am Bahnhof Lucien-L'Allier abfahren, drei davon jedoch erst ab Parc. An Wochenenden

The Greater Montreal region is served by several commuter rail lines, all of which are operated with push-pull trains on non-electrified routes and with a rather limited service. The trains are run by the agency 'Réseau de transport métropolitain' (RTM), which was founded in 2017, when it replaced the 'Agence métropolitaine de transport' to operate commuter rail and local buses in the outer areas; it was branded EXO (mostly written exo) in 2018, a prefix meaning 'outer'. The lines were listed as exo1 to exo6 until they were renumbered 11-15 in mid-2023, coinciding with the opening of the first section of the REM system (which, however, was not assigned any number!).

*On line 11 from Lucien-L'Allier to **Vaudreuil**, there are 13 trains a day, mostly at peak times and in the peak direction, but there are also 1-2 trains around noon. One train terminates at Beaconsfield, while only one rush-hour train a day continues to Hudson. On Saturdays, there are four and on Sundays three trains in each direction. Between Lucien-L'Allier and Vaudreuil, the EXO trains use CPKC trackage; these tracks run parallel to a pair of CN tracks which are also used by VIA Rail. Line 11 as well as lines 12 and 14 used to depart from Windsor Station, once Canadian Pacific's western terminal station in Montreal. The terminus was moved some 200 m west to its present location in 1996 to allow for the construction of an ice hockey arena on the old railway grounds. The station will be modernised in 2024/25, including the construction of a canopy over the platforms.*

*Line 12 to **Saint-Jérôme** has 14 trains a day, spread throughout the day and mostly starting at Lucien-L'Allier,*

Gare Centrale

Vendôme

pendeln fünf Züge zwischen Saint-Jérôme und De la Concorde, wo Anschluss an die Métro besteht. Die Fahrt mit EXO zwischen De la Concorde und Lucien-L'Allier (26,5 km) dauert etwa 40 Minuten! Die Saint-Jérôme-Linie nutzt bis Sainte-Thérèse die Gleise der CPKC, der Rest ist Eigentum von EXO.

Der Fahrplan der Linie 13 von Gare Centrale über den Fluss nach Osten auf CN-Gleisen bis **Mont-Saint-Hilaire** enthält nur 7 Züge pro Tag, die meisten davon während der Hauptverkehrszeit in der Hauptlastrichtung. Ähnliches gilt für die Linie 14 von Lucien-L'Allier über den Fluss nach Süden auf CPKC-Gleisen bis **Candiac** mit 9 Zügen pro Tag.

Auf der Linie 15 fahren täglich 8 Züge von **Mascouche** nach Ahuntsic, fünf davon im morgendlichen Berufsverkehr. Drei Züge fahren zur Hauptverkehrszeit weiter zum Gare Centrale, auch wenn der Umweg dorthin fast eine Stunde dauert! Mit Erweiterung von REM durch den Mont-Royal wird die Mascouche-Linie von Ahuntsic bis zum neuen Knoten Côte-de-Liesse verlängert. Wie auf den Linien 13 und 14 gibt es auch auf der Linie 15 keinen Wochenendverkehr! Die Mascouche-Linie verkehrt auf CN-Gleisen durch den Osten von Montréal bis nach Repentigny, von wo aus eine eigene 12,5 km lange eingleisige Strecke größtenteils im Mittelstreifen der Autoroute 640 errichtet wurde. Der neue Abschnitt wurde 2014 eröffnet, gleichzeitig wurde die Mascouche-Linie eingeführt; bis 2020 fuhren die Züge durch den alten elektrifizierten Mont-Royal-Tunnel ins Zentrum von Montréal, weshalb Zweisystemlokomotiven zum Einsatz kamen. Die Linie musste 2020 mit Schließung der Deux-Montagnes-Linie, die in das neue REM-Netz integriert wird, verkürzt werden (siehe S. 35).

but three trains only run between Parc and Saint-Jérôme. On weekends, five trains a day shuttle between Saint-Jérôme and De la Concorde, where interchange with the Métro is provided; the EXO journey between De la Concorde and Lucien-L'Allier (26.5 km) takes some 40 minutes! The Saint-Jérôme line runs on CPKC tracks to Sainte-Thérèse, while the rest of the line is owned by EXO.

Line 13 from Gare Centrale across the river and east on CN tracks to **Mont-Saint-Hilaire** only has 7 trains a day, most of which run during peak hours in the peak direction. Similarly, the timetable for line 14 from Lucien-L'Allier across the river and south on CPKC tracks to **Candiac** shows 9 trains a day, again primarily in the peak direction during peak hours only.

On Line 15, 8 trains a day depart from **Mascouche** for Ahuntsic, five of which serve the morning rush-hour demand; three rush-hour trains continue to Gare Centrale, although the detour takes almost an hour! Once the REM is extended through Mount Royal, the Mascouche line will also be extended from Ahuntsic to a new interchange at Côte-de-Liesse. Like on lines 13 and 14, there is no weekend service on line 15! The Mascouche line operates on CN trackage through eastern Montreal and up to Repentigny, from where it uses a purpose-built 12.5 km single-track route mostly aligned in the median of Autoroute 640. The new section opened in 2014 when the Mascouche line came into service. Until 2020, Mascouche trains shared the route into central Montreal via the old electrified Mont Royal tunnel, using dual-powered locomotives. The line had to be cut back when the Deux-Montagnes line was closed in order to be integrated into the new REM system (see p. 35).

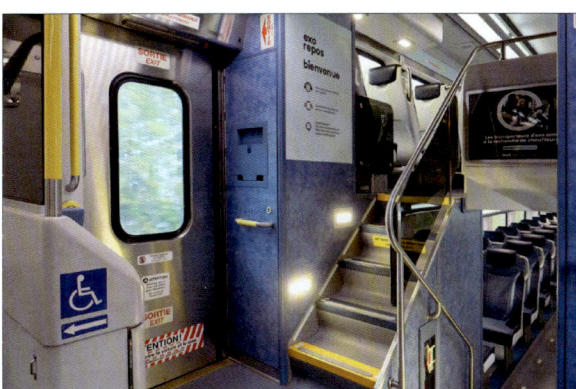

Unterdeck | *lower deck*

Pimisi – westliches Tunnelportal im Entwicklungsgebiet | western tunnel portal in a redevelopment area

OTTAWA, ON

Ottawa (bis 1855 *Bytown*), die Bundeshauptstadt Kanadas, liegt zwar in Ontario, aber an der Grenze zu Québec, also genau zwischen dem englisch- und französischsprachigen Teil des Landes; tatsächlich sind alle Straßen- und Stationsschilder zweisprachig. Die heutigen Stadtgrenzen wurden 2001 festgelegt und umfassen das gesamte bebaute Gebiet auf der Ontario-Seite des Ottawa River; hier leben 1,1 Mio. Menschen auf einer Fläche von 2.790 km². Die Metropolregion erstreckt sich jedoch über den Fluss bis in die Provinz Québec, wobei Gatineau mit etwa 295.000 Einwohnern zum Großraum von Ottawa gehört. Ottawa liegt 165 km westlich von Montréal und 350 km nordöstlich von Toronto.

Züge von *VIA Rail* verkehren achtmal täglich zwischen Toronto und Ottawa. Die Fahrt dauert etwa 4 Stunden und 30 Minuten. Von Montréal sind es etwas mehr als 2 Stunden, aber es gibt nur 4-5 Züge pro Tag. Der heutige Bahnhof von Ottawa liegt etwa 3,5 km östlich des Stadtzentrums und wird jetzt bequem mit der Station Tremblay der Stadtbahnlinie 1 erschlossen. Er wurde 1966 eröffnet und ersetzte damals die Union Station in der Innenstadt am Ostufer des Rideau-Kanals. Das Bahnhofsgebäude aus dem Jahr 1912 wurde später als Konferenzzentrum genutzt und ist heute der vorübergehende Sitz des kanadischen Senats.

Der gesamte öffentliche Nahverkehr in Ottawa wird von OC Transpo (ursprünglich kurz für „Ottawa-Carleton Regional Transit Commission") betrieben und umfasst zwei O-Train-Linien sowie zahlreiche Buslinien, von denen

Canada's federal capital, Ottawa (named Bytown until 1855), is located in Ontario along the Ottawa River, which forms the border with Quebec. As the seat of the officially bilingual federal government, located between the English- and French-speaking parts of the country, all its street and station signs are bilingual. Its present municipal boundaries were established in 2001 and now include the entire built-up area on the Ontario side of the Ottawa River, with a population of 1.1 million in an area of 2,790 km². The metropolitan area extends across the river into Quebec, with Gatineau adding some 295,000 inhabitants to the conurbation. Ottawa lies 165 km west of Montreal and 350 km northeast of Toronto.

VIA Rail operates between Toronto and Ottawa 8 times a day, with the journey taking approximately 4 hours and 30 minutes; from Montreal it is just over 2 hours, but there are only 4-5 trains per day. Ottawa's current train station lies some 3.5 km east of the city centre and is now conveniently served by O-Train Line 1's Tremblay station. Opened in 1966, it replaced a downtown Union Station on the east bank of the Rideau Canal; the 1912 station building was later used as a conference centre and is now the temporary home of the Senate of Canada.

All public transport in Ottawa is managed by OC Transpo (originally short for 'Ottawa-Carleton Regional Transit Commission'), and includes two O-Train lines and numerous bus routes, some of which use an exclusive

Hurdman – einziger Hochbahnhof auf der Linie 1 | *the only elevated station on line 1*

einige eine besondere Bustrasse, den „Transitway", nutzen. Eine einfache Fahrt mit Umsteigemöglichkeit kostet 3,75 $ (3,70 $ bei Zahlung mit einer PRESTO-Wertkarte). Für Besucher sind praktische Tageskarten an Fahrschein-automaten erhältlich: 1 Tag 11,25 $, 3 Tage 27,75 $, 5 Tage 44,50 $ bzw. 7 Tage 52,75 $.

Der städtische Schienennahverkehr begann in Ottawa bereits im Jahr 1870, als die *Ottawa City Passenger Railway Company* eine Pferdebahn zwischen New Edinburgh nördlich der Innenstadt und der Chaudière Bridge westlich des Stadtzentrums in Betrieb nahm. Ab 1891 betrieb die *Ottawa Electric Street Railway Company* die erste elektrische Straßenbahnlinie, sie fusionierte jedoch bereits zwei Jahre später mit der Pferdebahngesell-schaft zur *Ottawa Electric Railway Company*. Die O.E.R. blieb in Privatbesitz, bis sie schließlich 1950 von der Stadt übernommen wurde. Die städtische *Ottawa Transportation Commission* begann jedoch bald, Straßenbahnen durch Obusse zu ersetzen. Die letzte Straßenbahn fuhr 1959 auf der Britannia-Linie durch die westlichen Vororte, doch im selben Jahr wurde auch der Trolleybusbetrieb in Ottawa eingestellt.

Obwohl Ottawa im späten 19. Jahrhundert zu den Pionieren gehörte, war die Stadt eher zögerlich, als in den späten 1970er und 1980er Jahren in ganz Nordamerika zahlreiche neue Stadtbahn- und Metro-Betriebe entstan-den (in Kanada siehe Montréal, Edmonton, Calgary und Vancouver sowie in den benachbarten USA San Francisco, Washington DC, Portland, San José oder Sacramento). Stattdessen entschied sich Ottawa für den „Transitway", ein Netz besonderer und teilweise kreuzungsfreier Bustrassen. Die ersten Abschnitte wurden 1983 zwischen

'Transitway'. A single journey across the system costs $3.75 ($3.70 if paid with a PRESTO stored-value card). For visitors, convenient DayPasses are available from ticket machines: 1 day $11.25, 3 days $27.75, 5 days $44.50 or 7 days $52.75.

Urban rail transport in Ottawa started in as early as 1870 when the Ottawa City Passenger Railway Company started a horse-tram service from New Edinburgh north of downtown to the Chaudière Bridge to the west of the city centre. In 1891, the Ottawa Electric Street Railway Company launched the first electric tramway and two years later they merged with the horse-tram company to form the Ottawa Electric Railway Company. The O.E.R. remained in private hands until it was eventually taken over by the city in 1950. However, the public Ottawa Transportation Commission soon began to replace streetcars with trolleybuses. The last streetcar ran in 1959 on the Britannia line through the western suburbs, but that same year, trolleybus operation also ceased in Ottawa.

Though an early pioneer in the late 19th century, Ottawa was rather hesitant when the first urban rail boom came over North America in the late 1970s and 1980s, which saw numerous new-generation light rail and metro systems emerge in Canada (see Montreal, Edmonton, Calgary and Vancouver) as well as the neighbouring U.S.A. (e.g. San Francisco, Washington DC, Portland, San José, Sacramento). Instead, Ottawa opted for the 'Transitway', a network of dedicated and partly grade-separated busways. The first segments opened in 1983 between Lincoln Fields and Baseline in the southwest and between Lees and Hurdman in the east, and gradually

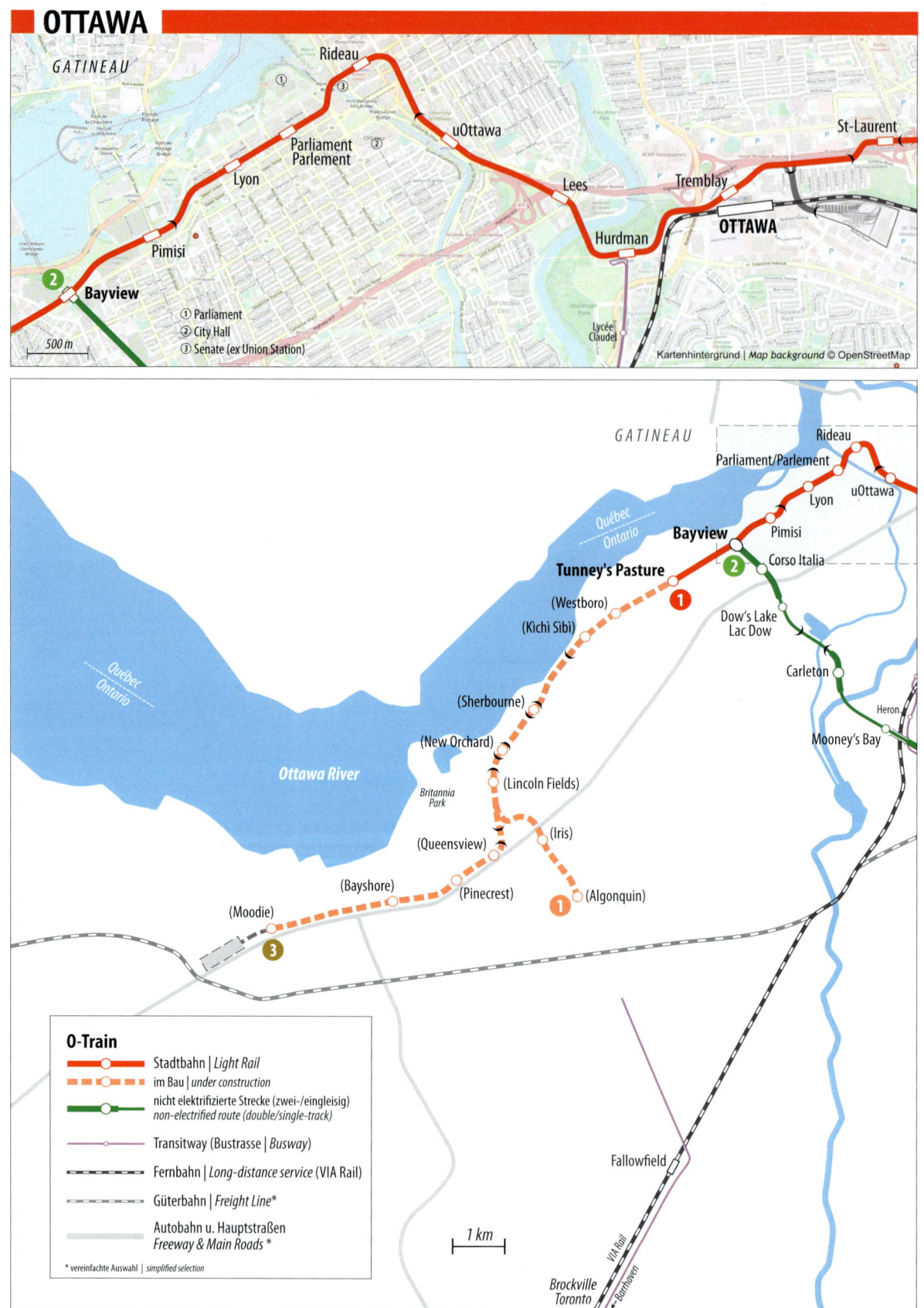

OTTAWA

GATINEAU

Rideau

uOttawa

Parliament
Parlement

Lyon

Lees

Tremblay

St-Laurent

Pimisi

Hurdman

OTTAWA

② Bayview

① Parliament
② City Hall
③ Senate (ex Union Station)

500 m

Kartenhintergrund | *Map background* © OpenStreetMap

GATINEAU

Québec
Ontario

Rideau

Parliament/Parlement

Bayview

Lyon

uOttawa

Tunney's Pasture

Pimisi

①

Corso Italia

(Westboro)

Dow's Lake
Lac Dow

(Kichì Sìbì)

②

Québec
Ontario

(Sherbourne)

Carleton

(New Orchard)

Heron

Ottawa River

Mooney's Bay

*Britannia
Park*

(Lincoln Fields)

(Queensview)

(Iris)

(Bayshore)

(Moodie)

(Pinecrest)

① (Algonquin)

③

Fallowfield

*Brockville
Toronto*

VIA Rail

Burthaven

1 km

O-Train

●━━●	Stadtbahn | *Light Rail*
○- -○	im Bau | *under construction*
●━━●	nicht elektrifizierte Strecke (zwei-/eingleisig) *non-electrified route (double/single-track)*
●──●	Transitway (Bustrasse | *Busway*)
├┤┼┤┤	Fernbahn | *Long-distance service* (VIA Rail)
┄┄┄	Güterbahn | *Freight Line**
▬▬▬	Autobahn u. Hauptstraßen *Freeway & Main Roads* *

* vereinfachte Auswahl | *simplified selection*

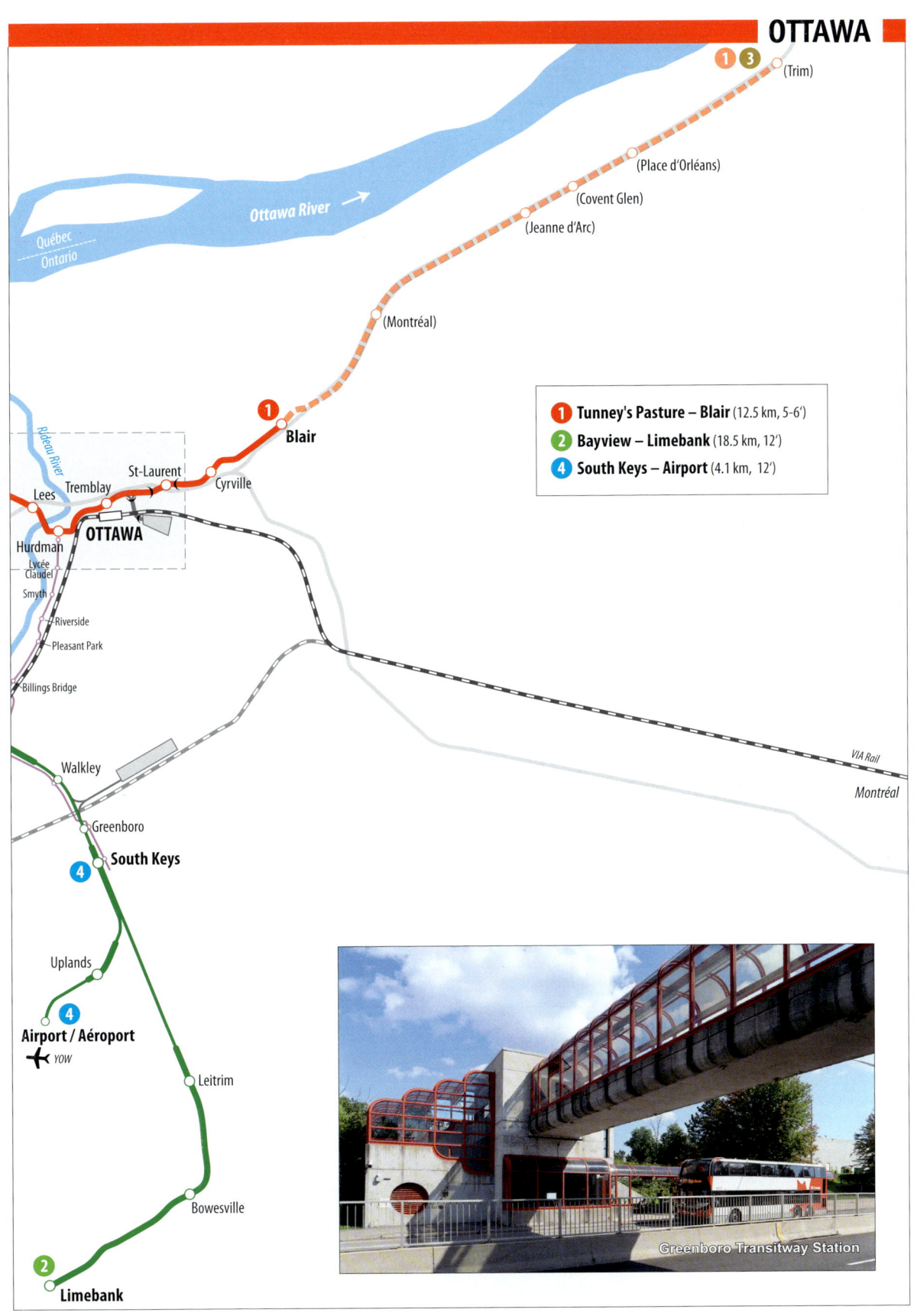

① ③ (Trim)

(Place d'Orléans)

(Covent Glen)

(Jeanne d'Arc)

Ottawa River →

Québec
Ontario

(Montréal)

① Blair

Rideau River

St-Laurent

Lees Tremblay Cyrville

OTTAWA

Hurdman

Lycée Claudel

Smyth

Riverside

Pleasant Park

Billings Bridge

VIA Rail

Montréal

Walkley

Greenboro

④ **South Keys**

Uplands

④ **Airport / Aéroport**
✈ YOW

Leitrim

Bowesville

② **Limebank**

①	**Tunney's Pasture – Blair** (12.5 km, 5-6')
②	**Bayview – Limebank** (18.5 km, 12')
④	**South Keys – Airport** (4.1 km, 12')

Greenboro Transitway Station

41

Blair – links eingehauste Treppenanlagen aus der Transitway-Zeit | *on the left, encased staircase from the Transitway period*

Lincoln Fields und Baseline im Südwesten und zwischen Lees und Hurdman im Osten eröffnet, woraus nach und nach die Durchmesserlinie 95 von Kanata und Fallowfield im Westen/Südwesten nach Orleans im Osten entstand. Durch das Stadtzentrum fuhren die Busse jedoch auf der Albert Street (Richtung Westen) bzw. der Slater Street (Richtung Osten) mit zahlreichen Straßenkreuzungen. Der südöstliche „Transitway" von Hurdman nach South Keys, heute die einzige verbliebene kreuzungsfreie Bustrasse, wurde in den 1990er Jahren auf einem ehemaligen Eisenbahngelände gebaut. Die 2011 eröffnete Bustrasse von Fallowfield nach Barrhaven Centre weist nicht nur mehrere Straßenkreuzungen auf, sondern sogar einen ebenerdigen Bahnübergang an der Strecke nach Toronto. Die meisten anderen Abschnitte wurden hingegen inzwischen zwecks Umbau zur Stadtbahn aufgegeben, darunter auch der erst 2017 fertiggestellte Abschnitt von Bayshore nach Moodie.

Ottawa unternahm 2001 einen ersten bescheidenen Versuch, eine Stadtbahn, den ursprünglichen O-Train, einzuführen, nämlich mit Dieseltriebwagen auf einer bestehenden CP-Eisenbahnstrecke zwischen Bayview und Greenboro, woraus später die Linie 2 (Trillium Line) wurde. Erst im Jahr 2012 schloss sich Ottawa schließlich mit dem Bau der Linie 1, die derzeit an beiden Enden verlängert wird, dem anhaltenden Stadtbahn-Boom in Kanada an.

the Transitway grew into a cross-city service (operated by route 95) from Kanata and Fallowfield in the west/southwest to Orleans in the east. Through the city centre, however, the buses travelled on Albert (westbound) and Slater (eastbound) Streets with numerous road intersections. The southeast Transitway from Hurdman to South Keys was built on former railway grounds in the 1990s and is the only surviving grade-separated busway in Ottawa. The busway from Fallowfield to Barrhaven Centre, opened in 2011, features several road intersections and even an at-grade crossing of the railway to Toronto, while most other sections have been closed for conversion to light rail, including the section from Bayshore to Moodie, which had only been completed in 2017.

Ottawa made a first humble attempt at urban rail in 2001 when it introduced the original O-Train, a DMU service on an existing CP railway line between Bayview and Greenboro, which would later become Line 2 (Trillium Line). Finally, in 2012, Ottawa City Council joined the ongoing urban rail boom in Canada with the approval of Line 1, which is currently being extended at both ends.

Cyrville

❶ Confederation Line

Im Dezember 2012 beschloss die Stadt Ottawa, einen Großteil des bestehenden „Transitway" in eine Stadtbahnlinie zu verwandeln. In der ersten Phase wurden ab 2013 die östliche Bustrasse von der University of Ottawa bis Blair und die westliche von LeBreton (heute Pimisi) bis Tunney's Pasture umgebaut. Durch die Innenstadt wurde jedoch eine völlig neue unterirdische Trasse anstelle der früheren Busspuren entlang der Albert Street und der Slater Street errichtet. Der Tunnelabschnitt umfasst drei U-Bahnhöfe: Lyon und Parliament unter der Queen Street sowie Rideau unter der Rideau Street im Einkaufsviertel von Ottawa.

Alle ehemaligen Busstationen wurden ausgebaut, wobei einige der ursprünglichen Elemente erhalten blieben. Die Station Hurdman wurde auf einem kurzen Hochbahnabschnitt errichtet, während die Station Tremblay (vormals Train) etwas nach Westen verlegt und die Trasse begradigt wurde. Der einst zur Unterquerung des Queensway (Teil des Trans-Canada Highway) gebaute Tunnel sowie der anschließende abgedeckelte Bahnhof St-Laurent wurden in die Stadtbahnlinie integriert. Zwischen Tremblay und St-Laurent zweigen zwei Gleise nach Süden ab und führen durch einen Tunnel unter der Belfast Road zum Betriebshof auf der Südseite der Eisenbahnanlagen.

Auf dem Westabschnitt der alten Bustrasse wurde die einzige Straßenkreuzung an der Booth Street beseitigt, indem die Stadtbahngleise in einem Einschnitt verlegt wurden und die neue Station Pimisi von beiden Seiten der neuen Straßenbrücke zugänglich gemacht wurde. Die umfassende Sanierung des Gebiets rund um diese Station ist noch im Gange (z.B. die neue Ottawa Public Library). An der Kreuzung der neuen Linie mit dem ursprünglichen

In December 2012, the Ottawa City Council decided to convert much of the existing Transitway into a light rail line. In the first phase, starting in 2013, the eastern busway from University of Ottawa to Blair and the western busway from LeBreton (now Pimisi) to Tunney's Pasture were rebuilt to accommodate the rail tracks. Through the city centre, however, a completely new underground alignment was chosen instead of the former dedicated surface bus lanes along Albert and Slater Streets. The tunnel section includes three underground stations, Lyon and Parliament beneath Queen Street, and Rideau under Rideau Street in Ottawa's shopping district.

All the former busway stations were transformed into more substantial structures, although some of the original elements have been retained. Hurdman station was built on a short elevated section and Tremblay (previously called Train) was relocated slightly west and the alignment straightened. The tunnel once built to cross under the Queensway (the Trans-Canada Highway) as well as the adjoining covered station at St-Laurent were integrated into the light rail line. Between Tremblay and St-Laurent, two tracks diverge south and into a tunnel beneath Belfast Road, leading to the depot

Confederation Line
- 12.5 km (Ⓤ 3.3 km) - 13 Stations (Ⓤ 4)

14-09-2019: Tunney's Pasture – Blair (12.5 km)
2025/26: Tunney's Pasture – Moodie / Algonquin (15 km)
Blair – Trim (12 km)

Parliament | Parlement

O-Train wurde die Station Bayview komplett von einer einfachen Bushaltestelle und einem schlichten Bahnsteig in einen bequemen Umsteigebahnhof umgebaut. Die meisten Buslinien, die früher den „Transitway" nutzten, fungieren heute als Zubringerlinien für den O-Train. Auch wenn für die Confederation Line Niederflur-Fahrzeuge gewählt wurden, kann man die Linie aufgrund ihrer gänzlich kreuzungsfreien Trassierung als Metro klassifizieren. Um zu verhindern, dass Fahrgäste die Gleise überqueren, sind an allen Bahnhöfen zwischen den Gleisen Zäune angebracht.

Wie die Eglinton Crosstown Line in Toronto könnte die Confederation Line gegebenenfalls auch ebenerdig mit Straßenkreuzungen verkehren, doch Ottawa hat sich vorerst dafür entschieden, den metro-artigen Ausbau auch auf der westlichen und östlichen Verlängerung fortzusetzen. Der Bau dieser Erweiterungen begann im Jahr 2019, direkt nach der Inbetriebnahme der ersten Linie. Auf der Oststrecke verkehren bislang Busse auf eigenen Fahrspuren der Stadtautobahn (Route 174), während der O-Train den Mittelstreifen dieser Straße nutzen wird. Dies erfordert den Bau einer Überführung östlich des Bahnhofs Blair sowie von komplett neuen Bahnhöfen, die von beiden Seiten der Schnellstraße entweder über Brücken oder Unterführungen zugänglich sein werden.

Auf der Weststrecke wird der O-Train auf der Trasse des bestehenden „Transitway" von Tunney's Pasture bis Dominion (zukünftige Station Kìchì Sìbì) weiterfahren, dann aber in einem flachen Tunnel entlang des Flusses und unter der Richmond Road verschwinden, bis er Lincoln Fields erreicht, wo sich die Weststrecke verzweigt. Die Zwischenstationen werden nicht unterirdisch, sondern teilweise offen zwischen zwei Tunnelabschnitten liegen. Ähnlich wird die dreigleisige Station Lincoln Fields direkt am Ende des

and maintenance facility on the south side of the railway line.

On the western segment of the old busway, the only road intersection at Booth Street was eliminated by putting the light rail tracks at a lower level and making the new Pimisi station accessible from either side of the new road bridge. Major redevelopment of the area around the station is still going on (e.g. the new Ottawa Public Library). At the intersection of the new line with the original O-Train, Bayview station was completely rebuilt from a simple bus stop and rail platform into a convenient interchange. Most of the bus routes formerly using the Transitway now act as feeder lines for the O-Train. Despite the low-floor light rail technology chosen for the Confederation Line, the final alignment allows it to be classified as a metro line, fully segregated from road traffic and without passengers crossing the tracks at any point. In fact, to prevent this, all the stations have fences between the tracks.

Like on Toronto's Eglinton Crosstown Line, light rail would leave the option of at-grade running with road intersections, but for now, Ottawa has chosen to continue the western and eastern extensions in metro style. The construction of these extensions started in 2019, right after the launch of the initial line. On the eastern leg, buses run on dedicated lanes on the urban motorway (route 174), while the O-Train will use the median of this road, requiring a new flyover just east of Blair station and the construction of completely new stations flanked by several road lanes on either side, and accessible from both sides via bridges or underpasses.

On the western leg, the O-Train will continue along the existing Transitway from Tunney's Pasture

Rideau – 26,5 m unter der Straßenoberfläche | 26.5 m below street level

unterirdischen Abschnitts angelegt. Von Lincoln Fields bis Algonquin wird der O-Train einen der ältesten „Transitway"-Abschnitte Ottawas nutzen. In Algonquin (vormals Baseline) wurde bereits 2010/11 ein Teil einer unterirdischen Station für die zukünftige Nutzung als Endstation der Linie 1 errichtet. Eine Verlängerung nach Barrhaven unter Nutzung der bestehenden Bustrasse wird in Erwägung gezogen.

Der Westast, auf dem die Linie 3 fahren soll, erhält einen weiteren kurzen Tunnel hinter der Busgarage Pinecrest von OC Transpo, bevor die Trasse auf die Nordseite des Highway 417 schwenkt, wo die Stationen Queensview und Pinecrest liegen werden. Letzterer war Ausgangspunkt eines weiteren „Transitway", der im Jahr 2009 Bayshore (die Station wird für den O-Train umgebaut) und erst im Jahr 2017 Moodie erreichte. Jenseits der Endstation der Linie 3

to Dominion (future Kìchì Sìbì station), but will then disappear into a shallow tunnel along the river and then Richmond Road before reaching Lincoln Fields, where the western leg will split into two branches. This section will not be fully underground, but will feature partly uncovered stations between the tunnel sections. Similarly, Lincoln Fields will be laid out with three tracks right at the end of the underground section. From Lincoln Fields to Algonquin, the O-Train will again make use of one of Ottawa's oldest Transitway sections. At Algonquin (formerly Baseline), part of a subsurface station was already built in 2010/11 for future use as the Line 1 terminus. An extension to Barrhaven taking advantage of the existing busway is being examined.

The western branch, intended to be served by Line 3,

St-Laurent

Tunney's Pasture > Bayview

Tunney's Pasture > Bayview

wird die „Moodie Light Maintenance and Storage Facility" entlang des Highway 417 angesiedelt. Langfristig könnte der O-Train über Kanata bis zur Hazeldean Road in Stittsville verlängert werden.

Die Confederation Line wird mit 39 Citadis Spirit-Straßenbahnen (Nr. 1101-1134, 1137-1141) von Alstom betrieben, die zwischen 2016 und 2019 ausgeliefert wurden. Die vierteiligen Fahrzeuge sind 100% niederflurig, 48,5 m lang und 2,65 m breit und meist in Doppeltraktion unterwegs. Sie wurden in Hornell, New York, hergestellt, aber in Kanada zusammengebaut. Weitere 33 Straßenbahnen sollen eine Taktverdichtung ermöglichen und auch den Mehrbedarf auf den Neubaustrecken abdecken. Die Züge verkehren halbautomatisch (ATO) mit dem SelTrac-Zugsteuerungssystem von Thales und erreichen eine Höchstgeschwindigkeit von 100 km/h.

will feature another short tunnel past the OC Transpo Pinecrest bus garage before the route gets aligned along the north side of Highway 417, serving Queensview and Pinecrest stations; the latter is the starting point of another Transitway which reached Bayshore in 2009 (the substantial station can be rebuilt for the O-Train) and Moodie only in 2017. Beyond the Line 3 terminus, the Moodie Light Maintenance and Storage Facility will extend alongside Highway 417. In the long term, the O-Train could be extended via Kanata to Hazeldean Road in Stittsville.

The O-Train Confederation Line is operated with a fleet of 39 Citadis Spirit trams (nos. 1101-1134, 1137-1141) from Alstom, delivered between 2016 and 2019. The 100% low-floor 4-section vehicles are 48.5 m long and 2.65 m wide and mostly run as double units. They were manufactured in Hornell, New York, but assembled in Canada. A further 33 trams are on order to increase service and operate on the extensions under construction. They are operated in semi-automatic mode using Thales' SelTrac train control system and reach a maximum speed of 100 km/h.

Lyon

Rideau

Pimisi

Tremblay > St-Laurent

Carleton > Mooney's Bay (Rideau River) – Coradia Lint   (2017 © MB-one/Wikipedia)

❷❹ Trillium Line

Der ursprüngliche 7,8 km lange O-Train wurde 2001 auf einer ungenutzten Eisenbahnstrecke der *Canadian Pacific Railway* (CPR) eingerichtet und war somit Teil des kanadischen Eisenbahnnetzes. Der vom O-Train genutzte südliche Abschnitt wurde 1855 von der *Bytown and Prescott Railway* (B&PR) eröffnet, die 1867 zur *St. Lawrence and Ottawa Railway* wurde und 1884 von der CPR übernommen wurde. Der nördliche Abschnitt der Strecke stammt aus dem Jahr 1871, als ein Abzweig zum Bahnhof Broad Street eröffnet wurde, der sich in der Nähe der heutigen Station Pimisi befand. Der Personenverkehr dorthin wurde 1920 eingestellt, als die Union Station im Stadtzentrum eröffnet wurde. Ab 1880 war der Abzweig auch mit der Prince of Wales Bridge (heute Chief William Commanda Bridge) verbunden, die von der heutigen Station Bayview über den Ottawa River nach Hull/Gatineau in Québec führte.

Der O-Train wurde als Pilotprojekt und entsprechend mit minimalem Investitionsaufwand umgesetzt. OC Transpo bestellte bei Bombardier drei 3-teilige Talent-Triebzüge der Baureihe 643 (man schloss sich dabei einer Bestellung der Deutschen Bahn an, die dieses Fahrzeug häufig auf nicht elektrifizierten Nebenstrecken einsetzt) und baute einfache Bahnsteige entlang der eingleisigen Strecke, die in Carleton auf halber Strecke zwischen Bayview und Greenboro einen Begegnungsabschnitt aufwies. Die Strecke verlief größtenteils im Einschnitt und hatte keine Bahnübergänge, verfügte jedoch über eine niveaugleiche Kreuzung mit der Hauptstrecke nach Toronto südlich des Bahnhofs Mooney's Bay sowie eine weitere nördlich des Endpunkts Greenboro mit der Walkley-Linie, auf der jedoch nur Güterverkehr

The original 7.8 km O-Train service was launched in 2001 on a disused railway line owned by the Canadian Pacific Railway (CPR), and which is thus part of the Canadian mainline network. The southern section used by the O-Train was opened in 1855 by the Bytown and Prescott Railway (B&PR), which became the St. Lawrence and Ottawa Railway in 1867 and was taken over by the CPR in 1884. The northern section of the line dates from 1871, when a spur was opened to Broad Street Station, which was located near today's Pimisi station. Passenger services there ceased in 1920 when Union Station opened in the city centre. From 1880, the spur was also linked to the Prince of Wales Bridge (today the Chief William Commanda Bridge) from today's Bayview station across the Ottawa River to Hull/Gatineau in Quebec.

The O-Train was implemented as a pilot project and with minimum investment. OC Transpo ordered three 3-car Talent class 643 DMUs from Bombardier (in fact joining a Deutsche Bahn order for this type frequently used in Germany on non-electrified regional branch lines) and built simple platforms along the line with a passing loop halfway between Bayview and Greenboro at Carleton. The line ran mostly below grade and had no level crossings, but featured a level intersection with the main line to Toronto just south of Mooney's Bay station and another with the freight-only Walkley Line just north of the Greenboro terminus. The service operated every 15 minutes with two trains, and a third in reserve.

In 2014, the line became the 'Trillium Line', named after Ontario's official flower. In 2015, the original trains were replaced by six 2-car Coradia LINT 41 sets from

Bayview

Airport/Aéroport (2023© OC Transpo)

stattfindet. Mit zwei Fahrzeugen wurde ein 15-Minuten-Takt angeboten, das dritte diente als Reserve.

Im Jahr 2014 bekam die Linie die Bezeichnung „Trillium Line", benannt nach der offiziellen Blume Ontarios, dem Dreizahn. Im Jahr 2015 wurden die ursprünglichen Fahrzeuge durch sechs zweiteilige Coradia LINT 41 von Alstom ersetzt, ebenfalls eine Baureihe, die häufig auf nicht elektrifizierten Nebenstrecken in Deutschland zu sehen ist. Zuvor war die Strecke ausgebaut worden, unter anderen mit neuen Begegnungsabschnitten zwischen Greenboro und Mooney's Bay sowie zwischen Bayview und Dow's Lake. Die Haltestellen wurden erweitert und mit Fahrkarten-schaltern ausgestattet.

Im Mai 2020 wurde die gesamte Strecke schließlich geschlossen, um sie erneut zu modernisieren und zur Limebank Road in Riverside South sowie zum Ottawa Macdonald-Cartier International Airport zu verlängern. Auf dem ursprünglichen Abschnitt bedeutete dies zusätzliche Stationen am Corso Italia (an der Gladstone Avenue) und in Walkley, eine Bahnsteigverlängerung an den bestehenden Haltestellen, eine neue Unterführung in Carleton sowie eine neue Brücke über den „Southeast Transitway" und die Eisen-bahnstrecke nach Toronto. Die Südverlängerung umfasst insgesamt 14,2 km, wovon 7,4 km auf dem alten CPR-Eisenbahnkorridor liegen, während 4 km Neubaustrecke in Richtung Südwesten durch landwirtschaftlich genutztes Gebiet nach Riverside South führen. Um Bahnübergänge zu vermeiden, wurden an der Lester und Leitrim Road zwei Brücken errichtet. Der 2,8 km lange Ast zum Flughafen zweigt etwa 1,2 km südlich der Station South Keys ab und endet an einem eingleisigen Hochbahnhof. Hier wird die Linie 4 als Shuttle zwischen South Keys und dem Flughafen verkehren, so dass die Fahrgäste zweimal umsteigen müssen, um in die Innenstadt zu gelangen.

Für die erweiterte Trillium Line bestellte OC Transpo sieben 4-Wagen-Züge der beliebten Baureihe FLIRT3 von Stadler. Diese Züge verfügen über dieselelektrische Motoren und könnten daher weiterhin eingesetzt werden, wenn sich OC Transpo eines Tages für die Elektrifizierung dieser Linie entscheidet.

Alstom, another type common on German non-electrified branch lines. By 2015, the route had been upgraded, with additional passing loops between Greenboro and Mooney's Bay as well as between Bayview and Dow's Lake. The stations were enhanced and equipped with fare gates.

In May 2020, the entire line was closed to allow for another upgrade and its extension to Limebank Road in Riverside South as well as to the Ottawa Macdonald-Cartier International Airport. On the original section this meant additional stations at Corso Italia (at Gladstone Avenue) and Walkley, platform lengthening at the existing stations, a new underpass at Carleton, and a new bridge spanning the Southeast Transitway and the railway line to Toronto. The southern extensions added a total of 14.2 km, 7.4 km of which follow the old CPR railway corridor, and 4 km is on a new alignment heading southwest through farmland to Riverside South. To avoid level crossings, two bridge structures were built at Lester and Leitrim Roads. The 2.8 km Airport branch diverges about 1.2 km south of South Keys station and ends at an elevated single-track Airport station. The Airport branch operates as Line 4, a shuttle service between South Keys and the Airport, thus obliging passengers to change trains twice to reach the city centre.

For the extended Trillium Line, OC Transpo purchased seven 4-car sets of Stadler's popular FLIRT3. These trains have diesel-electric engines, so they can still be used if OC Transpo eventually decides to electrify the line.

Trillium Line
- 22 km (Ø 0.6 km) - 13 Stations

15-10-2001: Bayview – Greenboro (7.8 km)
2024: Greenboro – Limebank (11.4 km)
South Keys – Airport (2.8 km)

Stadler Flirt3
(2022 © Reece Martin - RM Transit/Wikipedia)

Blick vom CN Tower nach Norden | *View north from the CN Tower*

TORONTO, ON

Mit rund 2,8 Mio. Einwohnern auf einer Fläche von 630 km² ist Toronto die größte Stadt Kanadas und die Hauptstadt der Provinz Ontario. Die städtische Bebauung erstreckt sich jedoch weit über die 1998 festgelegten Stadtgrenzen hinaus – „Greater Toronto" umfasst außerdem die „Regions" (Landkreise) Durham, York, Peel und Halton und hat eine Gesamtbevölkerung von 6,2 Millionen, während in der Metropolregion, der „Greater Toronto and Hamilton Area" (GTHA), dem Kern der als „Golden Horseshoe" (Goldenes Hufeisen) bekannten Region, etwa 8 Millionen Menschen leben.

Toronto liegt am Nordufer des Ontariosees und ist per Bahn mit vielen Teilen des Landes verbunden. Zwischen Windsor im Westen (am gegenüberliegenden Flussufer von Detroit) und Quebec City im Osten bietet die staatliche Bahngesellschaft *VIA Rail* einen für nordamerikanische Verhältnisse recht häufigen Zugverkehr: viermal pro Tag von Toronto nach Windsor (ca. 4h30), fünfmal nach London (~2h10/3h30), achtmal nach Ottawa (~4h45) und fünfmal nach Montreal (~5h). Um nach Quebec City zu kommen, muss hingegen in Montreal oder Ottawa umgestiegen werden. Eine direkte Verbindung gibt es jedoch zweimal pro Woche mit „The Canadian" über Winnipeg und Edmonton (ca. 2½ Tage) bis nach Vancouver (ca. 4 Tage). Der tägliche „Maple Leaf" von Amtrak verbindet Toronto mit New York City (875 km) in ca. 13 Stunden, mit Halt in Kanada in Oakville, Aldershot, Grimsby, St. Catharines und Niagara Falls (2h).

With some 2.8 million inhabitants in an area of 630 km², Toronto is the largest city in Canada and the capital of the province of Ontario. The urban area, however, spreads far beyond the city boundaries established in 1998 – Greater Toronto also includes Durham, York, Peel and Halton Regions with a combined population of 6.2 million, while the Greater Toronto and Hamilton Area (GTHA), the core of a region known as the 'Golden Horseshoe', is home to some 8 million people.

Toronto is located on the north shore of Lake Ontario, and is linked to many parts of the country by train. Between Windsor in the west (just across the river from Detroit) and Quebec City in the east, national rail operator VIA Rail runs a rail service which is quite frequent by North American standards, with four trains a day from Toronto to Windsor (~4h30m), five to London (~2h10m/3h30m), eight to Ottawa (~4h45m), and five to Montreal (~5h), while a trip to Quebec City requires a transfer at Montreal or Ottawa. A direct service, however, is provided twice a week by "The Canadian" all the way to Vancouver (~4 days) via Winnipeg and Edmonton (~2½ days). The daily international "Maple

TTC - www.ttc.ca
Metrolinx - www.metrolinx.com
GO Transit - www.gotransit.com
UP Express - www.upexpress.com

Der öffentliche Nahverkehr in der GTHA wird von Metrolinx koordiniert, einer Behörde, die 2006 gegründet wurde. Jede Stadt/Region betreibt jedoch ihr eigenes Nahverkehrsnetz, bislang ohne eine Art tariflichen Verkehrsverbund. Im Jahr 2009 führte Metrolinx die PRESTO Card ein, eine kontaktlose Smartcard, die in allen Bussen und Bahnen in der gesamten Region und auch in Ottawa akzeptiert wird. Die PRESTO Card kostet 6 $ und kann mit einem beliebigen Geldbetrag aufgeladen werden. Der Betrieb der Regional-/S-Bahnen von GO Transit untersteht direkt Metrolinx. Innerhalb der Stadt Toronto betreibt die TTC (*Toronto Transit Commission*) Busse und verschiedene Arten von städtischen Bahnen. Für das TTC-Netz ist eine Tageskarte für 13,50 $ in Form eines PRESTO-Tickets an Fahrkartenautomaten oder in Shoppers Drug Mart-Filialen erhältlich. Eine einfache Fahrt kostet 3,35 $ (3,30 $ mit PRESTO Card, inklusive Umsteigemöglichkeit innerhalb von 2 Stunden).

Für Straßenbahn- und U-Bahn-Freunde gehört Toronto sicherlich zu den Top-Städten in Nordamerika, da es alles bietet, von klassischer Straßenbahn über moderne Stadtbahn bis hin zur echten U-Bahn, außerdem ein weitreichendes Vorortbahnnetz, das derzeit zu einer richtigen S-Bahn ausgebaut wird. Auch in Toronto verkehrten einst Trolleybusse, allerdings nur von 1922 bis 1925 und erneut von 1947 bis 1993. Zwei Stadtbahnlinien, die 19 km lange „Line 5 – Eglinton" und die 10,3 km lange „Line 6 – Finch West", sollen demnächst in Betrieb genommen werden, während mehrere Strecken im Bau sind: die 9,2 km lange Eglinton West-Verlängerung, die 8 km lange U-Bahn-Verlängerung nach Scarborough, die 8 km lange

Leaf", operated by Amtrak, links Toronto to New York City (875 km) in approximately 13 hours, calling in Canada at Oakville, Aldershot, Grimsby, St. Catharines and Niagara Falls (2h).

Public transport in the GTHA is coordinated by Metrolinx, which was founded in 2006. Each city/region, however, operates its own local transport system, with no fare integration between them. In 2009, Metrolinx launched the PRESTO Card, a contactless smart card accepted on all buses and trains throughout the region, and in Ottawa, too. The PRESTO Card costs $6 and can be loaded with any amount of money. Metrolinx is directly responsible for GO Transit, the region's suburban/commuter rail service. Within the City of Toronto, the TTC (Toronto Transit Commission) runs buses and various types of urban rail lines. For the TTC network, a day pass is available for $13.50 in the form of a PRESTO Ticket from ticket vending machines or Shoppers Drug Mart stores. A single fare is $3.35 ($3.30 with PRESTO Card, including 2-hour transfer).

For tram and metro enthusiasts, Toronto is certainly one of the top cities in North America, offering everything from classic streetcar and modern light rail to genuine subway, plus an extensive commuter rail network which is being upgraded to become a proper S-Bahn/RER-style service. Trolleybuses also used to run in Toronto, but only from 1922 to 1925, and again from 1947 to 1993. Two light rail lines, the 19 km 'Line 5 - Eglinton' and the 10.3 km 'Line 6 - Finch West' are about to open, while some significant sections of new routes are under construction: the 9.2 km Eglinton West

Union Station (VIA Rail) – Haupthalle | *Main concourse*

Subway – Eglinton West (Cedarvale)

Yonge North-Verlängerung, die völlig neue 15,6 km lange Ontario Line sowie die 18 km lange Hurontario LRT – alias Hazel McCallion Line – im benachbarten Mississauga. Toronto gehört somit zweifellos weltweit zu den führenden Städten, was den Ausbau des städtischen Schienennahverkehrs angeht.

extension, the 8 km Scarborough Subway extension, the 8 km Yonge North Subway extension, the completely new 15.6 km Ontario Line, plus the 18 km Hurontario LRT - aka the Hazel McCallion Line - in neighbouring Mississauga. Toronto is thus without doubt one of the world's leading urban rail boom towns.

Streetcar – Fleet Street/Bathurst Street

GO Transit – Kitchener

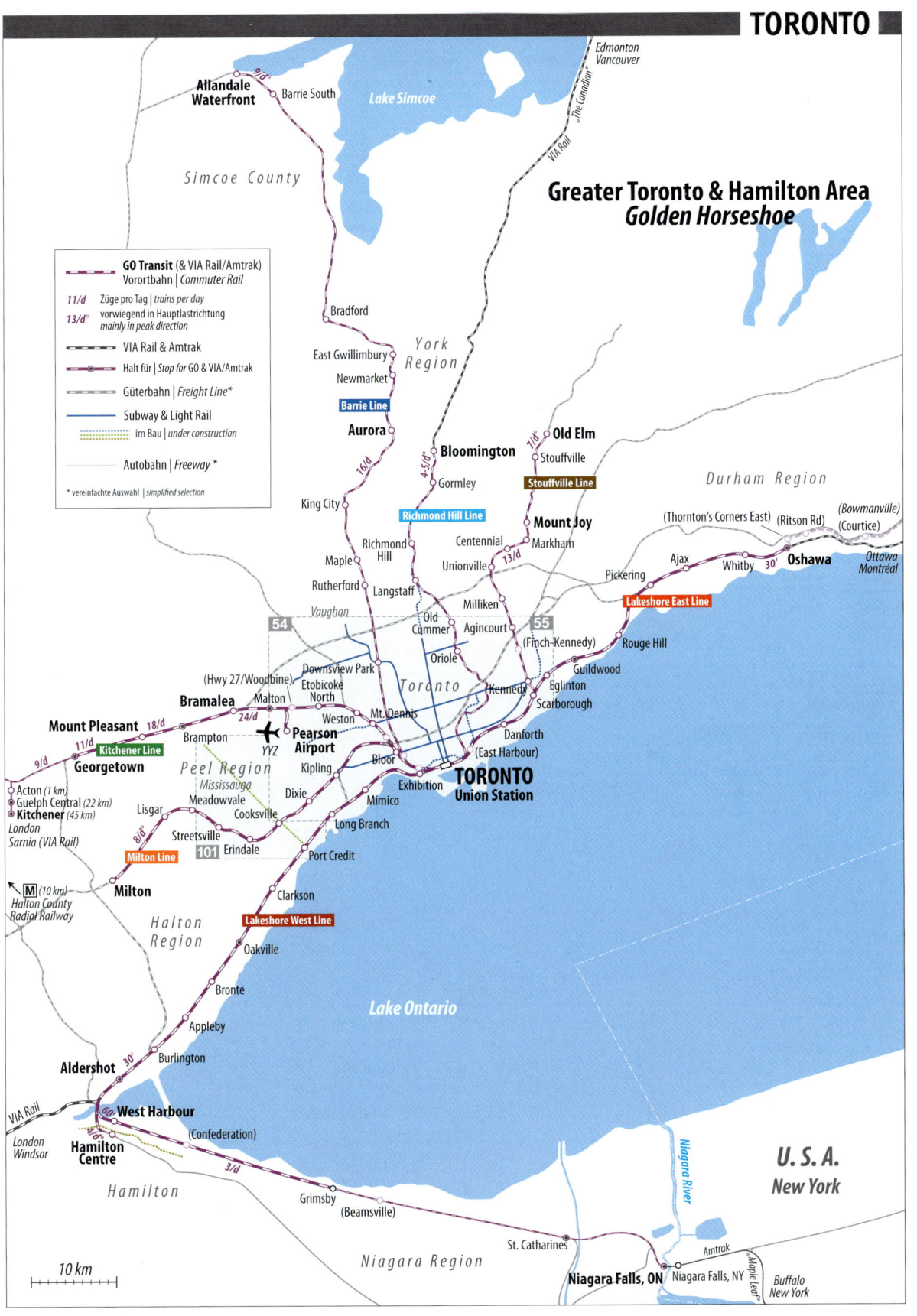

Greater Toronto & Hamilton Area
Golden Horseshoe

Legend:
- **GO Transit** (& VIA Rail/Amtrak) Vorortbahn | *Commuter Rail*
- *11/d* Züge pro Tag | trains per day
- *13/d°* vorwiegend in Hauptlastrichtung mainly in peak direction
- VIA Rail & Amtrak
- Halt für | *Stop for GO & VIA/Amtrak*
- Güterbahn | *Freight Line**
- Subway & Light Rail
- im Bau | *under construction*
- Autobahn | *Freeway **

* vereinfachte Auswahl | simplified selection

Lake Simcoe
Simcoe County
York Region
Durham Region
Peel Region
Mississauga
Vaughan
Halton Region
Lake Ontario
Hamilton
Niagara Region
U.S.A. New York

Allandale Waterfront
Barrie South
Bradford
East Gwillimbury
Newmarket
Barrie Line
Aurora
Bloomington
Gormley
King City
Richmond Hill Line
Richmond Hill
Maple
Rutherford
Langstaff
Old Elm
Stouffville
Stouffville Line
Mount Joy
Centennial
Markham
Unionville
Milliken
Agincourt
Old Cummer
Oriole
Kennedy
(Thornton's Corners East) (Ritson Rd) (Bowmanville) (Courtice)
Ajax
Whitby
Oshawa
Pickering
Lakeshore East Line
Rouge Hill
Guildwood
Eglinton
Scarborough
Danforth
(East Harbour)
TORONTO Union Station
Downsview Park
(Hwy 27/Woodbine)
Etobicoke North
Malton
Weston
Mt. Dennis
Bramalea
Mount Pleasant
18/d
Brampton
24/d
Kitchener Line
11/d
Georgetown
9/d
Acton (1 km)
Guelph Central (22 km)
Kitchener (45 km)
London Sarnia (VIA Rail)
Lisgar
Meadowvale
Cooksville
Streetsville
Erindale
Milton Line
8/d
Milton
M (10 km)
Halton County Radial Railway
★ Pearson Airport YYZ
Kipling
Dixie
Mimico
Long Branch
Bloor
Exhibition
Port Credit
Clarkson
Lakeshore West Line
Oakville
Bronte
Appleby
Burlington
Aldershot *30'*
West Harbour
(Confederation)
Hamilton Centre
3/d
Grimsby
(Beamsville)
St. Catharines
Niagara River
Niagara Falls, ON Niagara Falls, NY
Buffalo New York
Maple Leaf
Amtrak
VIA Rail London Windsor
"The Canadian" VIA Rail
Edmonton Vancouver
Ottawa Montréal

10 km

TORONTO

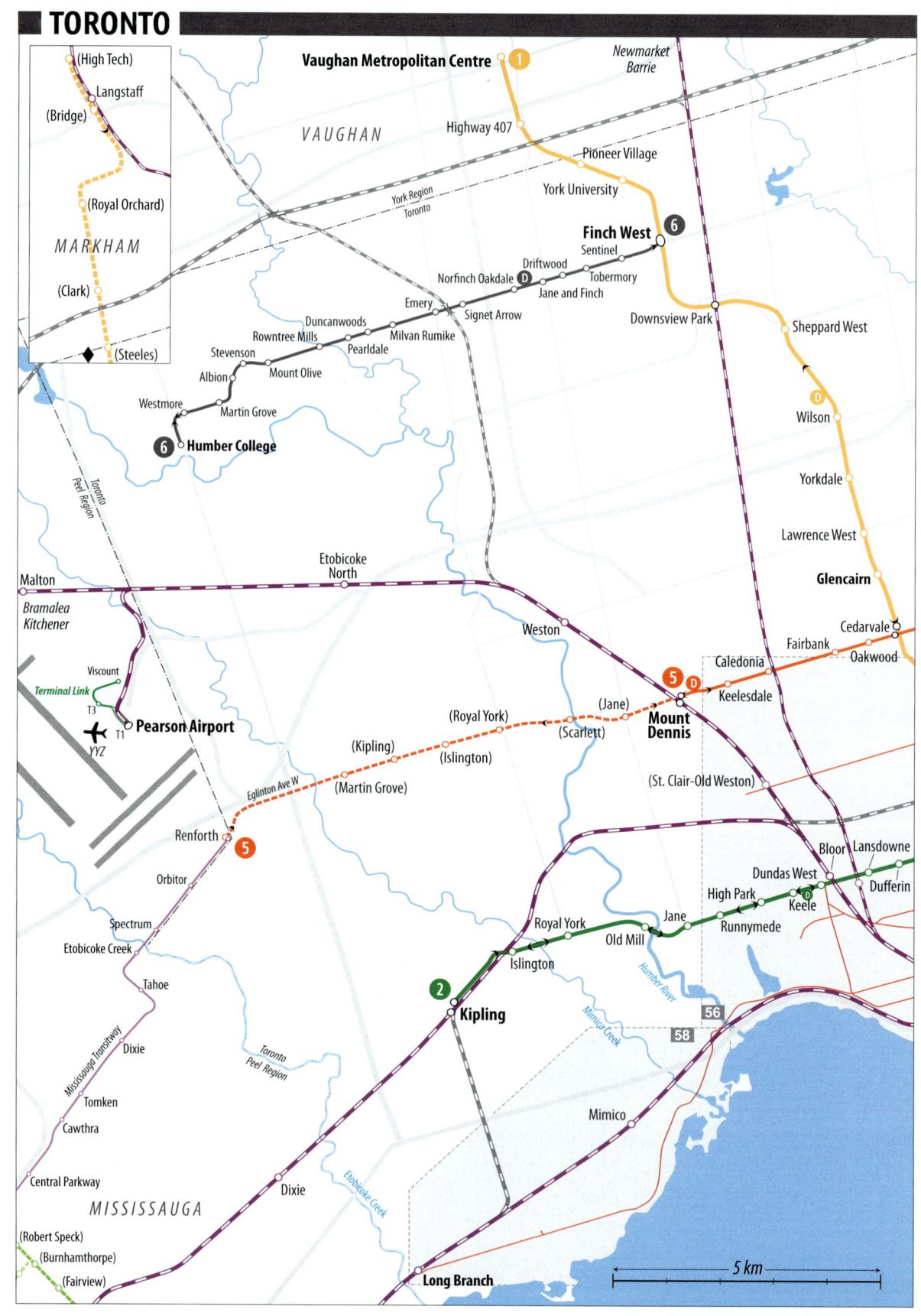

(High Tech)

Langstaff

(Bridge)

MARKHAM

(Royal Orchard)

(Clark)

(Steeles)

VAUGHAN

Vaughan Metropolitan Centre 1

Newmarket
Barrie

Highway 407

Pioneer Village

York University

Finch West 6

Sentinel

Driftwood

Norfinch Oakdale D   Tobermory

Jane and Finch

Emery

Signet Arrow

Duncanwoods

Rowntree Mills   Milvan Rumike

Stevenson   Pearldale

Albion   Mount Olive

Westmore

Martin Grove

6 Humber College

Downsview Park

Sheppard West

D

Wilson

Yorkdale

Lawrence West

Glencairn

Malton

Bramalea
Kitchener

Etobicoke
North

Weston

Cedarvale

Fairbank

Oakwood

Caledonia

5

D

Keelesdale

Mount
Dennis

Viscount

Terminal Link

T3

Pearson Airport

T1

YYZ

(Royal York)

(Jane)

(Scarlett)

(Kipling)

(Islington)

(Martin Grove)

Eglinton Ave W

(St. Clair-Old Weston)

Renforth

5

Orbitor

Spectrum

Etobicoke Creek

Tahoe

Mississauga Transitway

Dixie

Tomken

Cawtra

Central Parkway

MISSISSAUGA

(Robert Speck)

(Burnhamthorpe)

(Fairview)

Royal York

Jane

Old Mill

Runnymede

Islington

2

Kipling

Dixie

Humber River

Mimico Creek

High Park

Runnymede

Bloor   Lansdowne

Dundas West

Keele D   Dufferin

56

58

Mimico

Long Branch

Etobicoke Creek

Toronto
Peel Region

5 km

♦ (Steeles)

(opt.) (Cummer)

Old Cummer

Richmond Hill
Bloomington

Stouffville
Old Elm

proj.

(Sheppard East/
MacCowen)

① **Finch**

Agincourt

④ **Don Mills**

Scarborough Centre

McCowan

D

③ **

Bessarion

Leslie

Midland

North York Centre

Bayview

Oriole

④ **Sheppard-Yonge**

Ellesmere

(Lawrence East)

York Mills

Lawrence East

Oshawa
Eglinton

proj.

Lawrence

Scarborough

Aga Khan Park & Museum

Wynford

⑤

Birchmount Ionview

Kennedy

Sunnybrook Park

Sloane

Pharmacy Golden Mile

② ③ **

Science Centre (Flemingdon Park)

O'Connor Hakimi Lebovic

Laird

Eglinton Ave E

Leaside

Warden

Chaplin

Eglinton

(Thorncliffe Park)

Scarborough

Avenue

Mount Pleasant

Forest Hill

Victoria Park

Davisville D

57 58

St. Clair West

St. Clair

(Cosburn)

Woodbine

Main Street

Summerhill

Greenwood

Danforth

Rosedale

Chester

Coxwell

Dupont

Sherbourne

Broadview

Pape Donlands D

Spadina St. George Bay

Castle Frank

(Gerrard)

Bathurst Museum

Bloor-Yonge

Christie Ossington

Queen's Park

Wellesley

(Riverside/Leslieville)

College

Dundas (Moss Park)

(Queen/Spadina)

St. Patrick

Osgoode

(East Harbour)

(King/Bathurst)

Queen

King

(Corktown)

St. Andrew

Union

TORONTO
Union Station

Exhibition

Lake Ontario

① **Vaughan Metropolitan Centre – Finch**
② **Kipling – Kennedy**
③ **Kennedy – McCowan** **
④ **Sheppard-Yonge – Don Mills**
⑤ **Mount Dennis – Kennedy**
⑥ **Humber College – Finch West**

** außer Betrieb seit
out of service since 24-07-2023

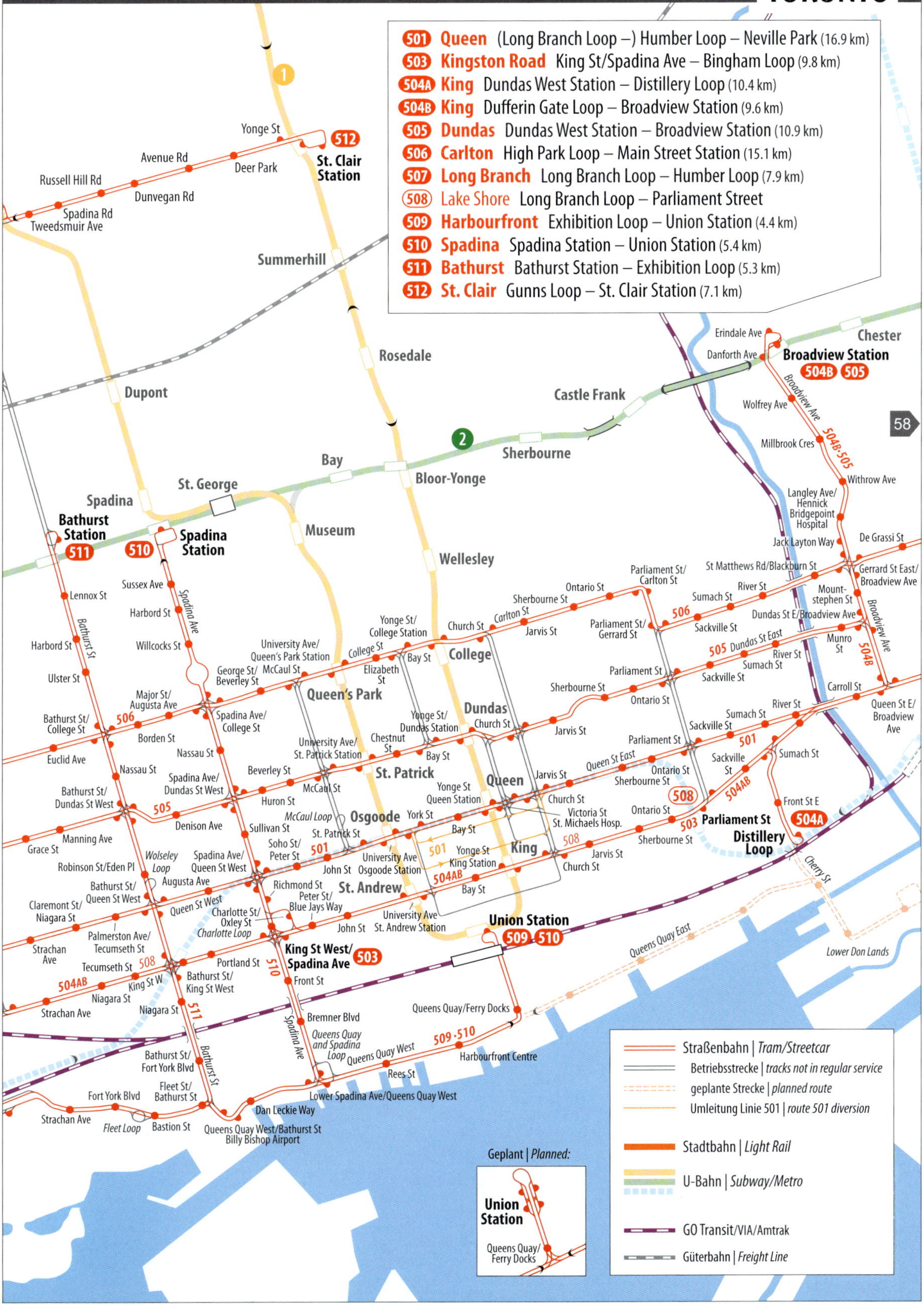

501 Queen (Long Branch Loop –) Humber Loop – Neville Park (16.9 km)
503 Kingston Road King St/Spadina Ave – Bingham Loop (9.8 km)
504A King Dundas West Station – Distillery Loop (10.4 km)
504B King Dufferin Gate Loop – Broadview Station (9.6 km)
505 Dundas Dundas West Station – Broadview Station (10.9 km)
506 Carlton High Park Loop – Main Street Station (15.1 km)
507 Long Branch Long Branch Loop – Humber Loop (7.9 km)
508 Lake Shore Long Branch Loop – Parliament Street
509 Harbourfront Exhibition Loop – Union Station (4.4 km)
510 Spadina Spadina Station – Union Station (5.4 km)
511 Bathurst Bathurst Station – Exhibition Loop (5.3 km)
512 St. Clair Gunns Loop – St. Clair Station (7.1 km)
Straßenbahn | Tram/Streetcar
Betriebsstrecke | tracks not in regular service
geplante Strecke | planned route
Umleitung Linie 501 | route 501 diversion
Stadtbahn | Light Rail
U-Bahn | Subway/Metro
GO Transit/VIA/Amtrak
Güterbahn | Freight Line
Geplant | Planned:
Union Station
Queens Quay/ Ferry Docks
St. Clair Station
Yonge St
Deer Park
Avenue Rd
Dunvegan Rd
Russell Hill Rd
Spadina Rd
Tweedsmuir Ave
Summerhill
Rosedale
Dupont
Bay
Bloor-Yonge
Sherbourne
Castle Frank
Chester
Broadview Station
Erindale Ave
Danforth Ave
Wolfrey Ave
Broadview Ave
Millbrook Cres
Withrow Ave
58
St. George
Spadina
Bathurst Station
Spadina Station
Museum
Wellesley
College
Queen's Park
Dundas
St. Patrick
Queen
Osgoode
King
St. Andrew
Union Station
King St West/ Spadina Ave
Parliament St
Distillery Loop
Cherry St
Lower Don Lands
Queens Quay East
Queens Quay West
Queens Quay/Ferry Docks
Harbourfront Centre
Rees St
Lower Spadina Ave/Queens Quay West
Queens Quay West/Bathurst St
Billy Bishop Airport
Dan Leckie Way
Fleet Loop
Bastion St
Fort York Blvd
Strachan Ave
Fleet St/ Bathurst St
Bathurst St/ Fort York Blvd
Queens Quay and Spadina Loop
Bremner Blvd
Front St
Bathurst St/ King St West
Niagara St
King St W
Tecumseth St
Strachan Ave
Palmerston Ave/ Tecumseth St
Portland St
Charlotte St/ Oxley St
Charlotte Loop
Queen St West
Claremont St/ Niagara St
Bathurst St/ Queen St West
Augusta Ave
Spadina Ave/ Queen St West
Wolseley Loop
Robinson St/Eden Pl
Grace St
Manning Ave
Bathurst St/ Dundas St West
Denison Ave
Spadina Ave/ Dundas St West
Nassau St
Euclid Ave
Bathurst St/ College St
Borden St
Major St/ Augusta Ave
Spadina Ave/ College St
Ulster St
Harbord St
Willcocks St
Lennox St
Sussex Ave
Bathurst St
Spadina Ave
George St/ Beverley St
McCaul St
University Ave/ Queen's Park Station
College St
Yonge St/ College Station
Elizabeth St
Bay St
Church St
Carlton St
Jarvis St
Sherbourne St
Ontario St
Parliament St/ Carlton St
Parliament St/ Gerrard St
St Matthews Rd/Blackburn St
River St
Sumach St
Sackville St
Dundas St E/Broadview Ave
Dundas St East
Munro St
Mount-stephen St
Gerrard St East/ Broadview Ave
De Grassi St
Jack Layton Way
Langley Ave/ Hennick Bridgepoint Hospital
Carroll St
Queen St E/ Broadview Ave
Front St E
Queen St East
University Ave/ St. Patrick Station
Chestnut St
Yonge St/ Dundas Station
Beverley St
Huron St
Sullivan St
McCaul Loop
Soho St/ Peter St
St. Patrick St
York St
University Ave/ Osgoode Station
John St
Yonge St/ Queen Station
Victoria St St. Michaels Hosp.
Yonge St/ King Station
Richmond St
Peter St/ Blue Jays Way
University Ave/ St. Andrew Station

TORONTO

Victoria Park

Main Street Station 506

Danforth Ave

Woodbine

Danforth

Coxwell

Gerrard St East/
Main St

Greenwood

Norwood Rd

Glenmount Park Rd

Golfview Ave

Bingham Loop
503

Donlands

Woodbine Ave

Kingston Rd

Malvern Ave

Kingsmount Park Rd

Main St

Pape

Bowmore Rd

Lee Ave

Waverley Rd

Coxwell Ave/
Gerrard St East

Beaton Ave

Elmer Ave

501
Neville Park Loop

57

Gerrard St East/
Coxwell Ave

Woodfield Rd

Woodbine Ave

Beech Ave

Silver Birch Ave

Greenwood Ave

Ashdale
Ave

Queen St East

Glen Manor Drive

Alton Ave

Gerrard St East

Dundas St/
Dixon Ave

Elmer Ave

Wineva Ave

Jones Ave

Leslie St

Woodbine
Loop

501

Woodbine Ave

Bellefair Ave

Logan
Ave

Carlaw
Ave

Marjory Ave

Queen St/
Kingston Rd

Lockwood Rd/
Sarah Ashbridge Ave

Queen-Coxwell Loop

501
507
Humber
Loop

506

Pape Ave

Coxwell Ave

2111
Lake
Shore
Blvd W

Greenwood Ave

Queen St East

Woodfield Rd

501·507

2155
Lake
Shore
Blvd West

Brooklyn Ave/
Caroline Ave

Leslie St

Alton Ave

508

Park Lawn Rd

Carlaw Ave 503

Jones
Ave

Russell Carhouse

Legion Rd

501

Pape Ave

Louisa St

Logan Ave

Burlington St

Empire
Ave

Mimico

Leslie Barns

Superior Ave

Boulton Ave/
Saulter St

Mimico Ave

Lake Shore Blvd West

(East Harbour)

Hillside Ave/
Norris Cres

Symons St/
Miles rd

Royal Oak Rd

1st St

3rd St

5th St

Islington Ave/
7th St

10th St

Kipling Loop

13th St

15th St

Kipling Ave/
Colonel Samuel Smith Park Dr

23rd St

27th St

29th St

Lake Shore Blvd West

31st St

37th St

Long Branch Ave

Long
Branch

501 507 508

Long Branch Loop

56

2

Flexity #4585 @ Bathurst Street (Fort York Blvd > Niagara St)

Toronto Streetcar

Mit einer Gesamtstreckenlänge von rund 83 km (nur Strecken mit regulärem Personenverkehr eingerechnet) verfügt Toronto über das größte klassische Straßenbahnnetz in Nordamerika. Das Netz wird ergänzt durch mehrere Verbindungsstrecken, die nicht im regulären Betrieb genutzt werden, aber für Umleitungen bei Gleisbauarbeiten oder anderen Störungen zur Verfügung stehen.

Das heutige Netz besteht aus 11 regulären Linien (504A und 504B getrennt gezählt) sowie der Linie 508, die nur während der Hauptverkehrszeit eingesetzt wird. Neben den zugewiesenen Liniennummern hat jede Linie auch einen Namen, der sich normalerweise auf die Straße bezieht, auf der die Linie die Innenstadt durchquert, z.B. „501 Queen"; eine Ausnahme bildet „506 Carlton", da diese Linie hauptsächlich auf der College Street durch die innere Stadt fährt. „504 King" wird als zwei separate Linien betrieben, die sich auf dem zentralen Abschnitt überlappen. Mit 16,9 km ist die Linie „501 Queen" die längste, auch nachdem die Linie „507 Long Branch", mit der sie 28 Jahre lang verknüpft war, im November 2023 wieder als eigenständige Linie eingeführt wurde. Heute fährt die Linie 501 nur spätabends bis Long Branch weiter. Die in der Liste fehlende Linie war die „502 Downtowner", die einst zwischen Bingham Loop und McCaul Loop im Stadtzentrum verkehrte, bevor ihre Fahrten 2019 in den Fahrplan der „503 Kingston Road" eingegliedert wurden. Die Linien 510 und 512 verkehren alle 5 Minuten, der Rest mindestens alle 10 Minuten.

Die meisten Straßenbahnlinien Torontos verdienen diese Bezeichnung, da sie weiterhin auf der Straße im Mischverkehr mit dem übrigen Verkehr unterwegs sind.

With a total route length of roughly 83 km (counting just the segments with regular passenger service), Toronto boasts the largest classic streetcar/tram system in North America. The network also has several links not used in regular service but available for diversions during track work or other disruptions.

The present system comprises 11 regular lines (counting 504A and 504B separately), plus route 508, which only operates during rush hour. Besides the assigned numbers, each route also has a name, usually the main road it runs along, such as '501 Queen'; an exception is '506 Carlton', which primarily uses College Street through the downtown area. Route '504 King' is operated as two separate lines, which overlap on the central portion of the route. At 16.9 km, route '501 Queen' is the longest, even after route '507 Long Branch', which had been part of route 501 for 28 years, was reinstated in November 2023; line 501 now only runs through to Long Branch in the late evening. The number missing from the list is the '502 Downtowner', which used to run between Bingham Loop and McCaul Loop in the city centre before its journeys were integrated into the '503 Kingston Road' timetable in 2019. Lines 510 and 512 operate every 5 minutes, while all the other lines run at least every 10 minutes.

Most of Toronto's streetcar routes deserve this designation as they continue to run on-street with other traffic. Only the following sections have a dedicated right-of-way, mostly in the median of the street: the entire '509 Harbourfront' route; the entire '510 Spadina' route; the entire '512 St. Clair' route; the

Flexity #4564 @ Dundas St/Yonge St

Nur die folgenden Abschnitte haben einen eigenen Gleiskörper, meist im Mittelstreifen der Straße: die Linien 509, 510 und 512 jeweils auf gesamter Länge, die Linie 501 auf dem Westabschnitt entlang des Queensway zwischen Glendale Avenue und Humber Loop und schließlich der neueste Abschnitt des Netzes, der kurze Abzweig zur Distillery Loop, der im Juni 2016 eröffnet wurde und am östlichen Rand der Sumach Street und der Cherry Street verläuft. Auf all diesen Abschnitten findet man auch Bahnsteige mit Unterständen und Infotafeln, während die meisten anderen Haltestellen nur durch eine an einer Stange am Straßenrand angebrachten Infotafel zu erkennen sind und von der Straße aus eingestiegen werden muss. Inzwischen wurden jedoch an mehreren Orten schmale Bahnsteige errichtet, die vom Autoverkehr umfahren werden müssen. Auf der Linie 504 entlang der Roncesvalles Avenue wurde 2010 ein Radweg mit erhöhten Abschnitten angelegt, die als Bahnsteige dienen (sogenannte „Bumpouts"). Straßenbahnhaltestellen sind in der Regel nach der nächsten Querstraße benannt und können demnach je nach Richtung unterschiedlich heißen. Während Straßenbahnen in Boston, San Francisco und Philadelphia hauptsächlich dank ihrer Tunnel durch die Innenstadt überlebt haben, wurden die unterirdischen Haltestellen in Toronto in erster Linie zwecks besserem Übergang zur U-Bahn gebaut. Im 600 m langen Tunnel unter der Bay Street zwischen der Union Station und dem Hafen liegt eine unterirdische Zwischenhaltestelle Queens Quay, eine einfache U-Strab-Station, in der die Fahrgäste die Gleise überqueren dürfen, weshalb Straßenbahnen Richtung Union Station vor der Einfahrt in die Station anhalten müssen.

'501 Queen' route on its western segment along The Queensway between Glendale Avenue and Humber Loop, and finally, the newest section of the network, the short branch to Distillery Loop, which opened in June 2016 and runs along the eastern side of Sumach and Cherry Streets. These sections with dedicated rights-of-way also feature proper platforms with shelters and info panels, whereas many of the other stops can only be identified by an info plate mounted on a pole on the side of the road, and with boarding from street level. At several locations, however, narrow boarding platforms have been built, with cars obliged to drive around them. On route 504 along Roncesvalles Avenue, a bike lane was established in 2010 featuring raised sections that function as streetcar platforms (so-called 'bumpouts'). Streetcar stops are usually named after the next intersecting street, and so the names may vary for each direction. While streetcars in Boston, San Francisco and Philadelphia have survived primarily because of their tunnels through the downtown area, Toronto's streetcar network also includes several underground stops, but they were essentially built to improve interchange with the Subway; the 600 m tunnel beneath Bay Street between Union Station and the harbourfront includes an intermediate underground stop at Queens Quay, a simple station in which passengers are allowed to cross the tracks, forcing inbound trams to stop before entering the station.

TRC #578 @ Yonge St/Queen St – Anfang des 20. Jahrhunderts | *in the early 20th century*   (City Of Toronto Archives)

● **Entwicklung des Straßenbahnnetzes**

Die **Toronto Street Railway** (TSR) eröffnete bereits 1861 die erste Pferdestraßenbahn der Stadt und des ganzen Landes. Sie fuhr von der Yorkville Town Hall im Bereich Bloor/Yonge Street über die Yonge Street und die King Street zum St. Lawrence Market an der Front/Jarvis Street. Bald darauf folgte eine zweite Linie entlang der Queen Street. Die TSR entschied sich für die ungewöhnliche Spurweite von 1495 mm (frühe Quellen sprechen auch von 1499 mm). In den 1870er und 1880er Jahren kam es zu erheblichen Erweiterungen, so dass die damalige Stadt Toronto 1890 bereits ein dichtes Straßenbahnnetz besaß. 1891 wurde die TSR von der **Toronto Railway Company** (TRC) abgelöst, die 1892 den elektrischen Straßenbahnbetrieb aufnahm. Bis 1894 wurden alle bestehenden Strecken elektrifiziert.

Die ebenfalls aus der Zeit der Pferdebahnen stammende *Metropolitan Street Railway* startete 1885 eine Überlandlinie von einem Punkt in der Nähe der heutigen U-Bahn-Station Summerhill nach Norden entlang der Yonge Street bis zur Eglinton Avenue. Der elektrische Betrieb auf dieser Strecke begann bereits 1890, und nach mehreren Verlängerungen nach Norden über Richmond Hill, Aurora und Newmarket erreichte die Bahn 1909 Sutton am Lake Simcoe. Zuvor war die Strecke 1904 Teil der *Toronto & York Radial Railway* geworden (T&YRR), die auch andere Überlandlinien in der Region um Toronto betrieb. Darunter befand sich auch die „Mimico Radial Line", die 1890 von der *Toronto and Mimico Electric Railway* eröffnet wurde und einst von Sunnyside bis nach Port Credit führte. Der Abschnitt bis Long Branch wurde später Teil der „Lake Shore Line (heute Linie 507). Auf der anderen Seite der Stadt eröffnete 1893 die *Toronto*

● *Evolution of the streetcar network*

*The **Toronto Street Railway** (TSR) opened the city's and the country's first horse-drawn streetcar in as early as 1861, running from Yorkville Town Hall at Bloor/Yonge Streets to St. Lawrence Market at Front/Jarvis Streets via Yonge and King Streets. This was soon followed by a second route along Queen Street. The TSR chose the unusual track gauge of 1495 mm (early sources also mention 1499 mm). Major expansion took place during the 1870s and 80s, and by 1890, a dense network of streetcar routes criss-crossed what was then the City of Toronto. In 1891, the TSR was succeeded by the **Toronto Railway Company** (TRC), which started electric streetcar service in 1892. By 1894, all the existing routes had been electrified.*

Also dating back to the horsetram era, the Metropolitan Street Railway started an interurban line in 1885 which ran from a point near today's Summerhill Subway station north along Yonge Street to Eglinton Avenue. Electric service on this route began in as early as 1890 and after several extensions north via Richmond Hill, Aurora and Newmarket it reached Sutton on Lake Simcoe in 1909. Prior to that in 1904, the line had become part of the Toronto & York Radial Railway (T&YRR), which also operated other interurban lines through the region around Toronto. Among them was the Mimico Radial Line, which was opened in 1890 by the Toronto and Mimico Electric Railway and once extended from Sunnyside all the way to Port Credit. The section up to Long Branch would later become part of the Lake Shore Line (now route 507). On the other side of town in 1893, the Toronto and Scarboro' Electric Railway (from 1904 part of the T&YRR) launched a

PCC #4614 & 4608, CLRV #4116 @ Sunnyside

(1995 © Bernhard Kußmagk)

and Scarboro' Electric Railway (ab 1904 Teil der T&YRR) eine Radiallinie entlang der Kingston Road, eine Vorgängerlinie der heutigen Linie 503.

Während sich das Stadtgebiet durch Eingliederung benachbarter Dörfer und Gemeinden ausdehnte, weigerte sich die private TRC, Strecken in diese neuen Gebiete zu bauen, weshalb die Stadt 1912 ihre eigene Straßenbahngesellschaft, die **Toronto Civic Railways** (TCR), gründete. Bis 1915 nahm die TCR mehrere Strecken in Betrieb, die später zu einem wichtigen Teil des Netzes wurden, z.B. auf der Gerrard Street East von der Greenwood Avenue zur Main Street; auf der Danforth Avenue von Broadview nach Osten bis zur Stadtgrenze an der Luttrell Avenue; auf der St. Clair Avenue West von der Lansdowne Avenue zur Yonge Street; entlang der Bloor Street West (bis zur Runnymede Road).

radial line along Kingston Road, a predecessor of today's route 503.

*As the city expanded by annexing neighbouring villages and townships, the private TRC refused to build new lines to these areas, and therefore the city formed its own streetcar company in 1912, the **Toronto Civic Railways** (TCR). By 1915, the TCR had opened several routes which would later become an important part of the network, e.g. on Gerrard Street East from Greenwood Avenue to Main Street; on Danforth Avenue from Broadview east to the city border at Luttrell Avenue; on St. Clair Avenue West from Lansdowne Avenue to Yonge Street; and along Bloor Street West (to Runnymede Road).*

The TRC's franchise was not extended, and it expired in 1921 when all streetcar services were united to form

PCC #4336 @ Carlton St/Yonge St   (1985 © B. Kußmagk)

ALRV #4212 @ The Queensway/Roncesvalles Ave
(2017 © Bernhard Kußmagk)

CLRV #4104 @ Exhibition Loop

(2017 © Robert Barrows)

Die Konzession der TRC wurde nicht verlängert und lief 1921 aus, woraufhin alle Straßenbahnlinien in der neuen städtischen *Toronto Transportation Commission* (seit 1954 **Toronto Transit Commission** – TTC) vereint wurden. Im Jahr 1927 übernahm die TTC auch den Betrieb einiger Radialstrecken von der T&YRR und errichtete Gleisverbindungen zu ihrem eigenen Netz. Nach dem Zweiten Weltkrieg, als die meisten nordamerikanischen Städte ihre Straßenbahnbetriebe aufgaben, erwarb Toronto zahlreiche PCC-Wagen in gutem Zustand aus Cleveland, Birmingham, Kansas City und Cincinnati. 1954 ersetzten Kanadas erste U-Bahn-Linie sowie einige daran anschließende Obuslinien die wichtige Straßenbahnstrecke entlang der Yonge Street, und 1966, mit der Eröffnung der Ost-West-U-Bahn, verschwanden die Straßenbahnen auch aus dem Straßenzug Bloor-Danforth; im selben Jahr beschloss sogar

*the new municipal Toronto Transportation Commission (since 1954 the **Toronto Transit Commission** - TTC). In 1927, the TTC took over operations of some of T&YRR's radial routes and connected them physically to their own network. After World War II, Toronto took advantage of the fact that most North American cities were abandoning their streetcar systems, and acquired many PCC cars in good condition from Cleveland, Birmingham, Kansas City and Cincinnati. By 1954, the important route along Yonge Street had been replaced by Canada's first Subway line and some connecting trolleybus routes, and in 1966, with the opening of the east-west Subway, streetcars disappeared from the Bloor-Danforth corridor; that same year, even Toronto decided to phase out streetcar operation by 1980. This decision encountered strong public opposition, and so in the end large parts of the*

Flexity #4404 (mit Stangenstromabnehmer | *with trolley pole*)
@ King St/Queen St (2017 © Bernhard Kußmagk)

Flexity #4482 (mit Stangenstromabnehmer | *with trolley pole*)
& CLRV #4191@ Main Street Station (2017 © Robert Barrows)

Flexity #4518 @ St. Clair West (Richtung Osten | *eastbound*)

Toronto, den Straßenbahnbetrieb bis 1980 ganz einzustellen. Diese Entscheidung stieß auf starken öffentlichen Widerstand, so dass am Ende große Teile des klassischen Straßenbahnnetzes erhalten blieben. In den späten 1970er Jahren bekam die TTC neue Fahrzeuge, die CLRVs und ALRVs, die das Bild des „Toronto Streetcar" über mehrere Jahrzehnte prägten. Bis zur Eröffnung der Harbourfront-Linie mit ihrem Tunnel an der Union Station im Jahr 1989 wurden jedoch keine neuen Strecken gebaut. Diese Strecke wurde 1997 entlang der Spadina Avenue nach Norden verlängert, also auf einer Strecke, wo der Straßenbahnbetrieb 1948 eingestellt worden war. Im Jahr 2000 wurde die Harbourfront-Linie nach Westen bis zur Bathurst Street verlängert und die heutige Linie „509 Harbourfront" eingeführt; die Exhibition Loop (bis 1996 weiter südlich gelegen) war erstmals im Jahr 1916 durch die Straßenbahn

classic streetcar network survived. The late 1970s saw the arrival of new rolling stock, the CLRVs and ALRVs, which would shape the image of the Toronto Streetcar for several decades. No new routes were built, however, until the Harbourfront line with its tunnel at Union Station opened in 1989. This route was extended north along Spadina Avenue in 1997, on a route where streetcar operation had ceased in 1948. In 2000, the Harbourfront route was extended west to Bathurst Street, introducing today's '509 Harbourfront' service; though located further south until 1996, Exhibition Loop had first been served by streetcars from Bathurst Street back in 1916. By the mid-2030s, a similar route is planned to serve the East Bayfront area now under redevelopment, including a completely rebuilt underground loop with four stop positions at Union Station. The latest addition to the

McCaul Loop

#4500 @ Roncesvalles Ave/Queen St West

![Queens Quay]

Queens Quay

von der Bathurst Street aus angeschlossen worden. Bis Mitte der 2030er Jahre ist eine ähnliche Strecke in das Entwicklungsgebiet East Bayfront geplant, gleichzeitig soll die unterirdische Schleife an der Union Station komplett umgebaut werden und vier Haltepositionen bekommen. Die jüngste Netzerweiterung war die Cherry Street-Strecke zur Distillery Loop im Jahr 2016, die möglicherweise auch zur Villiers Island in den Lower Don Lands verlängert wird. Am westlichen Seeufer soll die Exhibition Loop mit der Dufferin Gate Loop verbunden werden. Langfristig könnte die Waterfront-Linie entlang des Lake Shore Boulevard nach Westen verlängert werden.

Für ein Netz dieser Größe war und ist der Fuhrpark der Straßenbahn von Toronto meist recht homogen. Von den Anfängen der TTC-Ära bis 1965 fuhren auf Torontos Straßen rund 575 maßgeschneiderte Peter-Witt-Wagen.

system was the Cherry Street line to Distillery Loop in 2016, which may eventually also be extended to Villiers Island in the Lower Don Lands. Still on the waterfront, the Exhibition Loop is to be linked to the Dufferin Gate Loop. In the long term, the waterfront line may be extended west along Lake Shore Boulevard West.

For a system of this size, Toronto's streetcar network has long been operated with a rather homogenous fleet. From the early days of the TTC era until 1965, some 575 customised Peter Witt cars ran on Toronto's streets. These were joined from 1938 by a total of 745 PCC (Presidents' Conference Committee) streetcars, then the standard streetcar in North America. In a rebuilt form, some PCC cars remained in regular service until 1995, while others were replaced from 1979 by Toronto's standard 'Canadian Light Rail Vehicle' (CLRV), of which 196

Spadina

Union Station Loop

Flexity #4469 @ Bathurst St/Lakeshore Blvd West (Fleet St)

Ab 1938 kamen insgesamt 745 PCC-Wagen (Presidents' Conference Committee) hinzu, damals das Standard-Fahrzeug in Nordamerika. In umgebauter Form blieben einige PCC-Wagen bis 1995 im regulären Dienst, andere wurden ab 1979 durch Torontos Standardfahrzeug, das „Canadian Light Rail Vehicle" (CLRV), ersetzt, von dem bis 1981 insgesamt 196 Fahrzeuge geliefert wurden. 1988/89 folgten 52 Gelenkfahrzeuge, die „Articulated Light Rail Vehicles" (ALRV). Zwischen 2014 und 2019 wurden schließlich alle CLRVs und ALRVs von Torontos neuem Standardfahrzeug, dem Flexity Outlook von Bombardier (jetzt Alstom), abgelöst.

Der im Jahr 2009 bestellte Flexity Outlook musste für Toronto einige besondere Anforderungen erfüllen, z.B. Einrichtungsbetrieb, Stromversorgung (600 V DC) mithilfe eines Stangenstromabnehmers anstelle des weltweit genutzten Bügelstromabnehmers oder Betrieb auf Breitspur von 1495 mm anstelle der sonst üblichen 1435 mm Normalspurweite. Die zu 100% niederflurigen Fahrzeuge sind 30,3 m lang und 2,54 m breit und bestehen aus fünf Segmenten, um die engen Kurven zu bewältigen. Trotz der Verwendung einer Oberleitungsstange wurden die Flexity-Bahnen für eine zukünftige Umrüstung auch mit einem Bügelstromabnehmer ausgestattet. Auch wenn das erste Fahrzeug bereits im September 2012 aus dem Bombardier-Werk in Thunder Bay geliefert wurde, konnten die neuen Straßenbahnen erst im August 2014 in den regulären Betrieb gehen. Im Jahr 2015 wurde im Osten der Stadt ein neuer Betriebshof, die „Leslie Barns", für die neue Flotte eröffnet. Im September 2017 wurde auf der Strecke „509 Harbourfront" erstmals ein Bügelstromabnehmer anstelle der Oberleitungsstange eingesetzt, heute ist das auf allen Strecken der Fall. Trotz

vehicles were delivered until 1981, followed by a total of 52 'Articulated Light Rail Vehicles' (ALRVs) in 1988/89. Eventually, between 2014 and 2019, all the CLRVs and ALRVs were replaced by Toronto's new standard vehicle, the Flexity Outlook from Bombardier (now Alstom).

Ordered in 2009, Toronto's Flexity Outlook had to meet some special requirements, such as unidirectional operation, power supply (600 V DC) using a trolley pole rather than the typical pantograph, and operation on Toronto's broad gauge of 1495 mm instead of the typical 1435 mm standard gauge. The 100% low-floor tailor-made vehicles are 30.3 m long and 2.54 m wide, and made up of five sections to negotiate the tight curves. Despite the use of a trolley pole, the Flexity trams were equipped with a pantograph too to allow for future conversion. With the first vehicle delivered from Bombardier's

Flexity

Flexity #4461 @ St. Clair Ave West/Wychwood Ave

einiger Verzögerungen wurden bis Januar 2020 alle 204 bestellten Fahrzeuge (Nr. 4400-4603) ausgeliefert. Im Jahr 2021 bestellte die TTC bei Alstom weitere 60 Flexity-Straßenbahnen, um die Flotte zu vergrößern.

Torontos neue Stadtbahnlinien, die „5 – Eglinton" und die „6 – Finch West", werden von Fahrzeugen des Typs Flexity Freedom bzw. Citadis Spirit betrieben, die beide aufgrund ihrer unterschiedlichen Spurweite von 1435 mm und anderer technischer Unterschiede nicht auf dem Straßenbahnnetz eingesetzt werden können.

Thunder Bay plant in September 2012, the new trams were not able to enter regular service until August 2014. In 2015, a new depot for the new stock called Leslie Barns opened in the east of the city. In September 2017, route '509 Harbourfront' became the first to use the cars' pantograph instead of the trolley pole, but in the meantime all the routes have been adapted accordingly. Although with some delays, all 204 vehicles (nos. 4400-4603) ordered had been delivered by January 2020. In 2021, TTC ordered another 60 Flexity trams from what is now Alstom to increase the fleet.

Toronto's new Eglinton Crosstown route and the Finch West LRT are operated with Flexity Freedom and Citadis Spirit vehicles, respectively, neither of which can run on the streetcar network due to their different track gauge of 1435 mm, among other technical differences.

Warnlichter bei Halt | *Warning lights when stopping*

Flexity

Flexity #4523 @ Queen St East/Carlow Ave

Flexity #4532 @ Bathurst St (Bathurst Loop)

Flexity #4436 @ Exhibition Loop

Flexity #4479 @ Queen St East/Coxwell Ave

St. George

Toronto Subway & Light Rail

Nachdem im Jahr 2023 die Scarborough RT, eine Metro mittlerer Kapazität, stillgelegt wurde, umfasst Torontos Schnellbahnnetz drei richtige U-Bahn-Linien („Subway") sowie zwei neue Stadtbahnlinien. Die drei U-Bahn-Linien 1, 2 und 4 haben dieselbe Spurweite wie die Straßenbahn, nämlich 1495 mm, während die ehemalige Linie 3 und die neuen Linien 5 und 6 mit internationaler Standard-spurweite von 1435 mm gebaut wurden. Die Linien 1, 2 und 4 verfügen über eine Stromversorgung über seitliche Stromschiene (600 V DC), während die beiden Stadtbahn-linien mit Oberleitung (750 V DC) ausgerüstet sind; auf der Linie 3 waren zwei Stromschienen vorhanden. Während die Linien 2 und 4 noch mit automatischen Blocksignalen ausgestattet sind, wurde die Linie 1 mit einem automati-schen Zugbeeinflussungssystem nachgerüstet.

In Anlehnung an die Tradition der benannten Straßen-bahnlinien tragen auch die U-Bahn- und Stadtbahnlinien einen Namen, der sich von den Straßen ableitet, unter denen sie verliefen. Dies führte neben der „Bloor-Danforth Subway" zu dem etwas holprigen Namen der „Yonge-University-Spadina Subway", weshalb die TTC 2014 einfache Liniennummern einführte; die entsprechenden Linienfarben werden bereits seit den späten 1960er Jahren verwendet.

With the medium-capacity light metro Scarborough RT having closed permanently in 2023, Toronto's rapid transit network now comprises three proper Subway/ metro lines and two light rail lines. The three Subway lines (lines 1, 2 and 4) share the same broad gauge of 1495 mm as found on the city's streetcar system, whereas the former line 3 and the new lines 5 and 6 have the international standard track gauge of 1435 mm. Lines 1, 2 and 4 have a third-rail power supply system (600 V DC), whereas the two light rail lines use an overhead catenary (750 V DC); line 3 was operated with a special 2-rail power supply system. While lines 2 and 4 are still equipped with an automatic block signalling system, line 1 has been upgraded with an automatic train control system.

Following the tradition of the named streetcar lines, the Subway and light rail lines also have names derived from the streets they run under. Besides the Bloor-Danforth Subway, this has led to somewhat clumsy names such as the Yonge-University-Spadina Subway, and the TTC thus started implementing simple line numbers in 2014, while the associated line colours had been used since the late 1960s.

Sheppard-Yonge

St. Clair West

Line ① Yonge-University Subway

Kanadas erste Schnellbahnlinie wurde 1954 eröffnet, doch bereits fast 50 Jahre vorher wurden die ersten Vorschläge unterbreitet, um die stark befahrene Straßenbahnstrecke entlang der Yonge Street durch eine Art U-Bahn zu ersetzen. Die Yonge Street, die 60 km geradlinig von Toronto bis zum Lake Simcoe verläuft, ist seit dem 18. Jahrhundert ein wichtiger Verkehrsweg und teilt die Straßen der Stadt in einen Ost- und einen Westabschnitt.

In Boston fuhren bereits 1897 Straßenbahnen durch einen Innenstadttunnel. Bis zum Zweiten Weltkrieg zog Toronto den Bau von längeren Tunnelabschnitten für die Straßenbahn in Erwägung, nicht nur unter der Yonge Street, sondern auch in Ost-West-Richtung unter der Queen Street. Nach dem Zweiten Weltkrieg jedoch, als mit dem Bau begonnen werden sollte, wurde die Queen-Strecke vorerst aufgeschoben und das Yonge-Projekt zugunsten einer U-Bahn im Stil der New Yorker „Subway" geändert.

When Canada's first rapid transit line opened in 1954, it already had a history of nearly 50 years of different proposals to replace the busy streetcar route along Yonge Street with some sort of subway. Yonge Street, which runs straight for 60 km from Toronto to Lake Simcoe, has been an important corridor since the 18th century, and is the baseline dividing streets into east and west.

In Boston, streetcars started running through a downtown subway in as early as 1897. Up until World War II, Toronto considered building rather lengthy tunnel sections for its streetcars, not only beneath Yonge Street, but also east-west along Queen Street. After World War II, however, when construction was about to start, the Queen route was postponed and the Yonge project was modified in favour of a New York City-style Subway.

The initial route from Union Station to Eglinton Avenue was built underground at shallow depth in the city centre, but mostly in an open trench to the north

Line 1 (Yonge-University Subway)
- 38.8 km (Ⓤ 31.1 km), 38 Stations (Ⓤ 31)

30-03-1954: Eglinton – Union (7.4 km)
28-02-1963: Union – St. George (3.2 km)
31-03-1973: Eglinton – York Mills (4.1 km)
30-03-1974: York Mills – Finch (4.2 km)
28-01-1978: St. George – Wilson (9.4 km)
18-06-1987: + North York Centre
31-03-1996: Wilson – Downsview (2017: Sheppard West) (1.9 km)
17-12-2017: Sheppard West – Vaughan Metropolitan Centre (8.6 km)
~ 2030: Finch – High Tech (~ 8 km)

Glencairn

Queen

Die ursprüngliche Strecke von der Union Station zur Eglinton Avenue wurde im Stadtzentrum unterirdisch in geringer Tiefe errichtet, nördlich der Bloor Street dann jedoch größtenteils in einem offenen Einschnitt, der bis St. Clair etwa 50-100 m östlich der Yonge Street verläuft; mehrere Abschnitte wurden Ende der 1960er/Anfang der 1970er Jahre abgedeckt und überbaut. In der Innenstadt wurden U-Bahnhöfe an allen Kreuzungen mit Hauptstraßen etwa im Abstand von 500 m errichtet. Am U-Bahnhof Queen wurde unter der Nord-Süd-U-Bahn der komplette Rohbau für den oben erwähnten Straßenbahntunnel unter der Queen Street mitgebaut. Der U-Bahn-Betriebshof wurde neben der oberirdischen Station Davisville angelegt.

Ausgehend von der Union Station wurde die „Yonge Subway" Anfang der 1960er-Jahre verlängert, und zwar Richtung Norden auf einer parallelen Strecke nur 600 m westlich der ursprünglichen Linie. Zwischen Osgoode und Museum wurden die Streckentunnel im Schildvortrieb errichtet, um die Bäume entlang der University Avenue zu schützen; auf diesem Abschnitt liegen Torontos zwei richtige Röhrenstationen St. Patrick und Queen's Park. Die „University Subway" wurde zusammen mit der „Bloor-Danforth Subway" geplant, und die beiden Linien sind über ein völlig kreuzungsfreies Gleisdreieck zwischen den Stationen St. George, Bay und Museum miteinander verbunden. Nach Inbetriebnahme der Ost-West-Linie 1966 wurde sechs Monate lang ein verknüpfter Betrieb beider Linien getestet, danach wurden die beiden Linien jedoch betrieblich getrennt. Im U-Bahnhof St. George nutzt die Linie 1 den oberen Bahnsteig und die Linie 2 den unteren. Am ebenfalls doppelstöckigen U-Bahnhof Bay ist die untere Ebene seit nunmehr 57 Jahren außer Betrieb und steht etwa für Filmaufnahmen zur Verfügung.

of Bloor Street, running up to St. Clair some 50-100 m east of Yonge Street; several sections were covered and built over in the late 1960s / early 1970s. In the downtown core, stations were built some 500 m apart at the intersections with all major streets. At Queen station, a complete station box was built beneath the north-south Subway for the aforementioned Queen Street streetcar tunnel. The original Subway depot was established next to the surface station Davisville.

At the downtown end, the 'Yonge Subway' was extended in the early 1960s from Union Station, heading back north again with a parallel route just 600 m to the west of the original line. Between Osgoode and Museum, the running tunnels were bored to protect the trees along University Avenue, resulting in Toronto's two proper tube stations at St. Patrick and Queen's Park. The 'University Subway' was planned together with the 'Bloor-Danforth Subway', and therefore the two lines were linked via a fully grade-separated triangular junction between St. George, Bay and Museum stations. When the east-west line opened in 1966, an interlined service was tested for six months, after which the two lines were operationally separated. At St. George, line 1 uses the upper platform, and line 2 the lower. At Bay, which is also a bi-level underground station, the lower level has been out of service for 57 years and is available for other uses such as movie productions.

During the 1970s, both legs grew substantially with extensions into the suburbs. The eastern leg reached North York mostly through twin tube tunnels, and initially had only three intermediate stations on the 8.3 km extension to Finch; North York Centre station was added 13 years later to serve an emerging suburban town centre.

![Lawrence West station platform with train]

Lawrence West

In den 1970er Jahren wurden beide Äste weit in die Außenbezirke verlängert. Der östliche Ast erreichte North York größtenteils durch Doppelröhrentunnel und zunächst nur mit drei Zwischenstationen auf der 8,3 km langen Verlängerung bis Finch; der Bahnhof North York Centre wurde 13 Jahre später eingefügt, um ein aufstrebendes Stadtteilzentrum zu erschließen.

Der westliche Ast sollte im Stil der Blue Line von Chicago weitergeführt werden, nämlich im Mittelstreifen einer Stadtautobahn. Die Einwohner von Toronto lehnten das Straßenprojekt durch den Grüngürtel (Nordheimer und Cedarvale Ravines) jedoch strikt ab, weshalb die U-Bahn durch dieses Gebiet unterirdisch errichtet wurde und erst an der Station Eglinton West (ab 2024 Cedarvale) die Oberfläche erreicht. Ab hier verläuft die Strecke im Mittelstreifen der Allen Road nach Norden, mit vier

The western leg was modelled after Chicago's Blue Line, which was aligned in the median of an urban expressway. However, Torontonians successfully prevented the extension of the expressway south through the green corridor known as the Nordheimer and Cedarvale Ravines. As a result, the Subway only occupies the median of Allen Road north of Eglinton West (from 2024 Cedarvale), serving four stations; south of that station, the extension was built underground. Although only a short section follows Spadina Road, the extended line became known as the 'Yonge-University-Spadina Subway', often abbreviated to 'YUS'. Beyond the new terminus at Wilson, an extensive yard was built on land ceded by Downsview Airport. Wilson remained the terminus for 18 years before a short extension was added to Downsview (now Sheppard West) in 1996. A major

Lawrence West

Sheppard West

![Pioneer Village]

Pioneer Village

ebenerdigen Bahnhöfen. Obwohl nur ein kurzer Abschnitt der Spadina Road folgt, wurde die verlängerte Linie als „Yonge-University-Spadina Subway" bezeichnet, oft mit „YUS" abgekürzt. Hinter der neuen Endstation Wilson wurde auf einem vom Flughafen Downsview abgetretenen Gelände ein weitläufiger Betriebshof errichtet. Wilson blieb 18 Jahre lang Endbahnhof, bis 1996 eine kurze Verlängerung bis Downsview (heute Sheppard West) fertiggestellt wurde. Zwischen 2012 und 2014 wurde der stark überlastete U-Bahnhof Union umfassend umgebaut, indem ein separater Bahnsteig in Richtung Finch hinzugefügt wurde.

In den 1980er und 1990er Jahren gab es verschiedene Vorschläge, die beiden Äste im Norden zu verbinden und eine Ringlinie zu schaffen, doch letztendlich wurde einer Verlängerung in Richtung York University Vorrang eingeräumt. Seit 1998 bildet die Steeles Avenue die

reconstruction took place at Union station between 2012 and 2014, when a separate platform was added for Finch-bound trains to reduce overcrowding.

In the 1980s and 1990s, there were various proposals to link the two legs and form a circular line, but in the end an extension towards York University was given priority. Since 1998, Steeles Avenue has been Toronto's northern city border, and to receive provincial funding, the extension project needed to serve the wider metropolitan area. Eventually, the Subway line was extended across the border to the new town centre of Vaughan in York Region (TTC tickets are valid for the two stations outside Toronto!). While Highway 407 and Pioneer Village stations were built primarily as park+ride facilities, Downsview Park provides convenient interchange with GO Transit's Barrie Line, and Finch West is now an

Pioneer Village

Finch West

York University

nördliche Stadtgrenze Torontos. Um eine finanzielle Unterstützung von der Provinz Ontario zu erhalten, musste das Erweiterungsprojekt Teile der Metropolregion erschließen, weshalb die U-Bahn-Linie schließlich über die Stadtgrenze bis zum neuen Stadtzentrum von Vaughan in der York Region verlängert wurde (TTC-Tickets gelten für die beiden Stationen außerhalb von Toronto!). Während die U-Bahnhöfe Highway 407 und Pioneer Village in erster Linie als Park+Ride-Anlagen gebaut wurden, bietet Downsview Park einen bequemen Übergang zur Barrie Line von GO Transit. Am U-Bahnhof Finch West besteht nun eine Umsteigemöglichkeit zur neuen Stadtbahnlinie 6. Alle U-Bahnhöfe wurden in offener Bauweise errichtet, die Streckentunnel hingegen mit vier Tunnelbohrmaschinen.

Während der westliche Ast der Linie 1 möglicherweise seine endgültige Länge erreicht hat, steht der Baubeginn einer Verlängerung des östlichen Asts kurz bevor. Die Linie wird etwa 5 km lang unterirdisch weiter entlang der Yonge Street verlaufen, dann nach Osten abbiegen, um südlich der GO-Station Langstaff aus dem Tunnel aufzutauchen und kurz darauf an der High Tech Road zu enden. Wenn die „Yonge North Subway Extension" (8 km) fertiggestellt ist, wird Torontos „Line 1 Yonge-University" 47 km lang sein und 43 Stationen aufweisen.

interchange with the new Finch West light rail line 6. All the stations were built by cut-and-cover, but the running tunnels were excavated with four tunnel boring machines.

While the western leg of line 1 may have reached its definitive length for decades to come, the construction of an extension to the eastern leg is about to start. The line will continue underground along the Yonge Street corridor for some 5 km, then swing east to emerge from the tunnel south of Langstaff GO station before terminating shortly after at High Tech Road. When the 'Yonge North Subway Extension' (8 km) is completed,

Museum

Downsview Park

Yorkdale

Lawrence

Die „Yonge Subway" wurde mit Zügen der burgunderfarbenen G-Serie, die im englischen Gloucester produziert wurden, in Betrieb genommen. Die 17 m langen und 3,2 m breiten Wagen bildeten Züge mit bis zu 8 Wagen (136 m). Die letzten G-Züge wurden 1990 ausgemustert und durch die H-Serie ersetzt, die in Thunder Bay, Ontario, von Hawker Siddeley/UTDC/Bombardier hergestellt wurde. In den frühen 1960er Jahren wurde die Flotte um die M-Serie erweitert, die erstmals den Edelstahl-Look im New Yorker Stil trug. Die M- und nachfolgenden H-Wagen waren fast 23 m lang und nur 3,14 m breit, so dass ein Vollzug aus sechs Wagen bestand. M-Züge verkehrten bis 1999 und H-Züge bis 2014. Auf der Linie 1 wurden sie durch die T-Serie ersetzt, die immer noch auf der Linie 2 im Einsatz ist. Die Linie 1 wird jetzt mit der neuesten U-Bahn-Baureihe „Toronto Rocket" (TR) betrieben, die zwischen 2009 und

Toronto's 'Line 1 Yonge-University' will be 47 km long and serve 43 stations.

The 'Yonge Subway' started service with the burgundy-coloured G series built in Gloucester, England, with cars 17 m long and 3.2 m wide, forming trains of up to 8 cars (136 m). The last G trains were retired in 1990 and replaced by the H series, which were manufactured in Thunder Bay, Ontario, by Hawker Siddeley/UTDC/Bombardier. In the early 1960s, the fleet was expanded with the M series, which introduced a New York-style stainless steel look to Toronto's Subway rolling stock. The M and subsequent H cars were almost 23 m long and just 3.14 m wide, so a full-length train consisted of six cars. M trains ran until 1999 and H trains until 2014. On Line 1, they were replaced by the T series, which still operates on Line 2. Line 1 is now served by the TTC's

North York Centre

Toronto Rocket

Rosedale

2015 von Bombardier in Thunder Bay produziert wurde. Die Flotte besteht aus 76 Sechs-Wagen-Zügen (138 m) mit Übergängen zwischen allen Wagen. Die Züge werden manuell gefahren und waren bis 2022 am hinteren Ende des Zuges mit einem Zugbegleiter besetzt. Ebenfalls im Jahr 2022 wurde das Blocksignalsystem der Strecke auf automatische Zugbeeinflussung (ATC) umgerüstet.

newest type of Subway train, the 'Toronto Rocket' (TR), which was produced by Bombardier in Thunder Bay from 2009 to 2015. The fleet consists of 76 six-car trainsets (138 m), with gangways between all the cars. The trains are manually driven and until 2022 had a guard at the rear end of the train. Also in 2022, the line's block signal system was upgraded to automatic train control (ATC).

Finch

Dundas West

Line ② Bloor-Danforth Subway

Nach der Eröffnung der ersten U-Bahn-Linie im Jahr 1954 setzte Toronto die Planung weiterer Schnellbahnlinien fort, während der in den frühen 1960er Jahren geplante Straßenbahntunnel unter der Queen Street nicht mehr als vorrangig angesehen wurde, da die Zukunft der Straßenbahn ohnehin ungewiss war. Stattdessen wurde eine Ost-West-Linie entlang des nördlichen Randes der Innenstadt entworfen, um die Straßenbahnen auf dem Bloor-Danforth-Korridor zu ersetzen, der vor allem aus den östlichen Stadtteilen ein zunehmendes Fahrgastaufkommen verzeichnete. Dieses Projekt wurde mit einer zweiten Nord-Süd-Strecke durch das Stadtzentrum unter der University Avenue kombiniert und an der Union Station mit der bestehenden „Yonge Subway" verbunden.

Ähnlich wie die „Yonge Subway" wurde die neue „Bloor-Danforth Subway" größtenteils in offener Bauweise errichtet und nicht unter der Bloor und Danforth Street, sondern etwa 50-100 m nördlich davon quasi durch die Hinterhöfe. Auf diese Weise wurden Beeinträchtigungen während des Baus minimiert, und die Straßenbahnen konnten bis zur Eröffnung der U-Bahn im Februar 1966 weiterfahren. Der ursprüngliche westliche Endpunkt Keele ist ein Hochbahnhof, auch wenn die Züge dank eines Gefälles am westlichen Ende des Bahnhofs in einen Tunnel einfahren. Auf dem offenen Abschnitt zwischen Keele und Dundas West wurden mehrere Abstellgleise verlegt. Von Dundas West aus sind es 300 m zu Fuß zur GO-Station Bloor, wo jetzt auch der UP Express hält (von hier ist die Fahrt zum Flughafen wesentlich günstiger als von der Union Station). Ein direkter Übergang zwischen Subway und GO Transit ist geplant.

With the first Subway line opened in 1954, Toronto continued planning more rapid transit lines. However, the envisaged streetcar tunnel under Queen Street was no longer seen as a priority in the early 1960s when the future of streetcars was in doubt anyway. Instead, an east-west line was planned along the northern edge of the downtown core to replace the streetcars on the Bloor-Danforth corridor, which had seen increasing ridership especially from the eastern suburbs. This project was combined with a second north-south route through the city centre along University Avenue, which was linked to the existing 'Yonge Subway' at Union Station.

Similarly to the 'Yonge Subway', the new 'Bloor-Danforth Subway' was mostly built by cut-and-cover, and not beneath Bloor and Danforth Streets, but some 50-100 m further north through the backyards of the properties; in this way, disruptions during construction were minimised, and streetcars kept running until the opening of the line in February 1966. The initial western terminus Keele is

Line 2 (Bloor-Danforth Subway)
- 26.2 km (Ⓤ 21 km), 31 Stations (Ⓤ 28)

26-02-1966: Keele – Woodbine (12.5 km)
11-05-1968: Keele – Islington (5.4 km)
           Woodbine – Warden (4.3 km)
22-11-1980: Islington – Kipling (1.3 km)
           Warden – Kennedy (2.7 km)
~ 2030: Kennedy – Sheppard/McCowen (7.8 km)

Kipling > Islington

Die Linie 2 verläuft etwa 6 km geradlinig durch die Innenstadt, mit einfachen Haltestellen alle 600 m. Der U-Bahnhof St. George wurde zusammen mit der „University Subway" einige Jahre zuvor fertiggestellt, wobei die Linie 2 auf der unteren Ebene hält. Die folgende Station Bay hat einen ähnlichen Aufbau, hier fährt die Linie 2 auf der oberen Ebene, während die untere Ebene ungenutzt bleibt: „Lower Bay" war 1966 nur sechs Monate lang im regulären Fahrgastbetrieb, nämlich während einer Testphase des kombinierten Linienbetriebs – Züge von Woodbine verkehrten über „Lower Bay" Richtung Süden zur Station Museum und weiter auf der „Yonge Subway" bis Eglinton. Ebenso fuhren einige Züge von Keele über St. George und Museum bis Eglinton. Der Geisterbahnhof wird zeitweise als Filmdrehort genutzt. Alle Stationen der ursprünglichen „Bloor-Danforth Subway" verfügen über Seitenbahnsteige, mit Ausnahme von St. George und Bay, die wie die Station Yonge, Umsteigepunkt zur älteren U-Bahn-Linie und verkehrsreichste im Netz, Mittelbahnsteige aufweisen. Im U-Bahnhof Bloor-Yonge ist jedoch ein zusätzlicher Bahnsteig Richtung Osten geplant, so dass am bestehenden Mittelbahnsteig nur noch Züge Richtung Westen halten würden.

Der älteste und spektakulärste Teil der „Bloor-Danforth Subway" ist das Prince-Edward-Viadukt, eine Fachwerkbogenbrücke über den Fluss Don, die 1918 fertiggestellt wurde und ein Unterdeck für eine künftige Bahnverbindung erhielt, welche schließlich 48 Jahre später Wirklichkeit wurde. Auf einem 300 m langen Abschnitt können die Fahrgäste der Linie 2 einen Blick hinunter ins Don Valley genießen und gelegentlich einen Zug von GO Transit sehen. Eine ähnliche Vorleistung zwischen Sherbourne und Castle Frank konnte hingegen nicht genutzt werden,

an elevated station, although trains enter a tunnel at the western end of the station thanks to a slope in the terrain. The open section between Keele and Dundas West was used to lay some sidings. From Dundas West it is a 300 m walk to Bloor GO Station, which is now also a stop on the UP Express, and with a much cheaper fare to the airport than from Union Station. A direct connecting tunnel between the Subway station and the GO station is planned.

For some 6 km, the line runs straight through the downtown area, with plain stations every 600 m. St. George station was completed together with the 'University Subway' a few years earlier, with Line 2 stopping on the lower level. The following station, Bay, has a similar layout, but here with Line 2 on the upper level and the lower level disused; 'Lower Bay' was in regular service for only six months in 1966, during a trial period of 'interlined' operation which included trains from Woodbine to 'Lower Bay' and then south to Museum and on the 'Yonge Subway' to Eglinton. Similarly some trains from Keele travelled via St. George and Museum to Eglinton. The ghost station is sometimes used as a film location. All the stations on the initial 'Bloor-Danforth Subway' have side platforms except St. George and Bay, which have island platforms just like Bloor-Yonge, the interchange to the older Subway line and the busiest on the network. At Bloor-Yonge, however, an additional eastbound platform is planned, leaving the existing island platform for westbound trains only.

The oldest and most spectacular part of the 'Bloor-Danforth Subway' is the Prince Edward Viaduct, a truss arch bridge across the Don River, completed in 1918 with a lower deck for future rail use in mind, an option

Keele – Zugbegleiter im letzten Wagen | Train guard in last car

so dass für die U-Bahn eine neue, eingehauste Brücke über das Rosedale Valley, die sich nördlich der Straßenbrücke befindet, errichtet werden musste.

An der Broadview Avenue wird die Bloor Street zur Danforth Street, doch die U-Bahn schwenkt erneut etwa 100 m nach Norden und verläuft parallel zur Danforth Street bis zur ursprünglichen Endstation Woodbine. Zwischen Donlands und Greenwood bietet eine zweigleisige, kreuzungsfreie Ausfädelung eine Verbindung zum weitläufigen Betriebshof Greenwood Yard der Linie 2.

Die „Bloor-Danforth Subway" wurde nur zwei Jahre nach ihrer Inbetriebnahme an beiden Enden verlängert, es kamen sechs Stationen im Westen und drei im Osten hinzu. Die Westverlängerung setzt sich in einem eher flachen Tunnel 70 m nördlich der Bloor Street fort und weist drei offene Abschnitte auf; die meisten abgedeckelten

eventually used 48 years later. On a 300 m section, Line 2 passengers can enjoy a view down into the Don Valley and may spot an occasional GO Transit train. A similar provision between Sherbourne and Castle Frank could not be used, however, and the Subway therefore crosses the Rosedale Valley on a purpose-built, but completely enclosed bridge located just north of the road bridge.

At Broadview Avenue, Bloor Street becomes Danforth Street, but again, the Subway swings some 100 m north and continues parallel to Danforth Street all the way to the original terminus at Woodbine. Between Donlands and Greenwood, a double-track grade-separated triangular junction provides a link to Line 2's extensive Greenwood Yard.

The 'Bloor-Danforth Subway' was extended at both ends only two years after the initial segment had

Lansdowne

Ossington

![Old Mill](image of elevated subway station)

Old Mill

Abschnitte wurden nicht überbaut, sondern werden als Parkplätze oder Grünflächen genutzt. Eine 150 m lange Brücke überspannt den Humber River und führt direkt in den Bahnhof Old Mill, der ähnlich wie Keele aufgeständert ist, an seinem westlichen Ende jedoch in einen Tunnel übergeht. Vor Ankunft am Bahnhof Islington überqueren die Züge den Mimico Creek auf einer offenen Brücke. Die Ost-verlängerung verläuft weiter unterirdisch über Main Street bis kurz vor Victoria Park, dann größtenteils ebenerdig bis Warden, 12 Jahre lang östlicher Endpunkt der Linie 2 und großer Umsteigepunkt zwischen Bus und U-Bahn.

1980 wurde an beiden Enden der Strecke jeweils eine Station hinzugefügt. Zwischen Islington und Kipling wurde eine oberirdische Strecke entlang der Milton Line von GO Transit gebaut, während die Strecke von Warden bis Kennedy trotz einer bestehenden Güterbahntrasse

opened, adding six stations in the west and three in the east. The western extension continues on a rather shallow alignment 70 m north of Bloor Street and features three open sections, while most of the covered sections have not been built over, but are used as car parks or green areas. A 150 m bridge spans the Humber River and leads directly into Old Mill station, which, similar to Keele, is elevated but transitions into a tunnel at its western end. Before arriving at Islington, the trains cross Mimico Creek on an open bridge. The eastern extension continues underground from Woodbine through Main Street station, but the trains emerge from the tunnel just before arriving at Victoria Park, then run mostly at grade to Warden, the eastern terminus for 12 years; this station was laid out as a huge bus/Subway interchange.

Dufferin

Pape

![St. George station platform with escalator and stairs](St. George)

St. George

unterirdisch errichtet wurde. Mit 2,8 km ist Warden – Kennedy die längste Strecke zwischen zwei Stationen der Toronto Subway. Bei Inbetriebnahme des U-Bahnhofs Kennedy galt eine weitere Verlängerung in Richtung Scarborough als nicht vorrangig. Stattdessen wurde eine Art Stadtbahn vorgeschlagen, was schließlich zum Bau der 1985 eröffneten Scarborough RT (Linie 3) führte. Was damals eine preisgünstige Alternative darstellte, würde heute große Investitionen in die Modernisierung erfordern, weshalb die Stadt 2013 beschloss, die Linie 3 stillzulegen und stattdessen eine 7,8 km lange, vollständig unterirdische U-Bahn-Verlängerung auf einer östlicheren Trasse zu bauen, womit die meisten Fahrgäste eine schnellere und direkte Verbindung ins Stadtzentrum bekommen. An der künftigen Endstation Sheppard-McCowan könnte die

In 1980, one station was added at each end of the line. Between Islington and Kipling, a surface route was built alongside the GO Milton line, whereas the route from Warden to Kennedy was put underground despite an existing freight rail corridor. At 2.8 km, Warden – Kennedy is the longest distance between two stations on the Toronto Subway. When Kennedy station opened, a further extension towards the Scarborough town centre was not considered essential. Instead, some sort of light rail was proposed; this led to the construction of the Scarborough RT (Line 3), which opened in 1985. At the time an affordable alternative, Line 3 today would require heavy investment into its modernisation, and the city therefore decided in 2013 to abandon the RT and build a 7.8 km fully underground Subway extension

Greenwood

Sherbourne > Castle Frank

Warden

Linie 2 eines Tages auf eine verlängerte Linie 4 treffen. Die Bauarbeiten begannen Mitte 2021 und werden bis zum Ende des Jahrzehnts andauern.

Die Linie 2 startete mit Zügen der M- und H-Serie, wobei letztere durch die aktuelle, 1995 bis 2001 ausgelieferte T-Serie abgelöst wurde. Da auf den Linien 1 und 4 nun die neuen Toronto Rockets unterwegs sind, konnten alle T-Züge an die Linie 2 abgegeben werden; der Bestand umfasst insgesamt 370 Wagen (zwei wurden verschrottet), mit denen 61 Sechs-Wagen-Züge gebildet werden können. Am Ende jedes Zuges ist noch ein Zugbegleiter an Bord, der für das Öffnen und Schließen der Türen verantwortlich ist. Im Gegensatz zur Linie 1 verfügt die Linie 2 weiterhin nur über eine automatische Blocksignalisierung, die erst mit Ankunft neuer Fahrzeuge modernisiert wird.

instead on a more easterly route, providing a faster and more direct journey for most commuters. At the future terminus at Sheppard-McCowan, Line 2 may eventually meet an extended Line 4. Construction began in mid-2021 and will take until the end of the decade.

Line 2 started with M and H series trains, the latter having been replaced by the current T series, which was delivered from 1995 to 2001. With Lines 1 and 4 now operating the new Toronto Rockets, Line 2 has become the mainstay of the T series; the roster lists a total of 370 cars (2 having been scrapped) which can form 61 six-car trains. At the end of each train, there is a guard on board mainly responsible for opening and closing the doors. Unlike Line 1, Line 2 still operates with automatic block signalling, which will be upgraded upon the arrival of new rolling stock.

T-Series

Kennedy

Kennedy (2017 © Robert Barrows)

Line ③ Scarborough RT

Obwohl es sich ebenfalls um eine Metro-Linie handelte, war die Linie 3 nicht mit den anderen drei U-Bahn-Linien von Toronto (1, 2, 4) kompatibel – nicht nur wegen ihrer internationalen Spurweite (1435 mm), sondern auch wegen ihrer Antriebstechnologie. Sie war vielmehr ein Vorläufer des „Skytrain" von Vancouver, wurde jedoch nicht fahrerlos betrieben.

Als die damals unabhängige Gemeinde Scarborough in den 1970er Jahren auf dem Reißbrett ein neues Stadtzentrum plante, wurde auch der Bau einer Schienenanbindung in Erwägung gezogen. Anfangs dachte man an eine Art Stadtbahn von der Endstation Kennedy der „Bloor-Danforth Subway" in das neue Gebiet, mit einer möglichen Verlängerung bis zum Stadtzentrum von Malvern. Zu jener Zeit experimentierte die staatliche *Urban Transportation Development Corporation Ltd.* (UTDC) mit neuen Technologien und wählte das Scarborough-Projekt, um ihre Ergebnisse zu präsentieren. Als 1981 die Einführung des innovativen Systems beschlossen wurde, hatte der Bau der geplanten Stadtbahn am Bahnhof Kennedy bereits begonnen – direkt über dem U-Bahnhof war ein Hochbahnhof mitsamt einer aufgeständerten Wendeschleife entstanden. Die Schleife wurde zwar in die neuartige Bahn integriert, erwies sich jedoch als zu eng für einen sicheren Betrieb. Deshalb wurde der Hochbahnhof 1988 umgebaut und hatte seither nur ein Gleis mit Bahnsteigen auf beiden Seiten, während die Schleife danach nur noch zum Abstellen von Zügen genutzt wurde.

Nach Verlassen des Bahnhofs Kennedy nahmen die Züge eine scharfe Linkskurve hinunter bis auf das Straßenniveau und fuhren dann 3,9 km lang westlich der von GO

Although also a metro line, Line 3 was not compatible with the other three Subway lines (1, 2, 4), not just because of its international track gauge (1435 mm), but also because of its traction technology. It was in fact a predecessor of Vancouver's SkyTrain, though operated by a driver.

The idea of some sort of rail transport to this area came up in the 1970s when the then-independent municipality of Scarborough was planning a new town centre from scratch. Early proposals considered a sort of light rail line from the 'Bloor-Danforth Subway' terminus at Kennedy to the new area, with a possible extension to Malvern Town Centre. At the time, the state-owned Urban Transportation Development Corporation Ltd. (UTDC) was experimenting with new technologies and chose the Scarborough project to showcase its results. When the decision to implement the innovative system was taken in 1981, the construction of the planned light rail had already started at Kennedy, with an elevated station right above the Subway station and an elevated loop beyond it. The loop was incorporated into the new RT system but proved too tight for safe operation, and in 1988, the station was therefore rebuilt with a single track and platforms on either side, while the loop track was only used for stabling trains.

Line 3 (Scarborough RT)
- 6.4 km, 6 Stations

22-03-1985: Kennedy – McCowan
24-07-2023: Ende des Betriebs | *End of operations*

Kennedy — (2005 © Bernhard Kußmagk)

Kennedy > Lawrence East — (2005 © Bernhard Kußmagk)

Transit nach Stouffville genutzten Eisenbahn bis zur Station Ellesmere mit nur einer Zwischenstation, Lawrence East. Nach Ellesmere tauchten die „Rapid Transit"-Züge unter der Eisenbahn hindurch und fuhren schließlich als Hochbahn bis zum Ende der Linie weiter.

Die Linie 3 wurde mit einer Flotte von 7 Vier-Wagen-Zügen betrieben, die in Toronto als S-Serie klassifiziert waren, aber weitgehend mit den Mark I-Zügen in Vancouver identisch waren. Sie wurden von linearen Induktionsmotoren angetrieben, die von einer zwischen den Fahrschienen angebrachten Reaktionsschiene gesteuert wurden. Anstelle einer typischen Stromversorgung über seitliche Stromschiene, wie sie bei den meisten U-Bahnen zu finden ist, gab es auf einer Seite des Gleises eine separate positive und negative Stromschiene (+300 V/-300 V > 600 V DC). Wie in Vancouver war das System mit dem SelTrac-Betriebssystem ausgerüstet, es war jedoch stets ein Fahrer an Bord, der die Türen steuerte und den Betrieb überwachte.

Jahrelang war die Zukunft der Scarborough RT ungewiss – sollte sie modernisiert oder stillgelegt werden? Letztendlich brachte die Entscheidung, die Linie 2 von Kennedy nach Scarborough Centre und darüber hinaus zu verlängern, das Ende der Scarborough RT mit sich. Dieses war ursprünglich für November 2023 vorgesehen, doch nach einer Entgleisung im Juli 2023 wurde der Betrieb nicht wieder aufgenommen. Teile der Strecke sollen zu einer besonderen Bustrasse umgebaut werden. Bis dahin findet Schienenersatzverkehr statt; seit November 2023 fahren zahlreiche sonst in Scarborough endende Linien bis Kennedy weiter.

Upon leaving Kennedy station, the trains took a sharp curve left down to street level, where the line was aligned along the western side of the Stouffville GO line for 3.9 km all the way to Ellesmere, serving only one intermediate station at Lawrence East. After Ellesmere, the RT trains passed under the railway to climb onto a viaduct on the eastern side, which they followed for the rest of their journey.

Line 3 was operated with a fleet of 7 four-car trains, classified in Toronto as the S series, but largely identical to the Mark I trains in Vancouver. They were driven by linear induction motors controlled by a reaction rail placed between the running rails. Instead of a typical third-rail power supply system found on most metro systems, there was a separate positive and negative power rail on one side of the track (+300 V/-300 V > 600 V DC). Like in Vancouver, the system was equipped with the SelTrac operating system, but a driver was kept on board to control the doors and monitor operation.

For many years, the Scarborough RT had been suffering from an uncertain future as to whether it should be upgraded or abandoned. In the end, the decision to extend Line 2 from Kennedy to Scarborough Centre and beyond brought with it the end of the Scarborough RT. The line was initially planned to be retired in November 2023, but following a derailment in July 2023, it closed permanently earlier than expected. Parts of the route may be rebuilt into a busway. Until then, a bus replacement service is in operation; since November 2023, several bus routes, which used to terminate at Scarborough Centre, have been extended to Kennedy.

Midland – Hochbahn | *elevated guideway* (2017 © R. Barrows)

Kennedy – Sept. 2023: Ersatzverkehr | *Replacement bus*

Don Mills

Line ④ Sheppard Subway

Während die ersten beiden U-Bahn-Linien Torontos im Laufe der Jahrzehnte eine beträchtliche Länge erreicht haben, ist und bleibt die dritte U-Bahn-Linie, die „Sheppard Subway", eher eine Stummellinie.

Eine Linie entlang der Sheppard Avenue wurde erstmals 1985 vorgeschlagen. Sie sollte einst von Sheppard West am westlichen Ast der Linie 1 bis nach Scarborough im Osten verlaufen. Während die U-Bahnhöfe in offener Bauweise entstanden, wurden für den Bau der Streckentunnel Tunnelbohrmaschinen eingesetzt. Der Fluss Don wird auf einer eingehausten Betonbrücke östlich des U-Bahnhofs Leslie überquert. Die Stationen haben zwar die gleichen Abmessungen wie die der Linien 1 und 2, es werden jedoch nur zwei Drittel der Bahnsteiglänge genutzt, da auf der Linie 4 bislang nur Vier-Wagen-Züge im Einsatz sind. Um eine Überlastung wie am Umsteigebahnhof Bloor-Yonge zu verhindern, wurde am Umsteigebahnhof Sheppard-Yonge die (obere) Ebene der Linie 4 großzügig mit zwei Seitenbahnsteigen und einem Mittelbahnsteig gebaut, um bei Bedarf die Passagierströme trennen zu können; bei durchschnittlich 50.000 Fahrgästen pro Tag ist der Mittelbahnsteig bis heute nicht in Betrieb. Aktuelle Pläne sehen eine Ostverlängerung vor, um am Bahnhof Sheppard-McCowan in Scarborough auf die verlängerte Linie 2 zu treffen, doch die Finanzierung ist noch nicht gesichert.

Die „Sheppard Subway" begann mit Zügen der T-Serie mit vier Wagen, doch seit 2016 wird die Linie von sechs Vier-Wagen-Zügen der Baureihe „Toronto Rocket" betrieben, die im Betriebshof Davisville der Linie 1 beheimatet sind.

While Toronto's first two Subway lines have reached a considerable length over the decades, the third heavy rail metro line, the 'Sheppard Subway', has remained and will remain a relatively short stub line.

A line along Sheppard Avenue was first proposed in 1985, and was once intended to run all the way from Line 1's western leg at Sheppard West to Scarborough in the east. While the stations were built by cut-and-cover, tunnel boring machines were used to excavate the running tunnels. The Don River is crossed in an enclosed concrete bridge just east of Leslie station. Though built to the same dimensions as Lines 1 and 2, only two thirds of the platform length is used on Line 4 as only four-car trains are in service. To prevent overcrowding like at Bloor-Yonge, the Line 4 (upper) level at Sheppard-Yonge was built with two side platforms and an island platform to separate passenger flows if necessary; with an average of 50,000 passengers using the line every day, the island platform has not been finished yet. Current plans consider an eastern extension to meet the Line 2 extension at Sheppard-McCowan in Scarborough, but no funding has been secured yet.

The 'Sheppard Subway' started with T series trains made up of four cars, but since 2016, the line has been served by 6 four-car Toronto Rocket trains, which share Line 1's facilities at Davisville.

Line 4 (Sheppard Subway)
- 5.5 km, 5 Stations (Ⓤ)

22-11-2002: Sheppard-Yonge – Don Mills

Sheppard-Yonge

Bessarion

Leslie

Bayview

Bessarion

Cedarvale

Line ⑤   Eglinton Crosstown LRT

Entlang ihres östlichen Abschnitts von Sunnybrook Park bis Kennedy ähnelt die neue „Eglinton Crosstown Line" einer typischen modernen Straßenbahn französischer Prägung, mit einem eigenen Gleiskörper im Mittelstreifen der Eglinton Avenue. Der Rest der Linie, sowohl der 2024 zu eröffnende Abschnitt Mount Dennis – Laird als auch der im Bau befindliche westliche Abschnitt gleicht hingegen eher einer U-Bahn/Stadtbahn im Stil der „Confederation Line" in Ottawa, mit einer unterirdischen bzw. aufgeständerten Trassierung und mit Stationen in U-Bahn-Manier.

Ungefähr zu der Zeit, als die „Sheppard Subway" entworfen wurde, war eine ähnliche Linie entlang der Eglinton Avenue West geplant, um ein als York Centre geplantes Gebiet an der heutigen Station Mount Dennis zu erschließen. Nach den Erfahrungen mit der „Sheppard Subway" wurde die Eglinton-Strecke jedoch schließlich als Linie mittlerer Kapazität umgesetzt, nämlich mit modernen Straßenbahnfahrzeugen und oberirdischer Trassierung mit Straßenkreuzungen, wo eine vollständig kreuzungsfreie Trasse nicht für notwendig erachtet wurde.

Am derzeitigen westlichen Endpunkt Mount Dennis wurden an der Kitchener-Linie von GO Transit Bahnsteige hinzugefügt, um einen bequemen Übergang von/zur neuen Linie 5 zu schaffen; die Endstation liegt ebenerdig, doch ihr westliches Ende befindet sich in einem Tunnel, der Teil der künftigen Verlängerung nach Renforth ist. Auf dem Weg Richtung Osten passieren die Züge die Zufahrt zum Betriebshof und überqueren den Black Creek Drive auf einer Brücke, bevor sie in den ca. 10 km langen Tunnel unter der Eglinton Avenue einfahren. Dieser umfasst 12 unterirdische Stationen, von denen zwei eine Umsteigemöglichkeit zur

Along its eastern section from Sunnybrook Park to Kennedy, the new Eglinton Crosstown Line is like a typical French-style modern tramway, with a dedicated right-of-way in the median of Eglinton Avenue, whereas the rest of the line, the soon-to-open Mount Dennis — Laird section as well as the western extension under construction, is rather like a light metro in the style of Ottawa's Confederation Line, i.e. with an underground or elevated alignment, and with metro-style stations.

Around the time when the 'Sheppard Subway' was conceived, a similar line was designed along Eglinton Avenue West to serve an area planned as York Centre at what is now Mount Dennis station. But with the experience gained from the 'Sheppard Subway', the Eglinton route was eventually built as a medium-capacity line, using modern tram vehicles and surface running with road intersections where a fully grade-separated alignment was not considered necessary.

At Mount Dennis, platforms were added on the Kitchener GO line to create a convenient interchange with the new Line 5. The LRT station lies at grade, but with its western end in a tunnel which is part of the future extension to Renforth. Heading east, the trains pass the junction that links the line's depot, and cross

Line 5 (Eglinton Crosstown)
- 19 km (Ⓤ 11.5 km), 25 Stations (Ⓤ 15)

2024: Mount Dennis – Kennedy (19 km)
~ 2027: Mount Dennis – Renforth (9.2 km)

Linie 1 bieten (Eglinton West wird mit Eröffnung der Linie 5 in Cedarvale umbenannt). Ab 2013 wurden die eingleisigen Tunnelröhren vom westlichen Ende aus mit zwei Tunnelbohrmaschinen (Dennis und Lea) gegraben, zwei weitere (Don und Humber) begannen 2015 vom östlichen Ende aus. Alle Stationen wurden in offener Bauweise errichtet. Der Bau des größtenteils oberirdischen Abschnitts im Osten begann erst im Jahr 2017. Dieser Abschnitt umfasst auch die unterirdische Haltestelle Science Centre, wo gegen Ende des Jahrzehnts die neue Ontario Line in einem Hochbahnhof enden wird, sowie eine unterirdische Endstation am Knoten Kennedy.

Zwischen Baubeginn im Jahr 2011 und nun angepeilter Inbetriebnahme im Jahr 2024 kam es bei der „Eglinton Crosstown Line" zu erheblichen Verzögerungen und Rechtsstreitigkeiten. In der Zwischenzeit begannen zwei TBMs (Renny und Rexy) vom westlichen Ende aus mit dem Bohren zweier 6 km langer Röhren für die 9,2 km lange „Eglinton Crosstown West Extension" durch den Bezirk Etobicoke. Die Westverlängerung beginnt unterirdisch am Bahnhof Mount Dennis, geht dann aber in Hochlage über, verschwindet aber nach den Stationen Jane Street und Scarlett Road wieder im Untergrund bis zum Renforth Drive direkt hinter der Stadtgrenze zu Mississauga, wo ein Anschluss an die Busse auf dem „Mississauga Transitway" geschaffen wird. Zukünftig ist eine oberirdische Verlängerung zum Flughafen Pearson möglich.

Eine östliche Erweiterung, mit Projektnamen „Eglinton East Light Rail Transit" (EELRT, künftige Linie 7), ist als eigenständige 18 km lange oberirdische Stadtbahnlinie vom Bahnhof Kennedy über den University of Toronto Scarborough Campus (UTSC) zum Stadtzentrum von Malvern geplant, gegebenenfalls mit einer Verbindung zur zukünftigen Endstation der Linie 2 (und möglicherweise der Linie 4) Sheppard East/McCowan.

Die Linie 5 wird mit einer Flotte von 76 Flexity Freedom-Fahrzeugen (Nr. 6200-6275) von Bombardier betrieben, die in Thunder Bay, Ontario und Sahagún, Mexiko produziert wurden. Sie sind Eigentum von *Metrolinx* und werden von *Crosslinx Transit Solutions* gewartet, aber von der TTC betrieben. Nach einigen Verzögerungen wurden sie zwischen 2019 und 2022 ausgeliefert. Die 31 m langen und 2,65 m breiten Fahrzeuge verfügen nur über eine Fahrerkabine, da sie stets in Doppeltraktion unterwegs sind. Die Bahnsteige sind lang genug für drei Wagen. Für den U-Bahn-Abschnitt Mount Dennis – Laird sind die Fahrzeuge mit einem automatischen Zugsteuerungssystem (ATC) ausgestattet, das es ihnen ermöglicht, sich im Betriebshof fahrerlos zu bewegen. 750 V Gleichstrom werden über einen Stromabnehmer aus einer Oberleitung zugeführt.

Black Creek Drive on a bridge before descending into the approximately 10 km tunnel beneath Eglinton Avenue. There are 12 underground stations, two of which provide interchange with Line 1 (Eglinton West being renamed Cedarvale with the opening of Line 5). Starting in 2013, the single-track tube tunnels were dug from the western end by two tunnel boring machines (Dennis and Lea), with two more (Don and Humber) starting from the eastern end in 2015. All the stations were built by cut-and-cover. The construction of the eastern mostly surface section only began in 2017. This section also includes an underground stop at Science Centre, where by the end of the decade the new Ontario Line will terminate in an elevated station, as well as an underground terminus at Kennedy.

The Eglinton Crosstown Line has suffered severe delays and legal disputes since the start of construction in 2011 and the now envisaged launch of passenger service in 2024. In the meantime, two TBMs (Renny and Rexy) began to dig two 6 km tubes from the western end for the 9.2 km Eglinton Crosstown West Extension through the district of Etobicoke. This will start underground at Mount Dennis but soon transition to an elevated guideway between Jane Street and Scarlett Road, before continuing underground all the way to Renforth Drive just across the city border in Mississauga, where interchange with buses on the Mississauga Transitway will be provided. In the future, a surface extension to Pearson Airport is possible.

An eastern extension, the Eglinton East Light Rail Transit (EELRT, future Line 7), is planned as an independent 18 km surface light rail line from Kennedy station to Malvern Town Centre via the University of Toronto Scarborough Campus (UTSC), and with a link to the future terminus of Line 2 (and possibly Line 4) at Sheppard East/McCowan.

Line 5 is operated with a fleet of 76 Flexity Freedom vehicles (nos. 6200-6275) from Bombardier produced in Thunder Bay, Ontario and Sahagún, Mexico. They are owned by Metrolinx and maintained by Crosslinx Transit Solutions, but operated by the TTC. After some delays, they were delivered between 2019 and 2022. Each vehicle is 31 m long and 2.65 m wide, and has only one driver's cab as they will operate coupled end-to-end. Platforms have been built long enough for 3-car operation. For the metro-style Mount Dennis – Laird section they are equipped with an automatic train control (ATC) system which allows them to move in driverless mode within the depot. 750 V DC is collected by a pantograph from an overhead catenary.

Cedarvale

Flexity-Freedom (© Metrolinx)

Citadis Spirit (© Metrolinx)

Line ⑥ Finch West LRT

Während es sich bei der Linie 5, der Eglinton Crosstown Line, in erster Linie um eine unterirdische Stadtbahnlinie handelt, die auf dem östlichen Abschnitt teilweise als oberirdische Straßenbahn verläuft, ist die neue Linie 6 entlang der Finch Avenue West eher eine moderne Straßenbahn mit zwei tiefer liegenden Endstationen. Beide Linien haben 1435 mm Normalspur und sind daher nicht mit der klassischen Straßenbahn von Toronto kompatibel. Die Versorgung mit 750 V Gleichstrom erfolgt über eine Oberleitung.

Die Linie 6 beginnt unterirdisch an der bestehenden Station Finch West der U-Bahn-Linie 1, wobei der Bahnsteig der Linie 6 rechtwinkelig zum Bahnsteig der Linie 1 liegt. Östlich des Bahnhofs führen die Gleise etwa 100 m weiter, was eine zukünftige Verlängerung der Strecke nach Osten vereinfacht – als die Finch-Linie erstmals in den 2000er Jahren vorgeschlagen wurde, sollte sie ähnlich wie die Eglinton Crosstown zu einer Tangentiallinie werden und bis zum U-Bahnhof Don Mills der Linie 4 führen.

Gleich nach Verlassen der unterirdischen Station Finch West erreichen die Straßenbahnen auf einer Rampe die Oberfläche und fahren fast bis zum Ende der Linie auf dem Mittelstreifen der Finch Avenue West. 7,4 km lang geht es geradeaus, der Black Creek und der Humber River werden überquert, und der Highway 400, eine Stadtautobahn, wird unterquert. Der Betriebshof wurde unmittelbar nördlich der Strecke eingerichtet und ist aus beiden Richtungen zwischen den Haltestellen Jane & Finch und Norfinch Oakdale erreichbar. Nach Mount Olive umrundet die Linie 6 das Einkaufszentrum Albion Mall auf dessen Nordseite und fährt weiter nach Südwesten, immer noch der Finch Avenue West folgend, bis zur Haltestelle Westmore. Nachdem sie den Westmore Drive ebenerdig überquert hat, fährt die Straßenbahn in einen kurzen, gebogenen Tunnel ein, um die Kreuzung Finch West/Highway 27 ungehindert zu passieren. Der Rest der Strecke liegt im offenen Einschnitt, ebenfalls die Endstation Humber College, ein U-Bahnhof mit einem Mittelbahnsteig,

While line 5, the Eglinton Crosstown Line, is primarily an underground light rail line with some tram-style surface running on its eastern segment, the new line 6 along Finch Avenue West is rather a modern surface tram with below-ground termini at either end. Both lines have 1435 mm standard gauge and are thus incompatible with Toronto's legacy streetcar system. 750 V DC is supplied via an overhead catenary.

Line 6 starts underground at the existing Finch West station on Subway line 1, with the line 6 platform lying perpendicular to the older line 1 platform. East of the station, the tail tracks continue for some 100 m, allowing for a future eastern extension; when first proposed in the 2000s, the Finch line was to become a crosstown line much like the Eglinton Crosstown, running all the way to Don Mills station on line 4.

Upon leaving Finch West, the trams go up a ramp and reach their surface alignment in the median of Finch Avenue West, which they follow almost to the end of the line. For 7.4 km, the road continues straight ahead, crossing over Black Creek and the Humber River as well as under Highway 400, an urban expressway. The line's depot was established just north of the route, accessible from either direction between the Jane & Finch and Norfinch Oakdale stops. After Mount Olive the line skirts the Albion Mall on its northern side and continues southwest, still following Finch Avenue West, to Westmore. After crossing Westmore Drive at grade, the trams descend into a short curved tunnel to avoid the Finch West/Highway 27 intersection, and remain below grade in an open trench to the terminus at Humber College, which is a partially open-air metro-style station

Line 6 (Finch West)
- 10.6 km (Ⓤ 0.3 km), 18 Stations/Stops (Ⓤ 2)

2024: Humber College – Finch West (10.6 km)

Finch West (© Metrolinx)

der jedoch nicht vollständig überdacht ist. Eine Westverlängerung in Richtung Pearson Airport wurde vorgeschlagen.

Die meisten oberirdischen Haltestellen haben versetzte Bahnsteige nach den jeweiligen Straßenkreuzungen, nach denen sie benannt sind (um Verwechslungen mit bestehenden Bahnhöfen zu vermeiden, heißt die Haltestelle an der Weston Road Emery, an der Islington Avenue Rowntree Mills und an der Kipling Avenue Mount Olive). Mount Olive, Stevenson und Martin Grove haben Mittelbahnsteige, Westmore, Duncanwoods und Pearldale zwei gegenüberliegende Seitenbahnsteige. Wie auf der Linie 5 ist an allen Stationen das neue Ⓣ-Logo zu sehen.

Die Linie 6 wird mit 18 Fahrzeugen vom Typ Alstom Citadis Spirit betrieben. Die vierteiligen Straßenbahnen sind niederflurig, 48 m lang und 2,65 m breit. Die oberirdischen Bahnsteige sind lang genug für einen Wagen, während die beiden Endstationen Platz für Doppeltraktionen hätten. Die Fahrzeuge sind Teil einer größeren Bestellung, die auch Straßenbahnen für die Hurontario-Linie im benachbarten Mississauga umfasst. Die Fahrzeuge wurden in einem nur etwa 25 km entfernten Alstom-Werk in Brampton montiert. Die erste Bahn traf im Juli 2021 ein. Ähnliche Fahrzeuge verkehren auf der Confederation Line in Ottawa.

Die Linie 6 fährt während der Hauptverkehrszeiten alle 5-7 Minuten, sonst alle 7-10 Minuten. Eine Fahrt auf der gesamten Strecke dauert 34 Minuten.

with an island platform. A western extension toward Pearson Airport has been proposed.

Most of the surface stops have offset platforms located after the road intersections they are named after (to avoid confusion with existing stations, the stop at Weston Road is called Emery, at Islington Avenue Rowntree Mills, and at Kipling Avenue Mount Olive); Mount Olive, Stevenson and Martin Grove have island platforms, while Westmore, Duncanwoods and Pearldale have facing side platforms. As on line 5, the new Ⓣ logo is displayed at all stations and stops.

The Finch West line is operated with a fleet of 18 Alstom Citadis Spirit light rail vehicles. The four-section trams are low-floor, 48 m long and 2.65 m wide. The surface platforms were built long enough for single units, while the two termini could accommodate double units. The trams are part of a larger order which includes rolling stock for the Hurontario Line in neighbouring Mississauga. The vehicles were assembled at a new Alstom plant in Brampton, only some 25 km from Line 6's Maintenance and Storage Facility (MSF). The first tram arrived at the MSF in July 2021. Similar vehicles operate on Ottawa's Confederation Line.

Line 6 runs every 5-7 minutes during peak hours, and every 7-10 minutes during off-peak hours. A journey from end to end takes 34 minutes.

Westmore (Aug. 2023 © Grammin/YouTube)

Albion (Aug. 2023 © Grammin/YouTube)

King-Bathurst (© Metrolinx)

Ontario Line

Bei ihrer Fertigstellung Anfang der 2030er Jahre wird die neue Ontario Line 15,6 km lang sein und 15 Stationen haben. Obwohl sie als solche erst 2018 präsentiert wurde, reicht ihre Geschichte bis in die 1980er Jahre zurück, als die „Downtown Relief Line" (Innenstadtentlastungslinie) entworfen wurde, um den Knoten Bloor-Yonge und die „Yonge Subway" ins eigentliche Zentrum zu entlasten. Die Strecke sollte vom U-Bahnhof Pape an der „Bloor-Danforth Subway" nach Süden und dann nach Westen entlang der Queen Street verlaufen, d.h. auf einer Trasse, die in den 1950er Jahren für einen unterirdischen Straßenbahntunnel vorgesehen war. Letztendlich orientierte sich die Regierung von Ontario bei ihrem Projekt an der lange geplanten „Relief Line" und verlängerte sie an beiden Enden — wie bei der Canada Line in Vancouver wurde die neue Linie nach dem Hauptgeldgeber des Projekts benannt. Es ist jedoch wahrscheinlich, dass sie zukünftig als „Linie 3" bezeichnet wird, nachdem die Scarborough RT geschlossen worden ist.

Der Bau der neuen Ontario Line begann im März 2022 am künftigen westlichen Endpunkt Exhibition, einem Hochbahnhof direkt nördlich des bestehenden Bahnhofs von GO Transit, der gleichzeitig umgebaut wird. Die fahrerlosen Züge, die von Hitachi Rail STS Canada geliefert und von *Transdev Canada* betrieben werden, fahren dann in den 6 km langen Innenstadttunnel ein und halten an der Kreuzung King/Bathurst sowie an vier U-Bahnhöfen entlang der Queen Street; an allen Stationen ist ein Übergang zur Straßenbahn und an zwei auch zur U-Bahn-Linie 1 möglich. Fast fünf Jahre lang werden die Straßenbahnen zwischen York Street und Church Street von der Queen Street in die Richmond Street bzw. die Adelaide Street verlegt, teilweise auf neuen Gleisen.

When finished in the early 2030s, the new Ontario Line will be 15.6 km long and feature 15 stations. Though only proposed as such in 2018, its history dates back to the 1980s when a 'Downtown Relief Line' was suggested to reduce overcrowding at the Bloor-Yonge interchange and the 'Yonge Subway' into the CBD. The route was to run south from Pape station on the 'Bloor-Danforth Subway' and then west along the Queen Street corridor, an alignment which in the 1950s had been considered for a streetcar tunnel. Eventually, the Government of Ontario based its project on the long proposed Relief Line and extended it at either end — as with the Canada Line in Vancouver, the primary funder of the project gave the new line its name. It is likely, however, that with the Scarborough RT now closed, it will be become known as 'Line 3'.

The construction of the new Ontario Line started in March 2022 at the future western terminus Exhibition, an elevated station which will be located on the north side of the existing GO Transit station, which is being completely rebuilt at the same time. The driverless trains, which will be supplied by Hitachi Rail STS Canada and operated by Transdev Canada, will then descend into the 6 km downtown tunnel, with one station at the King/Bathurst intersection and four along Queen Street, all connecting to Toronto's streetcar system and two providing interchange with Subway line 1. For a period of

Ontario Line
- 15.6 km (Ⓤ ~9 km), 15 Stations (Ⓤ 8)

  ~2031: Exhibition – Science Centre (15.6 km)

Exhibition (© Metrolinx)

Im Gegensatz zur ursprünglichen „Relief Line" biegt die Ontario Line dann hinter dem U-Bahnhof Moss Park nach Süden zum U-Bahnhof Corktown ab, bevor sie nach Osten schwenkt und neben dem wichtigsten Eisenbahnkorridor Kanadas aus dem Tunnel auftaucht. Diese Trasse wurde gewählt, um die Anbindung an das als Lower Don Lands bekannte Entwicklungsgebiet über den künftigen GO Transit/Ontario Line-Knoten East Harbour zu verbessern, gleichzeitig soll auch der Knoten Union Station entlastet werden. Die Ontario Line wird an zwei weiteren Hochbahnhöfen neben der Eisenbahn halten, bevor sie nördlich der Gerrard Street East wieder im Untergrund verschwindet. Die Strecke wird mit Tunnelbohrmaschinen aufgefahren und folgt der Pape Avenue, schwenkt jedoch am U-Bahnhof Pape leicht nach Osten ab, um beim Bau Beeinträchtigungen auf dieser stark befahrenen Straße zu vermeiden. Die Ontario Line verläuft weiter unter der Pape Avenue und hält an einem U-Bahnhof zwischen Cosburn Avenue und Gamble Avenue. Sie überquert dann das Don Valley auf einer eigens dafür gebauten Brücke und fährt auf einem Viadukt weiter durch den Stadtteil Thorncliffe Park, wo auch der Betriebshof angesiedelt wird. Die Linie überquert dann den Westarm des Don River, hält am Hochbahnhof Flemingdale Park in der Nähe des Ontario Science Centre und endet wenig später in Hochlage an der Station Science Centre an der Kreuzung mit der Eglinton Avenue East, wo ein Übergang zur hier unterirdisch haltenden Linie 5 möglich ist. Von hier könnte die Ontario Line entlang des Don Mills-Korridors nach Norden verlängert werden.

almost 5 years, streetcars will be diverted between York and Church Streets from Queen Street onto Richmond and Adelaide Streets, partly on new tracks.

Unlike the original Relief Line, the 'Ontario Line' will then turn south after Moss Park station, serving Corktown station before turning east and emerging from the tunnel alongside Canada's busiest rail corridor. This alignment was chosen to improve connections to the redevelopment area known as Lower Don Lands via the future GO Transit/Ontario Line interchange at East Harbour, which is also intended to relieve the Union Station hub. The metro line will feature two more elevated stations adjacent to the railway before returning underground north of Gerrard Street East. Excavated by tunnel boring machines, the route will follow Pape Avenue, but swing slightly east at Pape station to prevent major disruptions on this busy road. Back under Pape Avenue, the Ontario Line will serve another underground station located between Cosburn and Gamble Avenues before crossing the Don Valley on a purpose-built bridge. It will then continue on a viaduct through Thorncliffe Park, where the line's maintenance and storage facility will also be established. The line will then cross the Don River West Branch before serving the elevated Flemingdale Park station near the Ontario Science Centre and terminating shortly after on a viaduct at Science Centre station at the intersection with Eglinton Avenue East, where interchange will be provided to Line 5, which has an underground station there. In the long term, the Ontario Line could be extended north from there along the Don Mills corridor.

(© Hitachi Rail/Metrolinx)

Exhibition – Lakeshore West Line

GO Transit

In der „Greater Toronto and Hamilton Area" findet man ein Regionalbahnnetz mit ganztägig verkehrenden Zügen, zumindest auf einigen seiner Strecken. Das als „GO Transit" (kurz für Government of Ontario Transit, heute zu Metrolinx gehörend) bezeichnete Netz besteht aus sieben Radiallinien mit unterschiedlichem Zugangebot. Von Oshawa auf der **Lakeshore East Line** verkehren halbstündlich Züge zur Union Station, die nach einem 5-minütigen Halt direkt auf der **Lakeshore West Line** nach Aldershot weiterfahren; einmal pro Stunde erreichen sie West Harbour in Hamilton und dreimal täglich Niagara Falls (2h15). Der Bahnhof Hamilton GO Centre wird hingegen nur von vier Zügen in der Hauptverkehrszeit bedient, sonst verkehrt dorthin ein Bus von Aldershot aus. Der Takt auf dem Lakeshore-Korridor wird während der Hauptverkehrszeiten noch verdichtet, wobei einige Züge auf dem inneren Abschnitt der Lakeshore West Line einzelne Stationen ohne Halt durchfahren. Auf der **Kitchener Line** verkehren den ganzen Tag über etwa einmal pro Stunde Züge bis Bramalea, 20 Züge pro Tag fahren weiter bis Mount Pleasant, 12 bis Georgetown und 9 bis nach Kitchener, allerdings mit längeren Pausen zwischen den einzelnen Fahrten. Die **Barrie Line** bietet 16 Züge pro Tag nach Aurora, von denen 9 vor allem während der Hauptverkehrszeiten weiter bis Allandale Waterfront in Barrie fahren. Ein ähnliches Angebot findet man auf der **Stouffville Line** mit 13 Zügen pro Tag bis Mount Joy, von denen 7 während der Hauptverkehrszeiten bis nach Old Elm weiterfahren. Mit nur 8 bzw. 4-5 Zügen pro Tag in Hauptlastrichtung weisen die **Milton Line** und **Richmond Hill Line** einen eher beschei-

The Greater Toronto and Hamilton Area boasts a regional rail network with trains running all day, at least on some of its lines. Known as 'GO Transit' (short for Government of Ontario Transit, now an operating division of Metrolinx), the network comprises seven radial lines, each with a different level of service. From Oshawa on the Lakeshore East Line *there are trains every half hour to Union Station, which after a 5-minute stop, continue directly on the* Lakeshore West Line *to Aldershot. Once an hour they run to West Harbour in Hamilton, and three times a day all the way to Niagara Falls (2h 15m). Hamilton GO Centre station is only served by four peak trains, and otherwise by bus from Aldershot. Service on the Lakeshore corridor is increased during peak hours, when some trains skip some stations on the inner section of the Lakeshore West Line. On the* Kitchener Line, *trains run about once an hour all day to Bramalea, 20 trains a day continuing to Mount Pleasant, 12 to Georgetown and 9 all the way to Kitchener, though with longer gaps between trains. The* Barrie Line *has 16 trains per day to Aurora, 9 of which continue to Allandale Waterfront in Barrie primarily during peak hours. Similarly, the* Stouffville Line *has 13 trains per day to Mount Joy, with 7 running all the way to Old Elm during peak hours. With only 8 and 4-5 trains, respectively, per day in the peak direction, the* Milton Line *and the* Richmond Hill Line *have a rather limited timetable. All the routes, however, are served by GO buses when no train service is available.*

GO Transit was first established by the provincial government in 1967 on the Lakeshore Line between

Downsview Park – Barrie Line (Umsteigemöglichkeit zur U-Bahn-Linie 1 | *Interchange with Subway Line 1*)

denen Fahrplan auf. In den Zeiten ohne Zugverkehr werden jedoch alle Strecken stattdessen mit GO-Bussen bedient.

GO Transit wurde 1967 von der Provinzregierung auf der Lakeshore-Linie zwischen Hamilton im Westen und Pickering im Osten eingeführt, zunächst mit einstöckigen Waggons. Der Regionalverkehr wurde 1974 auf die Georgetown Line über Malton und Brampton und 1978 auf die Richmond Hill Line ausgeweitet; im selben Jahr wurden erstmals Doppelstockwagen eingesetzt. In den 1980er Jahren wurde das GO-Netz mit den Strecken nach Milton (1981) sowie Bradford und Stouffville (1982) erweitert. Ab 1990 fuhren einige Züge während der Hauptverkehrszeit weiter nach Barrie, Guelph und Oshawa. Im Jahr 2007 wurde der ganztägige Betrieb nach Barrie South aufgenommen und im Jahr 2011 wurde die Georgetown Line bis Kitchener verlängert.

Im Jahr 2013 wurde auf den Lakeshore-Linien der ganztägige Halbstundentakt eingeführt. Metrolinx beginnt derzeit, mehrere Strecken zu modernisieren und zu elektrifizieren, um ein echtes S-Bahn-Netz zu schaffen. Die Züge sollen auf der Lakeshore West Line (bis Burlington) und auf der Lakeshore East Line sowie auf den inneren Abschnitten der Kitchener Line (bis Bramalea), der Barrie Line (bis Aurora) und der Stouffville Line (bis Unionville) alle 15 Minuten verkehren, während der Hauptverkehrszeiten noch häufiger. Im Rahmen dieses ehrgeizigen Projekts wurde 2023 ein neues Viadukt auf der Barrie Line zwischen Bloor und Davenport in Betrieb genommen, um Kreuzungen nicht nur mit Straßen, sondern auch mit einer Güterstrecke in der Nähe der Dupont Street zu beseitigen. Die Barrie Line wird bis Aurora zweigleisig ausgebaut und bis Allandale Waterfront elektrifiziert. Im Osten der Metropolregion wird das GO-Netz von Oshawa nach Bowmanville (20 km) erweitert,

Hamilton in the west and Pickering in the east, initially with single-deck coaches. Commuter rail service was introduced on the Georgetown Line via Malton and Brampton in 1974, and on the Richmond Hill Line in 1978; that same year, double-deck coaches started service on GO lines. During the 1980s, the GO network was expanded with trains running to Milton (1981), Bradford and Stouffville (1982). In 1990, some trains started to continue to Barrie, Guelph and Oshawa during rush hour. In 2007, regular service began to Barrie South, and in 2011, the Georgetown line was extended to Kitchener.

In 2013, a half-hourly all-day service was introduced on the Lakeshore lines. Metrolinx is now upgrading and electrifying several routes to provide a proper S-Bahn/RER-style service, with trains running every 15 minutes on the Lakeshore West (to Burlington) and East lines, as well as the inner sections of the Kitchener (to Bramalea), Barrie (to Aurora) and Stouffville (to Unionville) lines, with even more frequent service during peak hours. As part of this ambitious project, a new viaduct opened in 2023 on the Barrie Line between Bloor and Davenport to eliminate grade intersections not only with roads, but also with a freight line near Dupont Street. The Barrie Line will be double-tracked to Aurora and electrified all the way to Allandale Waterfront. In the east of the metropolitan region, the GO service is being extended from Oshawa to Bowmanville (20 km), which requires a new link between the two parallel railways. Within Toronto, after a new station opened at Mount Dennis (Kitchener Line) together with Line 5 (Eglinton Crosstown), the SmartTrack Stations Program envisages the construction of five new GO stations

Exhibition > Union Station (Bathurst Bridge)

wofür eine neue Verbindung zwischen den beiden parallelen Eisenbahnstrecken geschaffen werden muss. Innerhalb Torontos sieht das „SmartTrack Stations Program" nach der Eröffnung einer neuen Station Mount Dennis (Kitchener Line) zusammen mit der Linie 5 (Eglinton Crosstown) den Bau von fünf neuen GO-Stationen vor: Finch-Kennedy, East Harbour, King-Liberty, Bloor-Lansdowne und St. Clair-Old Weston.

Derzeit sind auf allen GO-Linien Wendezüge meist mit 10 bzw. 12 Doppelstockwagen von Bombardier unterwegs, die von MP40-Diesellokomotiven gezogen bzw. geschoben werden. Die Fahrzeuge werden im Willowbrook Yard westlich des Bahnhofs Mimico und in Whitby an der äußeren Lakeshore East Line gewartet. Der Großteil der von *GO Transit* genutzten Gleise wurde von der *Canadian National Railway* (CN) gekauft, die Milton Line ist jedoch

at Finch-Kennedy, East Harbour, King-Liberty, Bloor-Lansdowne and St. Clair-Old Weston.

For now, all the GO trains in operation are push-pull trains with mostly 10 or 12 bi-level coaches from Bombardier, hauled or pushed by MP40 diesel locomotives. The GO Transit rolling stock is maintained at the Willowbrook Yard west of Mimico station and at Whitby on the outer Lakeshore East Line. Most of the trackage used by GO Transit has been purchased from the Canadian National Railway (CN), while the Milton Line remains the property of CPKC (Canadian Pacific Kansas City Ltd.).

GO Transit also operates an extensive network of regional buses, but for now, their trains and buses are only integrated with some local transport services outside Toronto, while the TTC day pass is not valid on GO trains or buses. However, passengers can use the

Kitchener

Unterdeck | *Lower deck*

![Union Station > Bloor (Bathurst Bridge)]

Union Station > Bloor (Bathurst Bridge)

weiterhin Eigentum von CPKC (*Canadian Pacific Kansas City Ltd.*).

GO Transit betreibt außerdem ein umfangreiches Regionalbusnetz. Derzeit sind deren Züge und Busse jedoch tariflich nur mit einigen Nahverkehrsgesellschaften außerhalb Torontos integriert. Eine TTC-Tageskarte ist hingegen in GO-Zügen oder -Bussen nicht gültig. Die Fahrgäste können allerdings dieselbe PRESTO Card von Metrolinx verwenden, um den entfernungsabhängigen Fahrpreis zu entrichten. Es gibt keine Zugangssperren, Fahrscheinkontrollen finden stichprobenartig in den Zügen statt. Eine einfache Fahrt kostet z.B. von Union Station nach Port Credit 7,15 $, nach Aurora 10,15 $ und nach Kitchener 19,40 $, mit PRESTO Card etwas weniger. An Wochenenden sind ermäßigte Tageskarten erhältlich, jedoch nur online.

Metrolinx PRESTO Card to pay their fare which is calculated by the distance travelled. A 'proof-of-payment' policy is in place and tickets may be randomly checked on trains. A single fare from Union Station, e.g. to Port Credit is $7.15, to Aurora $10.15, and to Kitchener $19.40; it is slightly less if paid with a PRESTO Card. Reduced-fare passes are available on weekends, but can only be bought online.

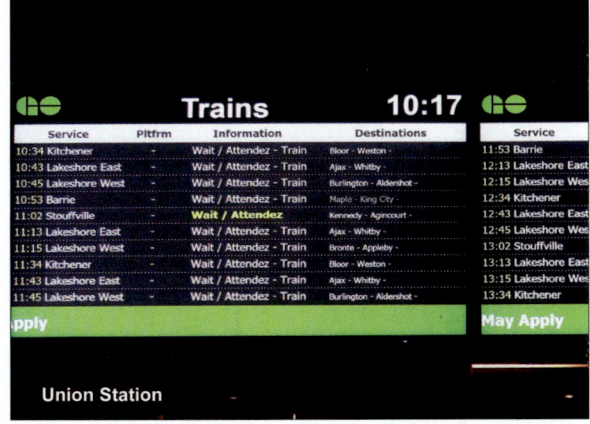

Union Station

Union Station (GO Bay Concourse)

Union Station (Skywalk)

UP Express

Der „Union Pearson (UP) Express" wurde am 6. Juni 2015 von Metrolinx eingeführt, um eine direkte Bahnverbindung zwischen Union Station und dem Pearson International Airport (23,3 km) zu schaffen. Es handelte sich erst um die zweite Flughafenanbindung per Bahn in Kanada, nachdem sechs Jahre zuvor die Canada Line in Vancouver eröffnet worden war. Der UP Express verfügt über einen eigenen Bereich und ein eigenes Gleis am westlichen Ende des Hauptbahnhofs von Toronto, teilt sich dann aber auf dem Weg durch den Nordwesten von Toronto die Gleise mit *GO Transit* und *VIA Rail*. Der UP Express hält an den GO-Bahnhöfen Bloor und Weston, weshalb diese jeweils an einem Ende über 75 m lange Hochbahnsteige für UP-Züge verfügen, während der Rest (310 m) für GO-Züge mit 12 Wagen als Niedrigbahnsteig ausgeführt ist. Nach Durchfahrt ohne Halt am Bahnhof Etobicoke North zweigt der UP Express niveaugleich nach Süden ab und erreicht den Flughafen auf einer 3 km langen, aufgeständerten und zweigleisigen Neubaustrecke. Im Flughafenbahnhof hält auch der „Terminal Link", ein kostenloser Peoplemover, der vom Terminal 1 zum Terminal 3 und weiter zum Bahnhof Viscount fährt, wo sich mehrere Parkmöglichkeiten befinden.

Der UP Express verkehrt alle 15 Minuten und erreicht den Flughafen von der Union Station in 25 Minuten. Während eine einfache Fahrt zur/von der Union Station 12,35 $ kostet, beträgt der Fahrpreis von/bis Bloor, wo man zur U-Bahn-Linie 2 (Station Dundas West) umsteigen kann, nur 5,65 $. Eine Fahrt von Weston zur Union Station kostet 5,65 $, genauso viel wie mit *GO Transit*. Am günstigsten

The Union Pearson (UP) Express was launched by Metrolinx on 6 June 2015 to provide a direct service between Union Station and Pearson International Airport (23.3 km). It became only the second airport rail link in Canada, with Vancouver's Canada Line having opened six years earlier. The UP Express has a dedicated area and track at the western end of Toronto's main railway station, but then shares tracks with GO Transit and VIA Rail as it heads northwest through Toronto, calling at Bloor and Weston; these two stations have 75 m long high platforms at one end for UP trains, while the rest (310 m) is low for the 12-car GO trains. Past Etobicoke North station, which is skipped, the UP Express diverges south in a flat junction and reaches the airport on a 3 km purpose-built double-track elevated line. The airport station is integrated with Terminal Link, the free airport people mover, which runs from Terminal 1 to Terminal 3 and on to Viscount station, where several parking facilities are located.

Union Station

Union Station

kommt man zum Flughafen mit der Expressbuslinie 900 (alle 10 Minuten) vom U-Bahnhof Kipling aus, da für diesen lediglich ein normales TTC-Ticket benötigt wird.

Der UP Express wird mit 18 Dieseltriebwagen betrieben, die von Nippon Sharyo in Japan hergestellt und in Illinois, USA, montiert wurden. Sie verkehren als 2-Wagen- (52 m) oder 3-Wagen-Einheiten (78 m). Sobald die Kitchener Line und der Flughafenabzweig elektrifiziert sind, können die Fahrzeuge auf elektrischen Antrieb umgerüstet werden.

The UP Express operates every 15 minutes and reaches the airport from Union Station in 25 minutes. While a single trip to/from Union Station costs $12.35, it is only $5.65 to/from Bloor, where transfer is available to Subway line 2 (Dundas West station). A trip from Weston to Union Station costs $5.65, the same as with GO Transit. The cheapest way to get to the airport is by express bus 900 (every 10 minutes) from Kipling Subway station, which only requires a standard TTC ticket.

The UP Express is operated with 18 DMUs (diesel multiple units) manufactured by Nippon Sharyo in Japan and assembled in Illinois, USA. They run as 2-car (52 m) or 3-car (78 m) units. Once the Kitchener Line and the airport branch have been electrified, the DMUs can be converted to electric operation.

Bloor

Port Credit (© Metrolinx)

MISSISSAUGA, ON

Ab ca. 2025 wird die 18 km lange **Hazel McCallion Line** (ursprünglich als „Hurontario LRT" bezeichnet, jetzt aber nach einem ehemaligen Bürgermeister von Mississauga benannt) entlang der Hurontario Street in Mississauga, einer Stadt in der Peel Region westlich von Toronto, verlaufen. Mississauga hat 720.000 Einwohner und wird halbstündlich von *GO Transit* mit den Bahnhöfen Port Credit und Clarkson an der Lakeshore West Line sowie, wenn auch nur während der Hauptverkehrszeiten, mit sechs Bahnhöfen von Dixie bis Lisgar an der Milton Line erschlossen.

Wie Torontos Linie 6 ist die Hazel McCallion Line eine moderne Straßenbahn französischer Prägung, die auf eigenem Gleiskörper in Mittellage der Hurontario Street verkehrt, jedoch über zahlreiche Bahnübergänge an Straßenkreuzungen verfügt. Sie beginnt an einer Haltestelle, die unter dem Bahndamm östlich des GO-Bahnhofs Port Credit gebaut wird, dem wichtigsten Umsteigepunkt für Fahrgäste, die nach Toronto möchten. Eine weitere Umsteigemöglichkeit besteht auch am GO-Bahnhof Cooksville der Milton Line, allerdings Richtung Toronto nur zu acht Zügen während der morgendlichen Hauptverkehrszeit zwischen 6:30 und 9:00 Uhr. Die restlichen 10 Haltestellen liegen gleichmäßig verteilt an wichtigen Querstraßen. In der Nähe des Highway 403 entsteht ein aufgeständertes Gleisdreieck, über das das Stadtzentrum von Mississauga angeschlossen ist, wo Anschluss an die Busse auf dem „Mississauga Transitway" besteht. Ursprünglich war eine Schleife um die Innenstadt geplant. Der Betriebshof wird südlich der Autobahn Highway 407 liegen, gleich hinter der Stadtgrenze im benachbarten Brampton (657.000 Einw.), wo sich auch die letzten drei Haltestellen der Linie befinden werden. Die Linie endet am Brampton Gateway Terminal

*Starting in around 2025, the 18 km **Hazel McCallion Line**, initially called the Hurontario LRT but now named after a former Mississauga mayor, will run along Hurontario Street in Mississauga, a city in Peel Region located just west of Toronto. Mississauga has a population of 720,000 and is served half-hourly by GO Transit trains via Port Credit and Clarkson stations on the Lakeshore West Line, and during peak hours only, via six stations on the Milton Line, from Dixie to Lisgar.*

Like Toronto's Line 6, the Hazel McCallion Line is a French-style modern tramway, running on a dedicated right-of-way in the middle of Hurontario Street, but with numerous level crossings at road intersections. It starts in a station built under the embankment of the railway just east of Port Credit GO station, the primary interchange for passengers travelling to/from Toronto. The line also intersects with GO Transit at Cooksville, but with only eight trains during the morning peak (6:30-9:00) going to Toronto on the Milton Line, this is only a secondary interchange. The rest of the 10 stops are evenly spaced and located at major intersections along the route. Near Highway 403, an elevated triangular junction will allow trams to serve the Mississauga City Centre, with connections to the buses on the Mississauga Transitway. Initially, a loop around the city centre had been planned. The Maintenance and Storage Facility will be located south of Highway 407, just across the city border in neighbouring Brampton (pop. 657,000), where the last three stops on the line will also be located. The line ends at Brampton Gateway Terminal on Steeles Avenue, the route of Brampton's Züm bus 511. It had initially been planned to continue 3.3 km north along Main Street South to Brampton GO station, but then

an der Steeles Avenue, auf der die Züm-Buslinie 511 von Brampton verkehrt. Ursprünglich sollte die Strecke 3,3 km weiter nach Norden entlang der Main Street South bis zur GO-Station Brampton führen, doch schließlich wurde eine Trasse durch das alte Stadtzentrum von Brampton abgelehnt.

Die Hurontario-Linie wird vom Konsortium Mobilinx gebaut, zu dem *Transdev* als zukünftiger Betreiber gehört. Die Infrastruktur und die Fahrzeuge sind Eigentum von Metrolinx. Die 44 Citadis Spirit-Fahrzeuge von Alstom wurden zusammen mit den gleichen Straßenbahnen für die Linie 6 Finch West bestellt. Die Fahrzeuge werden vor Ort in einem neuen Werk in Brampton hergestellt. Die meisten Haltestellen verfügen über 90 m lange Inselbahnsteige, die lang genug sind, um Doppeltraktionen aufzunehmen. Die Hazel McCallion Line soll während der Hauptverkehrszeiten alle 7½ Minuten und zu anderen Zeiten alle 12-15 Minuten verkehren, wobei die Fahrt von einem Ende zum anderen etwa 40 Minuten dauern wird.

Mississauga City Centre (© Metrolinx)

a route through Brampton's historic town centre was rejected.

The Hurontario line is being built by the Mobilinx consortium, which includes Transdev as the future operator. The infrastructure and rolling stock is owned by Metrolinx, who ordered 44 Citadis Spirit vehicles from Alstom together with the same trams for Line 6 Finch West. The vehicles are manufactured locally at a new plant in Brampton. Most stops will feature 90 m island platforms, long enough to accommodate 2-car trains. The Hazel McCallion Line is planned to run every 7½ minutes during peak hours and every 12-15 minutes at other times, taking some 40 minutes from end to end.

BRAMPTON

(Brampton Gateway Terminal/Steeles)
(County Court)
(Ray Lawson) D

(Derry)

Hazel McCallion Line

(Courtneypark)

(Britannia)

(Matheson)

(Bristol)

Hurontario Street

(Eglinton)

Milton

Mississauga City Centre
Square One

(Duke of York) proj.

Streetsville

Erindale

Erin Mills

Winston Churchill

Renforth
5
Orbitor
Spectrum
Etobicoke Creek
Tahoe

Mississauga Transitway

Dixie
Tomken
Cawthra
Central Parkway

MISSISSAUGA

(Robert Speck)
(Burnhamthorpe)
(Fairview)

Cooksville
(Dundas)
(Queensway)
(North Service)
(Mineola)

Port Credit

Toronto
Peel Region

Dixie

Etobicoke Creek

Toronto

Lake Ontario

Aldershot
Hamilton

5 km

King Street/Mary Street (© Metrolinx)

HAMILTON, ON

Hamilton liegt an der Westspitze des Ontariosees, etwa 60 km südwestlich der Innenstadt von Toronto und etwa 40 km von Mississauga entfernt. Die Hafenstadt hat knapp 600.000 Einwohner und ist Teil der „Greater Toronto and Hamilton Area". GO Transit-Züge verkehren etwa stündlich vom Bahnhof West Harbour nach Toronto, dazu kommen in der Hauptverkehrszeit einige Züge vom Bahnhof Hamilton GO Centre.

Der Bau einer modernen Straßenbahnlinie wurde 2015 von der Regierung Ontarios genehmigt, etwa zeitgleich mit der Hurontario-Linie in Mississauga. Hamiltons Projekt wurde jedoch 2019 gestrichen und zwei Jahre später wieder zum Leben erweckt. Während also der Bau in Mississauga im Jahr 2023 in vollem Gange war, werden die Arbeiten in Hamilton erst 2024 beginnen.

Bei der ersten Linie der Stadt, die als „Hamilton LRT" bezeichnet wird, handelt es sich um eine moderne Straßenbahn, die in den historischen Stadtkern entlang der King Street integriert wird. Die 14 km lange Linie beginnt an der McMaster University im Westen der Stadt und folgt von dort aus der Main Street in Richtung Stadtzentrum. Nach der Überquerung des Highway 403 wird es einen Abzweig nach Süden auf der Frid Street zum Betriebshof geben. Auf der Dundurn Street wechselt die Straßenbahn von der Main Street in die King Street, der sie durch die Innenstadt bis zum Gage Park folgt. Der zentrale Abschnitt der King Street soll ausschließlich von Straßenbahnen und Radfahrern genutzt werden, wobei zu bestimmten Zeiten Lieferverkehr erlaubt ist. Stattdessen wird die parallel verlaufende Main Street zukünftig dem Autoverkehr in beiden Richtungen zur Verfügung stehen. Am Gage Park kehrt die Linie auf ihrem Weg nach Osten bis zum Queenston Circle auf die

Hamilton lies at the western tip of Lake Ontario, some 60 km southwest of downtown Toronto and some 40 km from Mississauga. The port city has a population of almost 600,000 and is part of the Greater Toronto and Hamilton Area. GO Transit trains provide a link to Toronto roughly every hour from West Harbour station, complemented during peak hour by a few trains from Hamilton GO Centre station.

The construction of a modern tram line was approved by the Government of Ontario in 2015, around the same time as the Hurontario line in Mississauga. Hamilton's project, however, was cancelled in 2019 only to be revived two years later. So while the construction of Mississauga's line was in full swing in 2023, work will only be launched in Hamilton in 2024.

Known as the 'Hamilton LRT', the city's first line will be a modern tramway which will be integrated into the city's historic centre along King Street. The 14 km line will start at McMaster University in the west end, from where it will follow Main Street towards the city centre. After crossing Highway 403, there will be a junction for a branch south on Frid Street to the Maintenance and Storage Facility. On Dundurn Street, the trams will switch from Main Street to King Street, which they will follow through the city centre and all the way to Gage Park. The downtown section of King Street will be used exclusively by trams and cyclists, with only delivery traffic being allowed at certain times. Instead, the parallel Main Street will be converted to two-way traffic. From Gage Park, the line will return to Main Street on its way east to Queenston Circle, and finally follow Queenston Road to the terminus at Eastgate, a major

Main Street zurück und folgt schließlich der Queenston Road bis zur Endstation am Eastgate, einem großen Einkaufszentrum östlich des Red Hill Valley Parkway. In den frühen Plänen war die aktuell geplante Strecke als B-Line dargestellt, die durch eine A-Line entlang der James Street vom GO-Bahnhof West Harbour zum Flughafen sowie durch drei besondere Buslinien (BRT) ergänzt werden sollte. Die A-Line wurde später zu einem Ast der B-Line zum GO-Bahnhof West Harbour verkürzt, letztendlich aber gänzlich gestrichen. Daher wird die neue Straßenbahnlinie vorerst keinen direkten Übergang zu den Zügen von GO Transit bieten, da der Bahnhof Hamilton GO Centre etwa 400 m und der häufiger bediente Bahnhof West Harbour 1,2 km von der künftigen Straßenbahnhaltestelle an der King Street/James Street entfernt sind. Die Haltestellen werden eine Länge von 60 m aufweisen, so dass noch zu bestellende Straßenbahnen in Doppeltraktion eingesetzt werden können.

Bis heute wird das städtische Busnetz von Hamilton von der Hamilton Street Railway betrieben – ein Name, der an das frühere Straßenbahnnetz der Stadt erinnert. Es begann im Jahr 1874 mit Pferdebahnen auf der James Street und der King Street, und elektrische Straßenbahnen wurden bereits 1892 in Betrieb genommen. Das Netz wurde in den folgenden Jahrzehnten erweitert und umfasste 1940 sieben Linien, die jedoch bis 1951 alle stillgelegt und durch Busse bzw. Obusse ersetzt wurden; letztere verkehrten in Hamilton bis 1992.

shopping centre east of the Red Hill Valley Parkway. In the early plans, the currently planned route was shown as the B-Line, which was complemented by an A-Line along James Street from West Harbour GO station to the airport, as well as three BRT corridors. The A-Line was later shortened to become just a branch to West Harbour, but it was eventually shelved. So for now, the new tram line will not provide any direct interchange with GO Transit, with Hamilton GO Centre station some 400 m and the busier West Harbour station 1.2 km from the future tram stop at King/James Streets. Platforms will be built 60 m long to accommodate 2-car sets; the trams have yet to be ordered.

Local buses in Hamilton are today still operated by the 'Hamilton Street Railway', a name reminiscent of the city's former streetcar system. It started with horse trams in 1874 on James and King Streets, with electric trams being in operation in as early as 1892. The network was expanded over the following decades and by 1940 had seven lines; by 1951, however, they had all been abandoned and replaced by buses or trolleybuses. The latter continued to run in Hamilton until 1992.

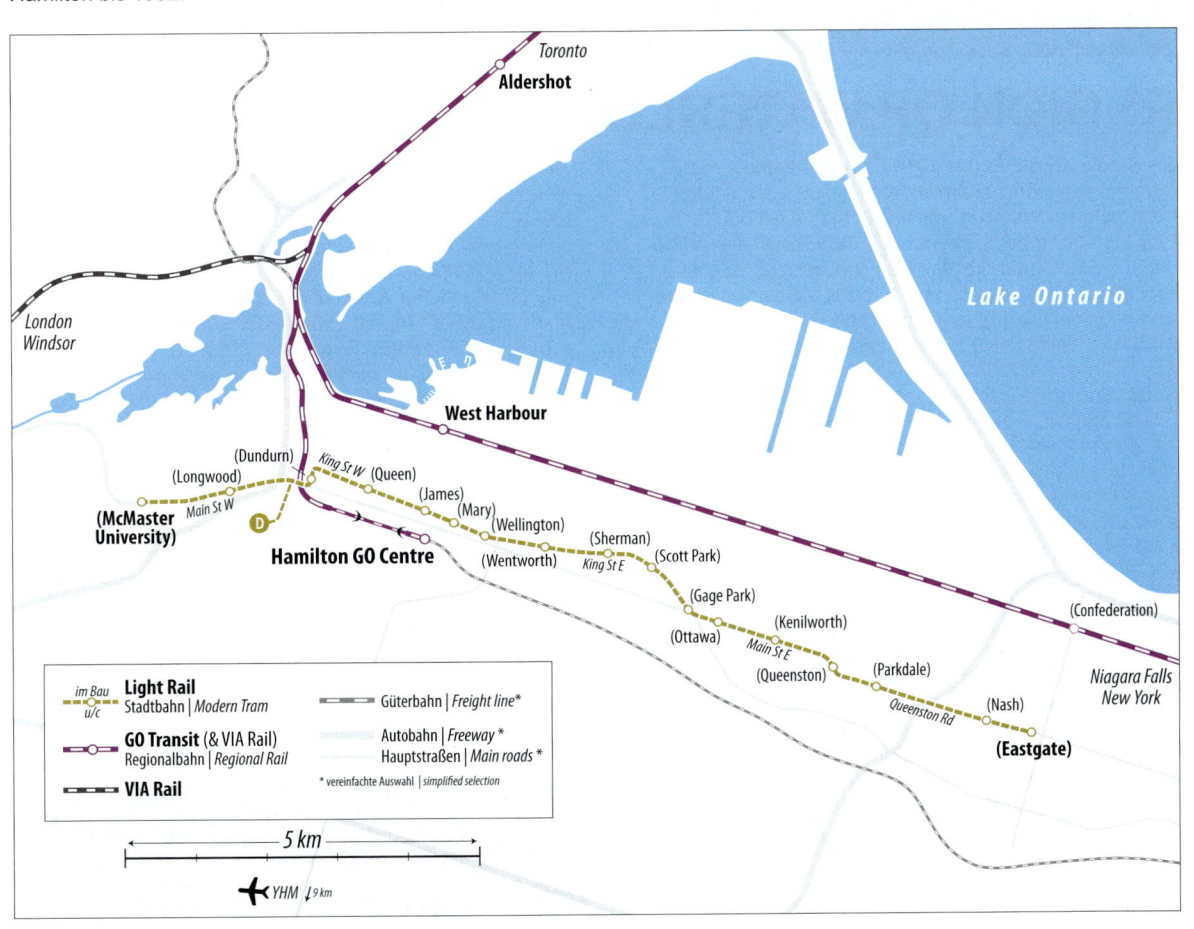

Grand River Hospital

REGION OF WATERLOO, ON

Die Städte Kitchener (bis 1916 *Berlin*), Waterloo und Cambridge bilden zusammen mit vier Landgemeinden die „Region of Waterloo" mit zusammen etwa 600.000 Einwohnern, wobei Kitchener (257.000 Einw.) die größte der drei Städte und Sitz des Regionalrates ist. Kitchener liegt etwa 90 km westlich von Toronto; die beiden Städte sind neunmal pro Tag durch die Züge von *GO Transit* (Kitchener Line; 1h45) miteinander verbunden, einmal pro Tag hält hier auch *VIA Rail* auf der Fahrt von Toronto nach Sarnia und umgekehrt.

Der öffentliche Nahverkehr in der Region Waterloo wird von *Grand River Transit* (GRT) betrieben, dazu gehört auch eine Stadtbahnlinie namens „ION Light Rail" bzw. Linie 301. Eine Einzelfahrt kostet 3,50 $ (2,92 $ bei Bezahlung mit einer EasyGO-Wertkarte). Eine Tageskarte ist an Fahrkartenautomaten für 8,50 $ erhältlich, man benötigt dazu jedoch eine EasyGO-Karte für 5,00 $.

Ab 1889 fuhren zwischen Waterloo und Berlin Pferdestraßenbahnen auf einer 4 km langen Strecke entlang der King Street, mit einem Abzweig zum Bahnhof. Die Strecke wurde 1895 elektrifiziert und blieb bis 1946 in Betrieb, bevor sie durch Obusse ersetzt wurde, die bis 1973 verkehrten.

Von 1904 bis 1955 betrieb die *Preston and Berlin Street Railway* (später CPR) eine elektrische Überlandbahn zwischen Preston (heute Teil von Cambridge) und der Stadt, die später in Kitchener umbenannt wurde.

The cities of Kitchener (until 1916 known as Berlin), Waterloo and Cambridge, together with four rural townships, form the Region of Waterloo with a combined population of approx. 600,000. Kitchener (pop. 257,000), the largest of the three cities, is the seat of the regional council. Kitchener lies some 90 km west of Toronto and is served by GO Transit's Kitchener Line 9 times a day (1h 45min) and VIA Rail's Toronto-Sarnia service once a day.

Public transport in the Waterloo Region is provided by Grand River Transit (GRT) and includes one LRT line known as 'ION Light Rail' or route 301. A single fare is $3.50 ($2.92 if paid with an EasyGO fare card). A Day Pass is available from ticket vending machines for $8.50 but requires an EasyGO fare card for $5.00.

Horse-drawn streetcars started running on a 4 km route along King Street between Waterloo and Berlin in 1889, with a spur to the railway station. The line was electrified in 1895 and operated until 1946, when it was replaced by trolleybuses, which lasted until 1973.

From 1904 until 1955, the Preston and Berlin Street Railway (and later the CPR) operated electric interurban trains between Preston (now part of Cambridge) and what would later become Kitchener.

ION Light Rail
- 16.3 km - 16 Stops

21-06-2019: Conestoga – Fairway (16.3 km)

Northfield – LOS = Line-of-sight operation | Fahren auf Sicht)

ION Light Rail

Nachdem die Region Waterloo im Jahr 2000 die Verant-wortung für den öffentlichen Nahverkehr in der Region übernommen hatte, wählte sie im Jahr 2009 die Stadtbahn (LRT – „Light Rail Transit") als bevorzugtes Verkehrsmittel der Zukunft. Der Bau der ersten Strecke wurde zwei Jahre später beschlossen, und noch bevor 2015 mit dem Bau begonnen wurde, erhielt die neue Bahn den Namen „ION", was auf eine kontinuierliche Bewegung wie bei einem elektrisch geladenen Atom anspielen soll.

Trotz der Bezeichnung als „Light Rail" hat die Stadtbahn von Waterloo wenig Ähnlichkeit mit der etwa zur gleichen Zeit gebauten „Confederation Line" in Ottawa. Sie weist vielmehr zwei recht unterschiedliche Trassierungen auf, nämlich Straßenbahn- und Eisenbahnabschnitte.

Die Linie startet im Norden von Waterloo am Einkaufs-zentrum Conestoga, führt erst nach Norden und dann nach Westen entlang des Mittelstreifens des Northfield Drive West, überquert den Conestoga Parkway und erreicht die Haltestelle Northfield. Hier wechseln die Fahrer vom Straßenbahnbetrieb (Fahrt auf Sicht) auf Eisenbahnbe-trieb, da der 4,6 km lange Abschnitt vor ihnen mit einem ATP-System (Automatic Train Protection) und Eisenbahn-signalen ausgerüstet ist. Auf diesem Abschnitt gibt es vier Bahnübergänge an Straßenkreuzungen sowie mehrere Fußgängerüberwege, die allesamt durch Schranken gesichert sind. Etwas südlich der Haltestelle Northfield mündet in das westliche Gleis (Richtung Süden) ein von Elmira kommendes Gütergleis; Güterzüge befahren diesen Abschnitt vorzugsweise nachts. Um eine Beeinträchtigung der Bahnsteige zu vermeiden, wurde an den nächsten

With the Region of Waterloo having taken over respon-sibility for transport in the area in 2000, it chose light rail transit (LRT) as the preferred technology for rapid transit in 2009. The initial route was approved two years later. Before construction started in 2015, the new system was named 'ION', suggesting continuous movement like an electrically charged atom.

Though labelled 'light rail', this system bears little resemblance to the Confederation Line in Ottawa built around the same time. Instead, it features two rather different types of alignment, namely tram and railway sections.

The route starts in the north of Waterloo at the Conestoga shopping centre, heading north and then west along the median of Northfield Drive West to cross Conestoga Parkway before arriving at the Northfield stop. At this point, the drivers switch from tram operation (line-of-sight) to railway operation, as the 4.6 km section ahead is equipped with an ATP (automatic train protection) system and railway signals. This section has four level crossings at road intersections plus several for pedestrians only, all protected with barriers. Just south of the Northfield stop, the western (southbound) track merges with a freight track coming from Elmira; freight trains may use this section but preferably at night. To prevent interference with the platforms, the next three stops feature gauntlet tracks. Near Waterloo Public Square, the freight track diverges east and the light rail line becomes a typical modern tramway, returning to line-of-sight operation and, unlike Toronto,

REGION OF WATERLOO

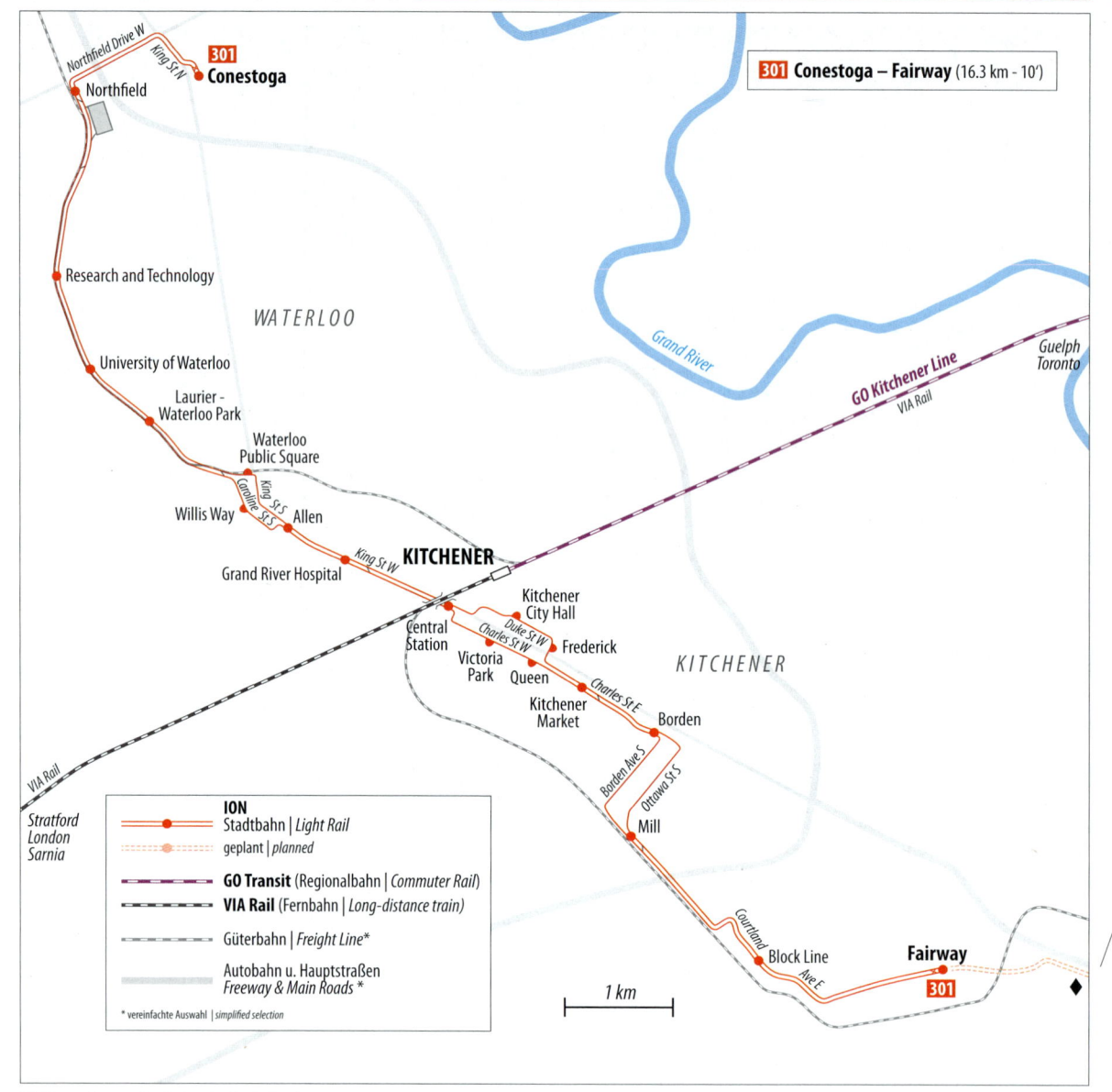

301 **Conestoga – Fairway** (16.3 km - 10')

Map labels:
- Northfield Drive W
- King St N
- **301** **Conestoga**
- Northfield
- Research and Technology
- WATERLOO
- University of Waterloo
- Laurier – Waterloo Park
- Waterloo Public Square
- Caroline St S
- King St S
- Willis Way
- Allen
- Grand River Hospital
- King St W
- **KITCHENER**
- Central Station
- Kitchener City Hall
- Duke St W
- Charles St W
- Frederick
- Victoria Park
- Queen
- Charles St E
- Kitchener Market
- Borden
- KITCHENER
- Grand River
- GO Kitchener Line
- VIA Rail
- Guelph Toronto
- Borden Ave S
- Ottawa St S
- Mill
- Stratford London Sarnia
- VIA Rail
- Courtland
- Block Line
- Ave E
- **Fairway**
- **301**

Legend:
ION
- Stadtbahn | Light Rail
- geplant | planned
- **GO Transit** (Regionalbahn | Commuter Rail)
- **VIA Rail** (Fernbahn | Long-distance train)
- Güterbahn | Freight Line*
- Autobahn u. Hauptstraßen Freeway & Main Roads *
- * vereinfachte Auswahl | simplified selection

1 km

Haltestellen, ähnlich wie bei der Lossetalbahn bei Kassel, ein 4-Schienen-Gleis verlegt. In der Nähe des Waterloo Public Square zweigt das Gütergleis nach Osten ab und die Stadtbahnlinie wird zu einer typischen modernen Straßenbahn, die wieder auf Sicht fährt und im Gegensatz zu Toronto mit Straßenbahnsignalen europäischer Art ausgerüstet ist. Durch das Stadtzentrum von Waterloo sind die Gleise in unterschiedlichen Straßen verlegt, treffen dann aber auf der King Street, wo 130 Jahre zuvor schon Pferdestraßenbahnen fuhren, wieder aufeinander. Kurz darauf passieren die modernen Straßenbahnen die Stadtgrenze zwischen Waterloo und Kitchener und unterqueren die Gleise der *Canadian National Railway* (CN), bevor sie das Stadtzentrum von Kitchener erreichen. Der Bahnhof liegt 600 m von der ION-Haltestelle Central Station entfernt, die zu einem wichtigen Verkehrsknotenpunkt werden soll.

Durch das Stadtzentrum von Kitchener spaltet sich die Straßenbahnlinie erneut auf und fährt dann auf dem

with European-style tram traffic signals. The route splits through the Waterloo city centre, but soon the two tracks align side by side again on King Street, where urban rail service began with horse-drawn streetcars 130 years earlier. Shortly after, the modern trams cross the border between Waterloo and Kitchener, reaching the latter's city centre after passing beneath the Canadian National Railway (CN) tracks. The city's railway station is a 600 m walk from the ION's Central Station stop, which is planned to become a major transport hub.

The tram line again splits through the Kitchener city centre, then continues along the median of Charles Street E (one block south from King Street E) before reaching the Borden stop. From there, the trams again operate on different streets in either direction, with the tram line on the side of the road and with numerous private driveway accesses besides the road intersections. After 850 m, however, the trams switch

Waterloo Public Square – Übergang von Eisenbahn- auf Straßenbahnabschnitt | *transition from railway to tram section*

Hwy 8

Hwy 401

Speed River

(Sportsworld)

(Pinebush)

(Preston)

Hespeler Rd

(Cambridge Centre Mall)

(Can-Amera)

Grand River

(Delta)

CAMBRIDGE

(Main)

(Downtown Cambridge)

Fairway

Mittelstreifen der Charles Street E (einen Block südlich der King Street E) weiter, bis sie die Haltestelle Borden erreicht. Ab hier verkehren die Trams je nach Richtung wieder auf unterschiedlichen Straßen, nun in Randlage, wobei es neben Straßenkreuzungen auch zahlreiche private Zufahrten gibt. Nach 850 m wechseln die Straßenbahnen jedoch wieder vom Straßenbahn- in den Eisenbahnbetrieb, auch wenn hier die Straßenbahngleise auf 1,2 km parallel zur Güterbahnstrecke liegen. Selbst die letzten 2,6 km bis zur Endstation Fairway sind mit Eisenbahnsignalen ausgerüstet, obwohl dieser Abschnitt enge Kurven aufweist; alle Bahnübergänge sind hier mit automatischen Schranken gesichert. Wie der nördliche liegt auch der südliche Endpunkt an einem großen Einkaufszentrum. Eine Fahrt auf der gesamten Strecke dauert 43 Minuten, was einer Durchschnittsgeschwindigkeit von 22 km/h entspricht. Während auf einigen eisenbahnähnlichen Abschnitten Geschwindigkeiten von bis zu 70 km/h zulässig sind, gibt es auf den Straßenbahnabschnitten übermäßig viele Schilder mit 10, 15 oder 20 km/h Höchstgeschwindigkeit. Die Straßenbahn verkehrt von 06:00 bis 18:00 Uhr im 10-Minuten-Takt, am frühen Morgen und abends bis Mitternacht alle 15 Minuten. Die meisten Haltestellen haben Mittelbahnsteige, und alle verfügen über eine individuell gestaltete Wand mit dem Namen der Station sowie den ION- und GRT-Logos.

In einer zweiten Phase soll die „ION Light Rail" nach Süden über Preston nach Cambridge verlängert werden, wiederum auf einer Trasse mit sowohl Straßenbahn- als auch Eisenbahnabschnitten. Derzeit verkehrt der „ION Bus" (Linie 302) in 35 Minuten auf der 17 km langen Strecke zwischen Fairway und der Innenstadt von Cambridge alle 10 Minuten und mit nur fünf Zwischenstopps.

from tram to railway operation again, although for the next 1.2 km the tram tracks do not interfere with the parallel freight line. Railway signalling continues for 2.6 km all the way to the Fairway terminus despite some rather tight curves; all the level crossings on this section are protected with automatic barriers. Like the northern terminus, the southern also lies adjacent to a large shopping centre. Overall, a ride on the entire line takes 43 minutes, resulting in an average speed of 22 km/h. While on some sections of the railway-type alignment speeds of up to 70 km/h are permitted, the tram sections have an excessive number of signs showing 10, 15 or 20 km/h maximum speed. Trams run every 10 minutes from 6 a.m. until 6 p.m., and every 15 minutes in the early mornings and until midnight. Most of the stops have island platforms, and all feature an individually designed wall with the station's name and the ION and GRT logos.

In the second stage, ION Light Rail is planned to be extended south to Preston and Cambridge, again on a mixed-type alignment. For now, ION Bus (route 302) serves the 17 km between Fairway and downtown

![Laurier - Waterloo Park – 4-Schienen-Gleis | 4-rail gauntlet track]

Laurier - Waterloo Park – 4-Schienen-Gleis | *4-rail gauntlet track*

„ION Light Rail" wird mit 15 Flexity Freedom-Fahrzeugen betrieben. Die Wagen 501-514 wurden vom Bombardier-Werk in Kingston, Ontario, in den Jahren 2017 und 2018 geliefert. Wagen 515 kam 2021 hinzu, als Ausgleich für die verspätete Lieferung der anderen 14 Straßenbahnen. Die 5-teiligen Fahrzeuge sind 100% niederflurig, 30,2 km lang und 2,65 m breit. Mit einer Länge von 80 m sind alle Bahnsteige lang genug für Doppeltraktionen. Die Stromversorgung mit 750 V Gleichstrom erfolgt über eine Oberleitung.

Cambridge in 35 minutes, running every 10 minutes and with only five intermediate stops.

ION Light Rail is operated with a fleet of 15 Flexity Freedom vehicles, with nos. 501-514 delivered from Bombardier's Kingston, Ontario plant in 2017 and 2018. Car no. 515 was supplied in 2021 to compensate for the late delivery of the other 14 trams. The 5-section 100% low-floor vehicles are 30.2 km long and 2.65 m wide. At 80 m, all platforms were built long enough to accommodate double units if required. 750 V DC is supplied via an overhead catenary.

Bay/Enterprise Square

EDMONTON, AB

Edmonton ist die Hauptstadt der Provinz Alberta und hat knapp über 1 Million Einwohner. In der gesamten Metropolregion leben rund 1,4 Mio. Menschen. Die Stadt erstreckt sich auf beiden Seiten des North Saskatchewan River und liegt 280 km nördlich von Calgary, 820 km nordöstlich von Vancouver und 2.700 km nordwestlich von Toronto (Luftlinie).

Zweimal pro Woche und pro Richtung hält in Edmonton der von *VIA Rail* betriebene „The Canadian" auf seiner 4.466 km langen Fahrt zwischen Toronto (61/64 Stunden) und Vancouver (27/33 Stunden). Früher hatte Edmonton einen CNoR-Bahnhof (*Canadian Northern Railway*) in der Innenstadt auf dem Gelände des CN Tower (Gebäude der *Canadian National Railway*, zwischen den LRT-Stationen Churchill und MacEwan), doch seit 1998 dient ein einfacher Bahnsteig 5 km nördlich der Innenstadt als Haltestelle; er liegt an einem Stummel der Westzufahrt zum ehemaligen Bahnhof. Entlang der Ostzufahrt verkehren seit 1978 die Züge der Stadtbahn. CPR-Züge (*Canadian Pacific Railway*) fuhren hingegen einst über die High Level Bridge von 1913 in die Innenstadt und endeten in einem Bahnhof an der Jasper Avenue/109th Street. Der Personenverkehr endete jedoch 1972, und der Bahnhof wurde 1978 abgerissen; die Brücke und ein Teil der CPR-Linie werden heute vom *High Level Bridge Streetcar* genutzt.

Der gesamte öffentliche Nahverkehr in Edmonton wird vom städtischen Unternehmen ETS (*Edmonton Transit Service*) durchgeführt, dazu gehören drei Stadtbahnlinien

Edmonton is the capital city of the province of Alberta and has a population of just over 1 million, which increases to 1.4 million when the entire metropolitan region is considered. It extends on both sides of the North Saskatchewan River, 280 km north of Calgary, 820 km northeast of Vancouver and 2,700 km northwest of Toronto (as the crow flies).

Edmonton is a stop twice a week in each direction for 'The Canadian', the 4,466 km cross-country service provided by VIA Rail between Toronto (61/64h) and Vancouver (27/33h). Edmonton used to have a downtown CNoR (Canadian Northern Railway) railway station on the site of the CN Tower (Canadian National Railway building, between the Churchill and MacEwan LRT stations) until services were relocated to a simple single-platform facility 5 km north of downtown on a stub of what was once the western access to the former station; alongside the eastern access, LRT trains started to run in 1978. CPR trains (Canadian Pacific Railway), however, used to enter the city centre via the 1913 High Level Bridge and terminate in a station at Jasper Avenue/109th Street, but passenger services ended in 1972 and the station was demolished in 1978; the bridge and part of the CPR line are now used by the High Level Bridge Streetcar service.

All public transport in Edmonton is managed by the municipal company ETS (Edmonton Transit Service),

ETS - *www.edmonton.ca/edmonton-transit-system-ets*

South Campus/Fort Edmonton – SD-160-#1039 (Foto J. Limanowka)

(LRT). Eine einfache Fahrt mit Stadtbahn und Bus kostet 3,50 $ (2,75 $ bei Bezahlung mit Arc-Karte; 90 Minuten), eine Tageskarte ist an Fahrkartenautomaten an LRT-Stationen für 10,25 $ erhältlich (an älteren Automaten als Tageskarte, an Arc-Automaten als 24-Stunden-Ticket). Der Flughafen-Bus 747 verkehrt nur halbstündlich oder stündlich ab/zur Stadtbahn-Station Century Park und kostet 5 $ extra.

Als 1978 der erste Abschnitt des heutigen Stadtbahn-netzes eröffnet wurde, gehörte Edmonton bei der Einführung eines modernen städtischen Schienenverkehrsmittels zu den Pionieren in Nordamerika. Aber auch Edmonton verfügte einst über ein elektrisches Straßenbahnnetz der ersten Generation, das von 1908 bis 1951 von der *Edmonton Radial Railway* (ERR) betrieben wurde. Der Name des Unternehmens entstand aus der Tatsache, dass alle Strecken vom Stadtzentrum ausgingen, insbesondere von der Kreuzung Jasper Avenue/101st Street, dem Standort der heutigen U-Bahn-Station Central. Die Straßen-bahnen erreichten das Südufer des North Saskatchewan River über die High Level Bridge, auf der früher drei Gleise lagen, ein zentrales Gleis für die CPR und zwei äußere Gleise für die Straßen-bahnen, während auf dem Unterdeck bis heute der Autoverkehr rollt. Zwischen 1939 und 2009 fuhren in Edmonton auch Obusse.

including three light rail (LRT) lines. A single journey across the system, including light rail and buses, costs $3.50 ($2.75 if paid with the Arc stored-value card; valid for 90 minutes), a day pass is available for $10.25 from ticket vending machines at LRT stations (from older machines as a day ticket, from Arc machines as a 24-hour ticket). The airport is served half-hourly or hourly by bus 747 from Century Park LRT station, which requires a separate $5.00 fare.

When the first section of today's light rail system opened in 1978, Edmonton was one of the pioneers in North America in implementing a modern urban rail system. But Edmonton also used to have a first-generation electric streetcar network, operated by the Edmonton Radial Railway (ERR) from 1908 to 1951. The name of the company came from the fact that all the routes radiated from the city centre, most notably from the intersection at Jasper Avenue and 101st Street, the location of today's Central underground station. The streetcars reached the south bank of the North Saskatchewan River via the High Level Bridge, which used to carry three tracks, a central track for the CPR and two outer tracks for the streetcars, and still has a lower deck for cars. Between 1939 and 2009, trolleybuses also operated in Edmonton.

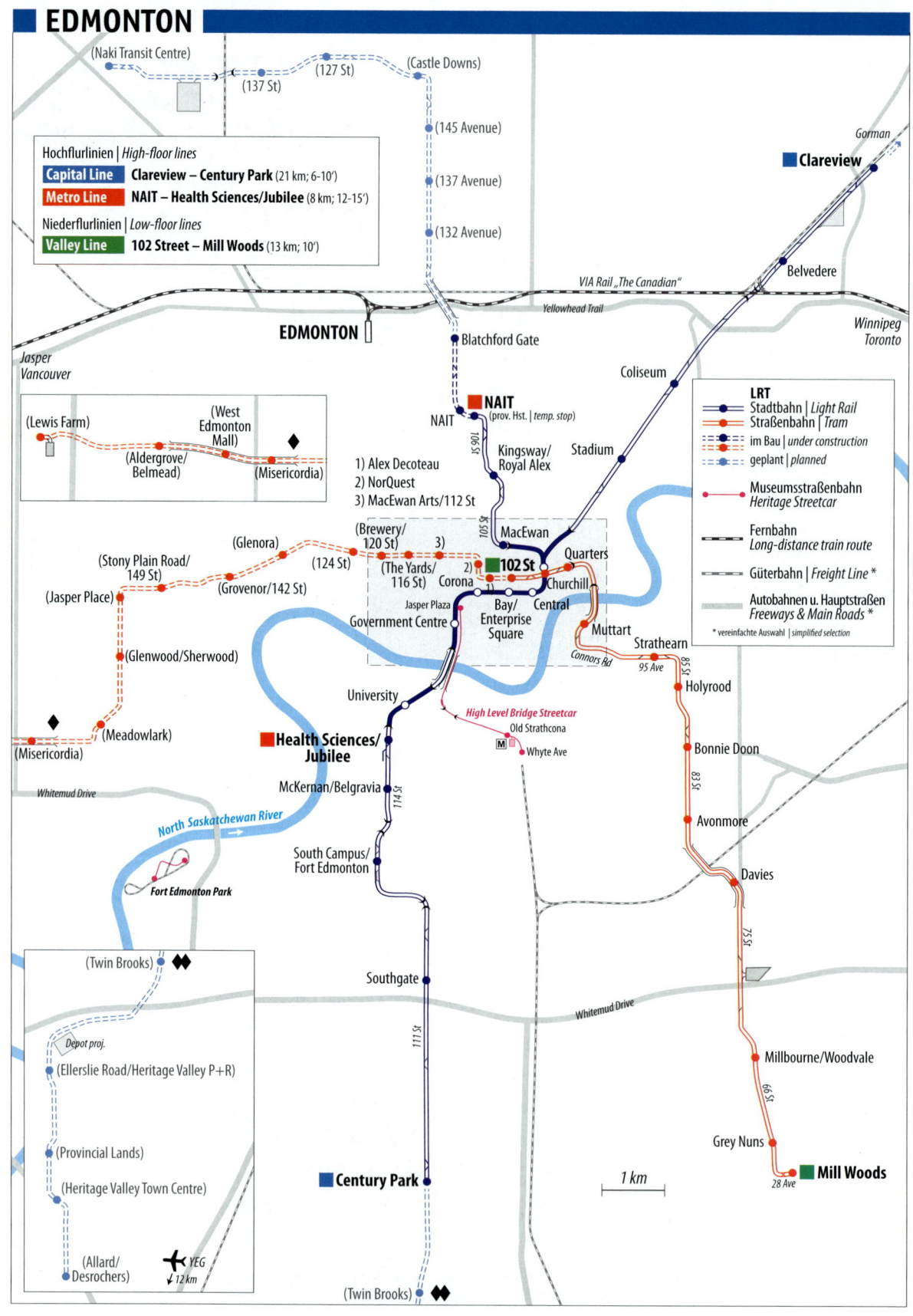

EDMONTON

Hochflurlinien | High-floor lines

Capital Line Clareview – Century Park (21 km; 6-10')
Metro Line NAIT – Health Sciences/Jubilee (8 km; 12-15')

Niederflurlinien | Low-floor lines

Valley Line 102 Street – Mill Woods (13 km; 10')

LRT

Stadtbahn | Light Rail
Straßenbahn | Tram
im Bau | under construction
geplant | planned

Museumsstraßenbahn
Heritage Streetcar

Fernbahn
Long-distance train route

Güterbahn | Freight Line *

Autobahnen u. Hauptstraßen
Freeways & Main Roads *

* vereinfachte Auswahl | simplified selection

(Naki Transit Centre)
(137 St)
(127 St)
(Castle Downs)
(145 Avenue)
(137 Avenue)
(132 Avenue)

Gorman

■ Clareview

Belvedere

Winnipeg
Toronto

VIA Rail „The Canadian"
Yellowhead Trail

EDMONTON

Blatchford Gate

■ NAIT
(prov. Hst. | temp. stop)

NAIT

Jasper
Vancouver

(Lewis Farm)
(West Edmonton Mall)
(Aldergrove/ Belmead)
(Misericordia)

Coliseum

Kingsway/
Royal Alex

Stadium

1) Alex Decoteau
2) NorQuest
3) MacEwan Arts/112 St

MacEwan

(Glenora)
(Brewery/ 120 St)
3)
(Stony Plain Road/ 149 St)
(124 St)
(The Yards/ 116 St)
2)
■ 102 St
Quarters

Corona
Churchill

(Grovenor/142 St)
Jasper Plaza
Bay/
Enterprise
Square
Central

(Jasper Place)
Government Centre

Muttart

(Glenwood/Sherwood)
Connors Rd
Strathearn

University
95 Ave
Holyrood

High Level Bridge Streetcar

Old Strathcona
M
Whyte Ave

(Meadowlark)
(Misericordia)

Whitemud Drive

■ Health Sciences/
Jubilee

McKernan/Belgravia

Bonnie Doon

114 St

North Saskatchewan River

Avonmore

Fort Edmonton Park

South Campus/
Fort Edmonton

Davies

(Twin Brooks)

Depot proj.

(Ellerslie Road/Heritage Valley P+R)

Southgate

Whitemud Drive

111 St

(Provincial Lands)

Millbourne/Woodvale

(Heritage Valley Town Centre)

Grey Nuns

■ Century Park

■ Mill Woods

1 km

28 Ave

(Allard/ Desrochers)

✈ YEG
↓12 km

(Twin Brooks)

LRT LIGHT RAIL TRANSIT

Das LRT-Netz von Edmonton besteht nun aus drei mit Namen bezeichneten Linien: die Capital Line und die Metro Line als Hochflurlinien, die beide den unterirdischen Abschnitt durch die Innenstadt durchfahren, sowie die Valley Line als Niederflurlinie, die das Stadtzentrum oberirdisch durchquert. Aufgrund der unterschiedlichen Fahrzeuge sind beide Teilnetze nicht miteinander kompatibel, beide sind allerdings normalspurig (1435 mm) und werden mit 600 V Gleichstrom über eine Oberleitung versorgt. 2024, nach Abschluss der Verlängerung der Metro Line bis Blatchford Gate, beträgt die Gesamtlänge 38,5 km. Mit zukünftigen Erweiterungen nach Norden, Westen und Süden wird das Stadtbahnnetz in den nächsten 10 Jahren um etwa 31,5 km anwachsen.

Der LRT-Betrieb beginnt um 5 Uhr morgens und dauert bis ca. 1 Uhr nachts. Während der Hauptverkehrszeit (06:00–09:00 Uhr, 14:00–18:00 Uhr) verkehren die Züge auf der Capital Line alle 6 Minuten, sonst tagsüber alle 10 Minuten, auf der Metro Line jedoch nur alle 12 bzw. 15 Minuten. Nach 18:00 Uhr und an Wochenenden verkehren beide Linien alle 15 Minuten. Die brandneue Valley Line verkehrt während der Hauptverkehrszeiten alle 5 Minuten und außerhalb der Hauptverkehrszeiten alle 10 Minuten. Eine Fahrt von einem Ende zum anderen dauert auf der Capital Line 44 Minuten, auf der Metro Line 17 Minuten und auf der Valley Line 31 Minuten.

Zahlreiche LRT-Stationen sind als „Transit Centre" angelegt, d.h. mehrere Zubringerbuslinien ermöglichen eine einfache Weiterfahrt in die weitläufigen Stadtteile. Die U-Bahn-Stationen in der Innenstadt verfügen alle über Zwischengeschosse und sind, mit Ausnahme von Corona, über unterirdische „Pedways" direkt mit angrenzenden Gebäuden verbunden.

The Edmonton LRT system now comprises three named lines, the high-floor Capital & Metro lines which share the underground section through downtown Edmonton, and the low-floor Valley Line, which runs through the city centre on the surface. Though incompatible for the type of trains used, both high-floor and low-floor lines are built with standard gauge (1435 mm) and use a 600 V DC overhead power supply. In 2024, with the completion of the Metro Line extension to Blatchford Gate, the network has a total length of 38.5 km. With extensions planned to the north, west and south, the Edmonton LRT system will grow by some 31.5 km over the next 10 years.

The LRT service starts at 5 a.m. and continues until around 1 a.m. Trains run every 6 minutes during peak times (6-9 a.m., 2-6 p.m.) and every 10 minutes during off-peak daytime service on the Capital Line, but on the Metro Line only every 12/15 minutes. After 6 p.m. and on weekends, each line operates every 15 minutes. The brand new Valley Line operates every 5 minutes during peak hours and every 10 minutes off-peak. A trip from end to end on the Capital Line takes 44 minutes, on the Metro Line 17 minutes and on the Valley Line 31 minutes.

Most LRT stations are laid out as Transit Centres, i.e. with several feeder bus routes providing easy onward travel into the spread-out neighbourhoods. The underground stations in the city centre all have mezzanines and, except for Corona station, are linked to adjacent buildings via subterranean 'pedways'.

McKernan/Belgravia – U2 #1034

◖◗● Capital & Metro Lines

Die ersten Vorschläge für ein Schnellbahnnetz entstanden in den frühen 1960er Jahren, mit einem Tunnel unter der 102nd Avenue und der Nutzung bestehender Eisenbahnkorridore auf den äußeren Abschnitten. Das Projekt reifte in den 1960er Jahren weiter, und nachdem Stadträte mehrere Städte in Europa besucht hatten, kamen sie zu dem Schluss, dass eine Stadtbahn die beste Lösung für Edmonton sei. Der Bau der Nordost-Linie begann im März 1974. Der erste Abschnitt hatte eine Gesamtlänge von 7,2 km, einschließlich eines 1,6 km langen Tunnels von der 95th Street bis zur U-Bahn-Station Central an Edmontons traditioneller zentraler Straßenkreuzung (im Gegensatz zu anderen nordamerikanischen Städten ist Edmonton nicht zentral in Quadranten unterteilt, weshalb quasi alle Straßen den Zusatz NW tragen!). Während der Tunnel östlich der 97th Street sowie die U-Bahn-Stationen Churchill und Central in offener Bauweise errichtet wurden, wurde der Rest mit einer Tunnelbohrmaschine als eingleisige Röhren aufgefahren. Die oberirdische Strecke zwischen dem Portal an der 95th Street und der ursprünglichen Endstation Belvedere wurde entlang der bestehenden CN-Bahnstrecke gebaut, die früher zum Hauptbahnhof von Edmonton führte. Auf diesem Abschnitt gibt es heute noch sechs Bahnübergänge, die alle durch automatische Schranken und ziemlich laute Glocken gesichert sind. Zur Unterfahrung der nördlichen Umgehungsbahn wurde ein kurzer Tunnel errichtet. Für die neuen Züge nutzte man zunächst die Cromdale Garage, eine Werkstatt aus der frühen Straßenbahnzeit (80th St/116th Ave). Die Stadtbahn wurde nach nur vier Jahren Bauzeit in Betrieb genommen,

The first proposals for a rapid transit system emerged in the early 1960s, and included a tunnel under 102nd Avenue while envisaging the use of existing railway corridors for the outer sections. The plan matured during the 1960s and after city councillors had visited several cities in Europe they came to the conclusion that light rail was the preferred option for Edmonton. The construction of the northeastern line started in March 1974. The initial segment had a total length of 7.2 km, including a 1.6 km tunnel from 95th Street to an underground station called Central at Edmonton's traditional central road intersection (unlike other North American cities, Edmonton is not centrally divided into quadrants, and therefore virtually all the streets and avenues are NW!). While the tunnel east of 97th Street as well as the underground stations Churchill and Central were built by the cut-and-cover method, the rest was excavated with a tunnel boring machine as single-track tubes. The surface stretch between the 95th Street portal and the initial terminus at Belvedere was built alongside the existing CN rail line which used to run into Edmonton's central railway station. This section still features six level crossings today, which are all protected by automatic barriers and rather noisy bells. A short tunnel was built to dive under the northern beltline railway. In the beginning, the Cromdale Garage, a workshop dating from the early streetcar period (located at 80th St/116th Ave), was used for the new trains. The LRT was opened for regular service only four years after the start of construction, just in time for the XI Common-

Health Sciences/Jubilee

Stadium

pünktlich zu den XI. Commonwealth Games im August 1978 und als die Stadt erst rund 500.000 Einwohner hatte. Alle Stationen verfügten über breite Mittelbahnsteige, die lang genug waren, um 125 m lange 5-Wagen-Züge aufzunehmen, auch wenn zunächst nur 2-Wagen-Züge eingesetzt wurden. Der ursprüngliche Endbahnhof Belvedere war eine einfache eingleisige Haltestelle. Drei Jahre nach Inbetriebnahme des ersten Abschnitts wurde mit dem Bau einer 2,1 km langen Verlängerung nach Clareview, dem heutigen nordöstlichen Endpunkt, begonnen, wobei die Station Belvedere erweitert wurde (sie wurde 1998 in ihrer heutigen Form umgebaut). Zwischen Belvedere und Clareview wurde ein neuer LRT-Betriebshof angelegt, der im Dezember 1983 als „D.L. MacDonald Yard" eröffnet wurde. In jüngerer Zeit, nämlich zwischen 2020 und 2022, wurde die Station Stadium komplett umgebaut und verfügt nun über einen zusätzlichen Seitenbahnsteig auf der Nordseite, der bei Großveranstaltungen im Commonwealth Stadium genutzt wird.

Der Bau einer westlichen Verlängerung vom U-Bahnhof Central unter der Jasper Avenue begann im Oktober 1980, wobei für die Streckentunnel wieder Tunnelbohrmaschinen zum Einsatz kamen; der Abraum wurde verwendet, um das Gelände für den neuen Betriebshof in Clareview zu planieren. Der erste Abschnitt war nur etwa 900 m lang und schloss zwei U-Bahn-Stationen, Bay und Corona (13 m tief) ein.

Die nächste Tunnelbau-Etappe umfasste nicht nur die 19 m tiefe U-Bahn-Station Grandin (heute Government Centre), sondern auch eine Kaverne für einen doppelten Gleiswechsel in Form einer Scherenkreuzung

wealth Games held in August 1978, and when the city had a population of just around 500,000. All the stations had wide island platforms long enough to accommodate 125 m long five-car trains, although initially only two-car trains were used. The original Belvedere terminus was a simple single-track station. With the first section in operation, construction started three years later on a 2.1 km extension to Clareview, today's northeastern terminus, including an enlarged Belvedere station (rebuilt in its present form in 1998). Between Belvedere and Clareview, a new LRT depot and workshop, known as the D.L. MacDonald Yard, was opened in December 1983. More recently, between 2020 and 2022, Stadium station was completely rebuilt and now features an additional side platform on the northern side used during special events at the Commonwealth Stadium.

Construction on a western extension from Central station under Jasper Avenue started in October 1980 using tunnel boring machines for the running tunnels; the spoil was used to level the terrain for the new yard at Clareview. The first segment of the southern extension was only some 900 m long and included two underground stations, Bay and Corona (13 m deep).

The next stage of tunnel construction included not only a 19 m deep underground station at Grandin (now Government Centre), but also a cavern for a scissors crossover beneath Jasper Plaza (between 109th and 110th Streets).

For the river crossing, the use of the High Level Bridge was discarded at an early stage due to the bridge's age and condition. For the LRT, a new 600 m box

Capital & Metro Lines

- 23.8 km (Ⓤ 5.1 km), 18 Stations (Ⓤ 6)
Capital Line - 20.5 km, Metro Line - 7.9 km

22-04-1978: Central – Belvedere (6.9 km)
26-04-1981: Belvedere – Clareview (2.1 km)
26-06-1983: Central – Corona (0.8 km)
03-09-1989: Corona – Grandin (Government Centre) (0.8 km)
23-08-1992: Grandin – University (1.6 km)
01-01-2006: University – Health Sciences (0.7 km)
25-04-2009: Health Sciences – South Campus (2.0 km)
24-04-2010: South Campus – Century Park (5.6 km)
06-09-2015: Churchill – NAIT (3.3 km)
~ 2024: NAIT – Blatchford Gate (1.6 km)
~ 2029: Century Park – Heritage Valley North (Ellerslie Rd)

NAIT – ursprüngliche Haltestelle | *original station*

Churchill – Verzweigungsbahnhof im Stadtzentrum | *junction in the city centre*

unter der Jasper Plaza (zwischen 109th und 110th Street).

Für die Flussquerung wurde eine Nutzung der High Level Bridge aufgrund ihres Alters und Zustands frühzeitig ausgeschlossen. Für die LRT wurde westlich parallel dazu eine neue 600 m lange Kastenträgerbrücke mit dem Namen Dudley B. Menzies Bridge errichtet, die auf dem Unterdeck einen Fuß-/Fahrradweg erhielt. Die anschließenden Streckentunnel am Südufer (650 m) wurden bergmännisch aufgefahren. Die Station University, deren Gleise 23 m unter dem Straßenniveau liegen, wurde in offener Bauweise errichtet. Bis 1994 stand nur das Gleis im Nordtunnel zwischen dem Süduferportal und der Station University zur Verfügung, was die Kapazität des neuen Endbahnhofs sehr einschränkte. Mit der Eröffnung des Abschnitts zur Universität im August 1992 stiegen die Fahrgastzahlen deutlich an, gleichzeitig ruhte jedoch der weitere Ausbau des Stadtbahnnetzes für mehrere Jahre.

Es dauerte 10 Jahre, bis eine weitere Verlängerung nach Süden beschlossen wurde. Ausgehend von der unterirdischen Station University erreichen die Züge mit 6% Steigung die Station Health Sciences/Jubilee, hinter der ein Wendegleis an der Westseite den hier endenden Zügen der Metro Line als Kehrgleis dient. Der Rest der Südstrecke wurde überwiegend ebenerdig mit mehreren Bahnübergängen gebaut, die durch Schranken geschützt waren, allerdings mit einem kurzen Tunnel zur Unterquerung der Belgravia Road. Der Bahnhof South Campus verfügt über ein mittiges Wendegleis und kann somit auch als Endstation dienen. Durch einen weiteren kurzen Tunnel gelangen die Züge auf den Mittelstreifen der 111th Street, der sie 4,4 km lang geradeaus nach Süden bis zum Endpunkt Century Park folgen. Auf diesem Abschnitt wurde nur eine einzige Station Southgate gebaut, obwohl mindestens eine weitere Station an der 40th Avenue nützlich wäre. Etwas südlich der Station Southgate überquert die Stadtbahn den Whitemud Drive auf einer 100 m langen Brücke. Der Bau einer weiteren Verlängerung nach

girder bridge was erected parallel to it on the western side; named the Dudley B. Menzies Bridge, it features a pedestrian/bicycle path on its lower deck. The adjoining running tunnels on the south bank (650 m) were dug with the sequential excavation method. University station, with tracks 23 m below street level, was built by cut-and-cover. Until 1994, only the track in the northbound tunnel between the south bank portal and University station was available, limiting the new terminus' capacity. With the opening of the University segment in August 1992, ridership rose significantly, but at the same time the further expansion of the LRT system was paused for several years.

It took 10 years for another southern extension to be approved. Starting from the underground University station, trains climb a 6% ramp to reach Health Sciences/Jubilee station, beyond which a western siding now caters to terminating Metro Line trains. The rest of the southern line was built primarily at grade with several level crossings, protected by barriers, although with a short tunnel to avoid an intersection with Belgravia Road. South Campus station features a central siding and may function as a terminus for some trains. Another short tunnel takes trains onto the median of 111th Street, which they follow straight south to Century Park for 4.4 km; on this section only one station was built at Southgate, when at least another station at 40th Avenue would be useful. Just south of Southgate station, the LRT crosses Whitemud Drive on a 100 m long bridge. A further extension south to Ellerslie Road and Heritage Valley (8 km) is at an advanced stage of planning, with construction on the first section up to Ellerslie Road having started in 2023. At the northern end of the Capital Line, the planning of a 1-station 2.9 km extension from Clareview to Gorman was started in 2009, with a future option to continue all the way to Fort Saskatchewan.

With the 'South LRT' completed in 2010, the focus switched to the 'Northwest LRT'. In view of this future

Süden zur Ellerslie Road und nach Heritage Valley (8 km) befindet sich in einem fortgeschrittenen Planungsstadium. Der Bau des ersten Abschnitts bis zur Ellerslie Road hat 2023 begonnen. Am nördlichen Ende der Capital Line wurde bereits 2009 mit der Planung einer 2,9 km langen Verlängerung von Clareview nach Gorman ohne Zwischenhalt begonnen; langfristig ist eine Weiterführung bis Fort Saskatchewan möglich.

Mit der Fertigstellung der „South LRT" im Jahr 2010 verlagerte sich der Schwerpunkt auf die „Northwest LRT". Im Hinblick auf diesen neuen Ast wurden 2013 Liniennamen eingeführt, indem die bestehende Linie (Linie 201) zur „Capital Line" und der neue Ast zur „Metro Line" wurde. Der erste 3,3 km lange Abschnitt wurde 2015 zwischen Churchill und dem Northern Alberta Institute of Technology (NAIT) eröffnet. Sie zweigt von der älteren Linie nördlich des Bahnhofs Churchill niveaugleich ab, umfährt dann den CN Tower an dessen Ostseite und schwenkt nach Westen (der Tunnelbau hatte bereits 2009 zusammen mit dem EPCOR Tower begonnen), um kurz vor der Station MacEwan die Oberfläche zu erreichen. Der Rest der Strecke verläuft ebenerdig zunächst im Mittelstreifen der 105th Street, dann abseits der Straße bis Kingsway und schließlich am östlichen Rand der 106th Street. Es steht durchgehend ein eigener eingezäunter Gleiskörper zur Verfügung, jedoch mit mehreren Bahnübergängen. Die Station MacEwan erschließt die Sporthalle Rogers Place und die MacEwan University, die beide auf ehemaligem Eisenbahngelände errichtet wurden. Der Endbahnhof NAIT erhielt nur einen 70 m langen provisorischen Bahnsteig. Um die Ecke entsteht derzeit ein neuer Bahnhof mit 120 m langen Seitenbahnsteigen, der zusammen mit der Erweiterung bis Blatchford Gate noch im Jahr 2024 eröffnet werden soll. Die Blatchford-Verlängerung erschließt ein Stadtentwicklungsgebiet auf dem Gelände des ehemaligen Edmonton City Centre Airport, der 2013 geschlossen wurde.

In zukünftigen Etappen wird die Metro Line weiter nach Norden geführt und auf einer spektakulären Schrägseilbrücke den Yellowhead Trail und die weitläufigen Gleisanlagen des CN Walker Yard überqueren, um die 113A Street zu erreichen. Die Linie wird dann an der 153rd Avenue nach Westen abbiegen und schließlich am Nakî Transit Centre an der Campbell Road enden. Langfristig könnte die Linie bis ins benachbarte St. Albert verlängert werden. Alle Stationen dieser Erweiterung werden ebenerdig liegen, lediglich die Stationen an der 137th Avenue und an

MacEwan > Kingsway/Royal Alex

branch, line names were introduced in 2013, with the existing line (route 201) becoming the Capital Line and the new branch the Metro Line. The initial 3.3 km section opened in 2015 between Churchill and the Northern Alberta Institute of Technology (NAIT). It diverges from the older line in a flat junction just north of Churchill station, and then skirts the CN Tower on the eastern side before turning west (tunnel construction started in 2009 together with the EPCOR Tower) and surfacing just before arriving at MacEwan station. The rest of the line is at grade, lying on a dedicated right-of-way throughout but with several level crossings, first in the median of 105th Street, then off-road to Kingsway and finally along the eastern side of 106th Street. MacEwan station serves the Rogers Place indoor arena and MacEwan University, both built on former railway land. The terminus at NAIT has a 70 m temporary platform, with a new station featuring 120 m side platforms being built around the corner which will open together with the extension to Blatchford Gate in 2024. The Blatchford extension will serve new developments on the site of the former Edmonton City Centre Airport, which closed in 2013.

In future stages, the Metro Line will continue north, crossing Yellowhead Trail and the extensive CN Walker Yard on a spectacular cable-stayed bridge before reaching 113A Street. The line will then turn west at 153rd Avenue and eventually terminate at the Nakî Transit Centre at Campbell Road; in the long term it could be extended into neighbouring St. Albert. All the stations on this extension will be at grade, except the ones at 137th Avenue and 127th Street, which will lie in a trench at intersections with busy roads.

Government Centre

Kingsway/Royal Alex

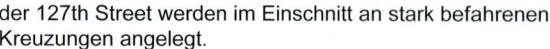

U2 – modernisiert | *refurbished*

SD-160

der 127th Street werden im Einschnitt an stark befahrenen Kreuzungen angelegt.

LRT-Hochflurfahrzeuge

Edmonton war die erste nordamerikanische Stadt (vor Calgary und San Diego), die Frankfurts beliebte U2-Wagen von Duewag und Siemens bestellte. Die Fahrzeuge von Edmonton sind weitgehend identisch mit der ursprünglichen Frankfurter Version (mit Ausnahme der ursprünglichen Einstiegsstufen bei den Wagen in Frankfurt). Die Gelenkfahrzeuge sind 23 m lang (24,3 m über Kupplungen) und 2,65 m breit. Sie besitzen zwei angetriebene Drehgestelle sowie ein nicht angetriebenes Drehgestell unter dem Gelenk und werden mit 600 V Gleichstrom betrieben, der über Oberleitung zugeführt wird. Bei einer Fußbodenhöhe von 978 mm über Schienenoberkante ist ein stufenloser Einstieg an allen Stationen möglich. Die U2-Wagen kamen in drei Lieferungen nach Edmonton, 14 rechtzeitig zur Eröffnung des Betriebs im Jahr 1978 (Nr. 1001–1014), drei weitere im Jahr 1979 (Nr. 1015–1017) und schließlich 20 weitere 1981-82 (Nr. 1018-1037). Ihre Höchstgeschwindigkeit beträgt 80 km/h. Ab 2008 wurden alle U2-Fahrzeuge schrittweise aufgearbeitet und modernisiert, um ihre Lebensdauer um rund 20 Jahre zu verlängern. Sie sollen nun bis 2030 ersetzt werden.

Für die Süderweiterung und um dem steigenden Fahrgastaufkommen Rechnung zu tragen, nahm ETS 2008 eine erste Serie von 37 SD-160-Fahrzeugen (Nr. 1038-1074) von Siemens in die Flotte auf. In den Jahren 2012-13 folgte eine zweite Serie mit 20 Wagen (Nr. 1075-1094) für die Metro Line. Mit 24,8 m über Kupplung haben die SD-160 ähnliche Abmessungen wie die U2-Wagen. Sie basieren auf den bewährten SD-100- und frühen SD-160-Fahrzeugen, die damals in Denver, Salt Lake City, San Diego und Calgary im Einsatz waren, wurden jedoch mit einer moderneren Front geliefert.

Während der Hauptverkehrszeit verkehren auf der Capital Line Züge mit fünf Wagen, auf der Metro Line sind jedoch bis zur Inbetriebnahme der Verlängerung bis Blatchford Gate vorerst nur Züge mit drei Wagen möglich.

LRT High-floor vehicles

Edmonton was the first North American city (before Calgary and San Diego) to order Frankfurt's popular U2 cars manufactured by Duewag and Siemens. Edmonton's cars are largely identical to the original Frankfurt version (except for the step inside the Frankfurt cars). The cars are 23 m long (24.3 m over couplers) and 2.65 m wide; they are articulated with two powered bogies, plus one unpowered bogie under the articulation. They run on 600 V DC taken from an overhead power line. With a floor height of 978 mm above the top of the rail, they allow stepfree boarding at all stations. They came to Edmonton in three batches, 14 in time for the opening of the system in 1978 (nos. 1001-1014), three more in 1979 (nos. 1015-1017), and finally 20 more in 1981-82 (nos. 1018-1037). Their maximum speed is 80 km/h. Starting in 2008, all U2 vehicles were gradually refurbished and modernised to extend their lifespan by some 20 years. They are now planned to be replaced by 2030.

For the southern extension and to cater for increasing ridership, ETS added a first batch of 37 SD-160 vehicles (nos. 1038-1074) from Siemens to the fleet in 2008. A second batch of 20 cars (nos. 1075-1094) followed for the Metro Line in 2012-13. At 24.8 m over couplers, the SD-160s have similar dimensions to the U2s. They are based on the proven SD-100 and early SD-160 trains then in use in Denver, Salt Lake City, San Diego and Calgary, but were delivered with a more modern front.

During peak hours, 5-car trains operate on the Capital Line, but for now only 3-car trains are possible on the Metro Line until it is extended to Blatchford Gate.

NAIT – SD-160 #1082

Government Centre > University – U2 #1014+1037+1033+1024 @ Dudley B. Menzies Bridge & High Level Bridge

Die „**Edmonton Radial Railway Society**" (ERRS) betreibt historische Straßenbahnen über die High Level Bridge sowie im Freilichtmuseum Fort Edmonton Park.

Der Verein besitzt eine große Auswahl an historischen Straßenbahnen aus Edmonton und anderen Betrieben in Kanada sowie einige Importe, z.B. aus Melbourne oder Osaka. Zur Sammlung gehörte einst auch ein Stadtbahn-Prototyp aus Hannover (Nr. 601), der jedoch 2016 nach Deutschland zurückgegeben wurde. Der High Level Bridge Streetcar verkehrt von der Jaspar Plaza (nahe der LRT-Station Corona und in der Nähe des ehemaligen CPR-Bahnhofs) über die Brücke nach Strathcona (3 km), wo es ein kleines Museum gibt, das von Mai bis Oktober samstags von 10:00 bis 14:00 Uhr geöffnet ist.

Weitere Informationen finden Sie auf der Website des Vereins ERRS:

*The **Edmonton Radial Railway Society** (ERRS) operates heritage streetcars across the High Level Bridge and in Fort Edmonton Park, a living history museum.*

The association owns a large selection of historic streetcars from Edmonton and other cities in Canada, as well as some imports, e.g. from Melbourne and Osaka. The collection once also included a prototype Stadtbahn car from Hanover (no. 601), but this was returned to Germany in 2016. The High Level Bridge Streetcar operates from Jaspar Plaza (near Corona LRT station and close to the site of the former CPR railway station) across the bridge to Strathcona (3 km), where there is a small museum open on Saturdays 10:00-14:00, May-October.

For more information visit the ERRS's website:

www.edmontonstreetcars.ca

Fort Edmonton Park – Edmonton #42 (1912)

High Level Bridge – Edmonton #33 (1912)

Grey Nuns – Flexity Freedom #1003

● Valley Line

Bei der Valley Line entschied sich Edmonton für einen neuen Ansatz und schuf eine moderne Straßenbahn europäischer Prägung. Dabei werden Niederflurfahrzeuge eingesetzt, die oberirdisch durch die Innenstadt fahren. Rund um die Haltestellen soll das städtische Umfeld aufgewertet und die Bebauungsdichte erhöht werden, denn auch Edmonton hat sich in den letzten Jahrzehnten immer mehr durch Einfamilienhaussiedlungen ausgedehnt.

Auf diese Weise wurde die „Southeast LRT" ähnlich wie eine moderne französische Straßenbahn konzipiert, mit Tunneln und Viadukten nur dort, wo es nötig war. Nach der Genehmigung im Jahr 2009 dauerte es jedoch 14 Jahre, bis die Valley Line Wirklichkeit wurde. Die kürzlich eröffnete Linie beginnt im Stadtzentrum an der 102nd Street, von wo aus sie entlang der 102nd Avenue nach Osten verläuft und am Churchill Square, dem Hauptplatz der Stadt, Anschluss an die Hochflurlinien bietet. Es wird erwartet, dass sich das Gebiet rund um die Haltestelle Quarters in naher Zukunft erheblich verändert. Die Straßenbahn fährt dann in einen 500 m langen Tunnel unter der 95th Street, um die Jasper Avenue nicht niveaugleich kreuzen zu müssen. Nach Verlassen des Tunnels überquert die Tram den North Saskatchewan River auf der neu errichteten Tawatinâ-Brücke, einer Schrägseilbrücke mit einem Fußgängerweg auf dem Unterdeck, die die frühere Cloverdale-Fußgängerbrücke ersetzte. Auf der Südseite des Flusses verläuft die Valley Line entlang oder in der Mitte von Hauptstraßen (Connors Road, 95th Avenue, 83rd Street), bis sie ein 1,4 km langes Viadukt erreicht, auf dem die Argyll Road, die Güterbahnstrecke der Canadian Pacific sowie die 75th Street überquert werden. Auf diesem Abschnitt liegt der Hochbahnstation Davies, der jetzt von Parkplätzen umgeben ist, wo

For the Valley Line, Edmonton opted for a new approach by creating a European-style tramway or 'urban-style LRT'. This uses low-floor vehicles, runs on the surface through the city centre and aims at encouraging urban development around stations, thus increasing the density along the corridors to stop the ever-increasing urban sprawl.

In this way, the 'Southeast LRT' was conceived much like a modern French tramway, with tunnels and elevated structures only where necessary. It was approved in 2009, but ultimately took 14 years to become reality. The recently opened line starts in the city centre at 102nd Street from where it runs east along 102nd Avenue, providing interchange with the high-floor lines at Churchill Square, the city's main square. The area around the Quarters stop is expected to see significant redevelopment in the near future. The trams then enter a 500 m tunnel under 95th Street, thus avoiding an intersection with Jasper Avenue. Upon leaving the tunnel, the trams cross the North Saskatchewan River on the purpose-built Tawatinâ Bridge, a cable-stayed bridge with a pedestrian walkway on the lower deck which replaced the former Cloverdale footbridge. On the south side of the river, the Valley Line runs alongside or in the median of major roads (Connors Road, 95th Avenue, 83rd

Valley Line

- 13.2 km (⑪ 0.5 km), 12 Stops

04-11-2023: 102nd Street – Mill Woods (13.2 km)
~ 2027: 102nd Street – Lewis Farms (14 km)

Davies
– Bus 73A

Mill Woods > Grey Nuns
– Flexity Freedom #1016

aber eine Neubebauung vorgesehen ist. Die Strecke führt weiter nach Süden entlang der 75th Street, die dort zur 66th Street wird, wo sie den Whitemud Drive in der Nähe des Straßenbahnbetriebshofs überquert. Die Straßenbahn biegt an der 28th Avenue nach Osten ab und endet kurz danach im Zentrum von Mill Woods.

Die Valley Line wird mit einer Flotte von 26 Flexity Freedom-Niederflurstraßenbahnen (Nr. 1001-1026) betrieben, die von Bombardier (heute Teil von Alstom) stammen. Die 7-teiligen Fahrzeuge sind 42 m lang, 2,65 m breit und können in Doppeltraktion eingesetzt werden. Das erste in Kingston, Ontario, hergestellte Fahrzeug kam im Sommer 2018 per Bahn an, das letzte im Jahr 2020.

Der Bau einer 14 km langen westlichen Verlängerung der Valley Line wurde im Jahr 2021 begonnen und soll etwa 2027 abgeschlossen sein. Diese weist erneut einen eher urbanen Charakter auf und führt entlang der 102nd Avenue, 107th Street und 104th Avenue, dann entlang der nicht ins Straßenraster passenden Stony Plain Road, bevor sie im Stadtteil Jasper Place nach Süden in die 156th Street abbiegt und über die Meadowlark Road die 87th Avenue erreicht. Ab der 164th Street beginnt ein fast 2 km langes Viadukt mit zwei Hochbahnhöfen, Misericordia und West Edmonton Mall, das in erster Linie gebaut wird, um niveaugleiche Kreuzungen an der stark befahrenen 170th und 178th Street zu vermeiden. Die Straßenbahn überquert dann die Ringautobahn (Anthony Henday Drive), bevor sie am östlichen Rand des Stadtteils Lewis Farms endet, wo auch eine kleine Abstellanlage errichtet wird.

Für die Westverlängerung der Valley Line bestellte ETS im Jahr 2021 beim südkoreanischen Hersteller Hyundai 40 Niederflurfahrzeuge, die ab 2025 ausgeliefert werden sollen.

Street) until it reaches a 1.4 km viaduct built to cross Argyll Road, the Canadian Pacific freight line and 75th Street. This features an elevated station at Davies, which is currently surrounded by car parks, but is intended for transit-oriented development. The line continues due south along 75th Street which becomes 66th Street as it crosses Whitemud Drive near the LRT depot. Trams turn east at 28th Avenue just before terminating in the Mill Woods town centre.

The Valley Line is served by a fleet of 26 Flexity Freedom low-floor trams (nos. 1001-1026) manufactured by Bombardier (now part of Alstom). They are 42 m long (7 sections), 2.65 m wide, and can operate as double units. Produced in Kingston, Ontario, the first vehicle arrived by rail in summer 2018, the last in 2020.

The construction of the Valley Line's western leg was launched in 2021 for completion in around 2027. The 14 km western extension again features a rather urban alignment along 102nd Avenue, 107th Street, 104th Avenue and then the out-of-grid Stony Plain Road, before turning south into 156th Street in the Jasper Place neighbourhood and reaching 87th Avenue via Meadowlark Road. At 164th Street, the trams will ascend an almost 2 km long viaduct with two elevated stations, Misericordia and West Edmonton Mall, built primarily to avoid intersections with the busy 170th and 178th Streets. The trams will then cross the orbital freeway (Anthony Henday Drive) before terminating at the eastern edge of the Lewis Farms neighbourhood where a small stabling facility will also be built.

For the expanded Valley Line service, ETS ordered 40 low-floor vehicles from Hyundai (South Korea) in 2021, with delivery starting in 2025.

Mill Woods

Grey Nuns > Millbourne/Woodvale – Flexity Freedom #1014

![6th Street SW (Transit Mall) – Siemens S200 #2449 – Haltestellen mit wechselnder Farbbeleuchtung | stops with changing colour lighting]

6th Street SW (Transit Mall) – Siemens S200 #2449 – Haltestellen mit wechselnder Farbbeleuchtung | *stops with changing colour lighting*

CALGARY, AB

Mit 1,3 Millionen Einwohnern ist Calgary die größte Stadt in Alberta; in der „Metropolregion" kommen lediglich etwa 200.000 Einwohner hinzu. Calgary liegt ca. 280 km südlich der Provinzhauptstadt Edmonton, 225 km nördlich der US-Grenze, 675 km östlich von Vancouver und 2.700 km westlich von Toronto (Luftlinie).

Obwohl hier Bahnstrecken aus allen Richtungen zusammenlaufen und die Stadt von Ost nach West durchqueren, ist Calgary derzeit nicht per Bahn erreichbar. Zwischen Calgary und Banff in den Rocky Mountains (130 km) sind neue Gleise für den Personenverkehr geplant, außerdem wird eine Hochgeschwindigkeitsverbindung zwischen Calgary und Edmonton (Prairie Link) in Erwägung gezogen. Bis 1990 hielt am zentral gelegenen Bahnhof von Calgary „The Canadian", bevor dieser auf die Strecke über Edmonton verlegt wurde. Später nutzte den Bahnhof gelegentlich „The Rocky Mountaineer". Den Flughafen Calgary erreicht man von der Innenstadt aus mit der Buslinie 300 und von der LRT-Station McKnight-Westwinds mit der Buslinie 100 jeweils halbstündlich.

Der gesamte öffentliche Nahverkehr in Calgary wird von der städtischen Gesellschaft *Calgary Transit* durchgeführt, dazu gehören zwei Stadtbahnlinien (und eine dritte im Bau), bekannt als „CTrain". Eine einfache Fahrt im gesamten Netz, einschließlich Stadtbahn und Busse, kostet 3,60 $ (90 Min.), eine Tageskarte ist für 11,25 $ erhältlich (an Fahrkartenautomaten an CTrain-Stationen oder in der

With a population of 1.3 million, Calgary is the largest city in Alberta, with its 'Metropolitan Region' only adding some 200,000 inhabitants. It lies some 280 km south of the provincial capital of Edmonton, 225 km north of the U.S. border, 675 km east of Vancouver, and 2,700 km west of Toronto (as the crow flies).

Although railway routes converge there from all directions and bisect the city from east to west, Calgary is currently not reachable by passenger train. New passenger tracks are planned between Calgary and Banff in the Rocky Mountains (130 km), while a high-speed link between Calgary and Edmonton (Prairie Link) has also been proposed. Until 1990, Calgary's centrally located station was served by 'The Canadian' before it was rerouted via Edmonton. Later, 'The Rocky Mountaineer' occasionally used the station. Calgary's airport is served half-hourly by bus route 300 from downtown and by bus route 100 from the LRT station McKnight-Westwinds.

All public transport in Calgary is managed by the municipal company 'Calgary Transit', including two light rail lines (and a third under construction) known as the 'CTrain'. A single journey across the system, including light rail and buses, costs $3.60 (90 min.), and a day pass is available for $11.25 (from ticket vending machines

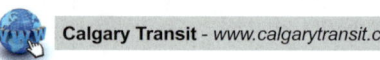 **Calgary Transit** - www.calgarytransit.com

City Hall <> Bridgeland/Memorial – Brücke über den Bow River | *bridge over the Bow River*

My Fare-App). Der CTrain-Abschnitt zwischen City Hall und Downtown West-Kerby ist „Free Fare Zone", kann also gratis genutzt werden.

Als der erste Abschnitt des heutigen Stadtbahnnetzes im Jahr 1981, also drei Jahre nach Edmonton, eröffnet wurde, gehörte Calgary bei der Einführung eines modernen städtischen Schienenverkehrsmittels zu den Pionieren in Nordamerika. Calgary verfügte einst auch über ein elektrisches Straßenbahnnetz der ersten Generation, das von 1909 bis 1950 von der *Calgary Municipal Railway* betrieben wurde. Im Stadtzentrum war die 8th Avenue der Hauptkorridor der Straßenbahn, von dem aus die einzelnen Strecken auf drei Brücken über den Bow River nach Norden, durch drei Eisenbahnunterführungen nach Süden und auf zwei Brücken über den Elbow River nach Südosten führten. Das Unternehmen wurde 1946 in *Calgary Transit System* umbenannt, als mit der schrittweisen Umstellung von Straßenbahnen auf Obusse begonnen wurde, die bis 1975 auf den Straßen von Calgary zu sehen waren.

at CTrain stations or on the My Fare app). The CTrain section between City Hall and Downtown West-Kerby is a 'free fare zone'.

When the first section of today's light rail system opened in 1981, i.e. three years after Edmonton, Calgary was one of the pioneers in North America in implementing a modern urban rail system. Calgary also used to have a first-generation electric streetcar network, which was operated by the Calgary Municipal Railway from 1909 to 1950. In the city centre, 8th Avenue was the main streetcar corridor from where routes radiated north via three bridges across the Bow River, south via three underpasses to cross the railway line, and southeast via two bridges across the Elbow River. The company was renamed Calgary Transit System in 1946 when the gradual conversion from streetcar to trolleybus operation began. Trolleybuses remained on Calgary's streets until 1975.

Heritage Park – Calgary #15

CTrain
- 57.3 km (Ⓓ 3.6 km) - 41.5* Haltestellen | *stations* (Ⓓ 1)
Red Line: 34.2 km
Blue Line: 25 km

25-05-1981: Anderson – 8th Street SW (12.3 km)
27-04-1985: 8th Street SW – 10th Street SW** (0.4 km)
        City Hall – Whitehorn (9.6 km)
17-09-1987: 8th Street SW – University (5.4 km)
31-08-1990: University – Brentwood (1.0 km)
09-10-2001: Anderson – Fish Creek-Lacombe (3.6 km)
15-12-2003: Brentwood – Dalhousie (2.7 km)
28-06-2004: Fish Creek-L. – Somerset-Bridlewood (2.7 km)
17-12-2007: Whitehorn – McKnight-Westwinds (2.7 km)
15-06-2009: Dalhousie – Crowfoot (3.9 km)
27-08-2012: McKnight-Westwinds – Saddletowne (2.8 km)
10-12-2012: 8th Street SW – 69th Street SW (7.8 km)
23-08-2014: Crowfoot – Tuscany (2.4 km)

* Einrichtungshaltestellen im Stadtzentrum halb gezählt
Single-direction stops in the city centre counted as half a station
** 2012 durch Downtown West - Kerby ersetzt
Replaced in 2012 by Downtown West - Kerby

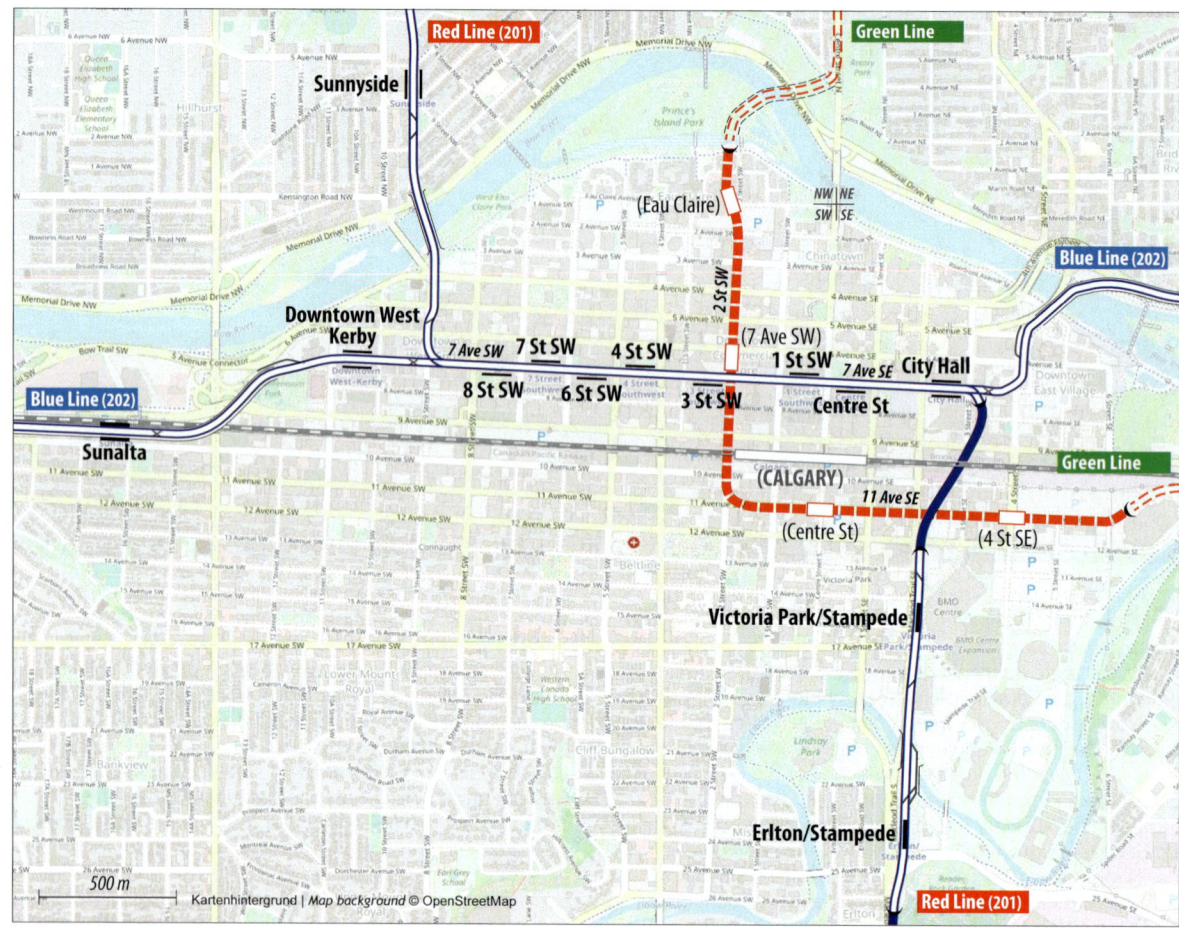

◯◯ CTrain – Red & Blue Lines

Das Stadtbahnsystem von Calgary, der CTrain, besteht derzeit aus zwei farblich gekennzeichneten Linien, der Red Line und der Blue Line, obwohl auch deren Streckennummern weiterhin verwendet werden (201 bzw. 202). Die beiden Linien teilen sich durch die Innenstadt von Calgary einen straßenbündigen Abschnitt entlang der 7th Avenue. Wie die älteren Linien in Edmonton nutzen beide Linien in Calgary Hochflurfahrzeuge, die auf Gleisen mit Normalspur (1435 mm) fahren und über eine 600-V-DC-Oberleitungsstromversorgung verfügen. Die beiden Linien haben eine Gesamtstreckenlänge von 57,3 km, die sich in den nächsten 10-15 Jahren deutlich erhöhen kann, wenn alle aktuellen Projekte umgesetzt werden. Dazu gehört die Green Line, deren Bau im ersten Abschnitt im Jahr 2023 begann und deren Fertigstellung frühestens im Jahr 2027 erfolgen wird. Auf der Green Line werden jedoch Niederflurfahrzeuge zum Einsatz kommen, die die Innenstadt unterirdisch durchqueren werden.

Der CTrain-Betrieb beginnt gegen 4:30 Uhr und dauert bis 1:00 Uhr nachts. Während der Hauptverkehrszeiten (05:30-09:30 Uhr, 14:30-18:00 Uhr) verkehren die Züge alle 6 Minuten, tagsüber und abends außerhalb der Hauptverkehrszeiten jedoch nur alle 15 Minuten.

Die meisten CTrain-Stationen sind als „Transit Centre" ausgelegt, d.h. mit mehreren Zubringerbuslinien, die

The Calgary light rail system, the CTrain, currently comprises two colour-coded lines, the Red and Blue Lines, although their route numbers are also still used (201 and 202, respectively). The two lines share a surface section through downtown Calgary, the transit mall along 7th Avenue. Like Edmonton's original LRT, the two lines use high-floor vehicles running on standard-gauge tracks (1435 mm) and with a 600 V DC overhead power supply. The two lines now have a combined route length of 57.3 km, which may increase significantly over the next 10-15 years if all the current projects are realised. Among these is the Green Line, the first segment of which started construction in 2023 with completion in 2027 at the earliest. The Green Line will use low-floor vehicles and run underground through the city centre.

CTrain service starts at around 4:30 a.m. and continues until 1 a.m. Trains run every 6 minutes during peak times (5:30-9:30 a.m., 2:30-6 p.m.), but only every 15 minutes during off-peak daytime service and in the evening.

Most CTrain stations are laid out as Transit Centres, i.e. with several feeder bus routes providing convenient onward travel into the spread-out neighbourhoods. The shared stations in the city centre along the transit mall have staggered platforms, with four stops westbound and five eastbound.

Hochflurlinien | High-floor lines
Red Line (201) Tuscany – Somerset-Bridlewood (32.2 km; 6–15′)
Blue Line (202) 69 Street SW – Saddletowne (23 km; 6–15′)

Niederflurlinien | Low-floor lines
Green Line Eau Claire – Shepard (20 km; im Bau | under construction)

(160 Ave N)
(144 Ave N)
(Stonegate)
(North Pointe)
(128 Ave NE)
(96 Ave N)
(Country Hills Blvd)
Harvest Hills Blvd
(Beddington Blvd)
(88 Ave NE)
60 Street NE
Saddletowne
(64 Ave N)
Martindale
Calgary International Airport
YYC
McKnight-Westwinds
Oliver Bowen Maintenance Facility
(Thorncliffe)
Metis Trail NE
Centre Street
(40 Ave N)
Whitehorn
Tuscany
(28 Ave N)
Rundle
Crowfoot
36 Street NE
Marlborough
Dalhousie
SAIT / AUArts Jubilee
(16 Ave N)
(9 Ave N)
Bridgeland/ Memorial
Crowchild Trail
Brentwood
Zoo
Barlow/ Max Bell
University
Lions Park
Banff Trail
Franklin
Bow River
Sunnyside
City Hall
Memorial Drive
17 Ave SE
Shaganappi Point
Sunalta
Ramsay/Inglewood)
(85 St SW)
Sirocco
Westbrook
Victoria Park/ Stampede
(26 Avenue SE)
69 Street
45 Street
Erlton/Stampede
(Highfield)
39 Avenue
Chinook
(Lynnwood/Millican)
Heritage Park
(Ogden)
Heritage
Haysboro depot
(South Hill)
14 Street SW
Southland
(Quarry Park)
Anderson
Anderson Shops
(Douglas Glen)
Bow River →
(Shepard)
Canyon Meadows
Fish Creek - Lacombe
(Prestwick)
Shawnessy
(McKenzie Towne)
Somerset-Bridlewood
(Auburn Bay/ Mahogany)
Elbow River
(Silverado)
(Hospital)
(Seton)
(210 Avenue S)
5 km

CTRAIN
Hochflur-Stadtbahn | High-Floor Light Rail
geplant | planned
Niederflur-Stadtbahn | Low-Floor Light Rail
im Bau | under construction
geplant | planned
Eigene Bustrasse | Dedicated Busway
Parkeisenbahn | Heritage Railway
Museumsstraßenbahn | Heritage Streetcar
Güterbahn | Freight Line *
Autobahnen u. Hauptstraßen *
Freeways & Main Roads *
* vereinfachte Auswahl | simplified selection

Anderson – U2 #2024

eine einfache Weiterreise in die weitläufigen Stadtteile ermöglichen. Die von beiden Linien bedienten Haltestellen im Stadtzentrum entlang der „Transit Mall" sind versetzt angeordnet, mit vier Haltestellen in Richtung Westen und fünf Haltestellen in Richtung Osten.

Die ersten Vorschläge für eine moderne Schnellbahnlinie, die das Universitätsgebiet im Nordwesten mit den südlichen Stadtteilen verbinden sollte, wurden 1966 vorgestellt. Das Projekt wurde später überarbeitet und der Bau eines Stadtbahnnetzes schließlich 1977 vom Stadtrat genehmigt, als in Edmonton bereits ein ähnliches Netz im Bau war. Im Gegensatz zu Edmonton hat Calgary auf den Tunnelbau im Stadtzentrum verzichtet und stattdessen eine „Transit Mall" geschaffen, d.h. einen 2,1 km langen Abschnitt entlang der 7th Avenue zwischen der 10th Street SW und der 3rd Street SE, der nur von Stadtbahnen, Bussen, der Polizei und anderen Einsatzfahrzeugen befahren werden darf. Die Straße ist breit genug, so dass haltende Busse die LRT-Züge nicht behindern, allerdings wurden inzwischen ohnehin alle Buslinien in Parallelstraßen verlegt. Zwischen 2005 und 2011 wurden die versetzten Seitenbahnsteige, die ursprünglich nur lang genug für einen 3-Wagen-Zug waren, allesamt modernisiert, für 4-Wagen-Züge verlängert und vollständig in die Bürgersteige integriert; die Hochbahnsteige sind über Rampen an beiden Enden stufenlos zugänglich. Einige Bahnsteige wurden dabei einen Block weiter nach Osten verlegt. Von Anfang an wurde jedoch die langfristige Option eines Tunnels unter der 8th Avenue in Betracht gezogen, insbesondere beim Bau des Calgary Municipal Building in den frühen 1980er Jahren.

Als erster der vier CTrain-Äste wurde die **Südlinie** nach Anderson, dem Standort des Stadtbahn-Betriebshofs,

The first proposals for a modern rapid transit system were presented in Calgary in 1966, with a line linking the University area in the northwest to the southern districts of the city. The plan was later revised, and the construction of a light rail system was eventually approved by the City Council in 1977 when Edmonton was already building a similar system. Unlike Edmonton, Calgary ruled out tunnelling beneath the city centre, and instead created a 'transit mall', a 2.1 km section along 7th Avenue between 10th Street SW and 3rd Street SE reserved for LRT trains, buses, police and other emergency vehicles. This road is wide enough that buses stopping would not obstruct the LRT trains, though in the meantime, the buses have all been diverted onto parallel streets. Between 2005 and 2011, the offset side platforms, initially long enough for a 3-car train, were all refurbished, lengthened for 4-car trains and fully integrated into the pavements with stepless access via ramps at either end. Some of the platforms were relocated one block further east. From the beginning, however, a long-term option for a tunnel under 8th Avenue was taken into account, most notably when the Calgary Municipal Building was built in the early 1980s.

The first of the four CTrain legs to open was the **South Line** to Anderson, the site of the LRT depot and workshops. The route turns south right after City Hall station at 3rd Street SE. Trains then go down a ramp which used to lead to a tunnel portal just before 9th Avenue SE; in 2015, the Central Library was built above the ramp, so that trains now disappear under the library into the tunnel just after leaving City Hall station. The now 600 m long tunnel was necessary to cross the CN rail corridor and align the CTrain with MacLeod Trail,

39th Avenue > Erlton/Stampede – S200 #2453 – *tunnel portal @ 34th Avenue*

in Betrieb genommen. Die Strecke biegt direkt nach der Haltestelle City Hall an der 3rd Street SE nach Süden ab. Auf einer Rampe erreichten die Züge kurz vor der 9th Avenue SE das ursprüngliche Tunnelportal, bis 2015 die Rampe abgedeckt und darüber die Zentralbibliothek errichtet wurde, so dass die Züge seither unmittelbar nach Verlassen der Haltestelle City Hall im Tunnel verschwinden. Der nun 600 m lange Tunnel war notwendig, um den CN-Eisenbahnkorridor zu unterfahren und die Stadtbahn auf den MacLeod Trail zu führen, dem sie auf ihrem Weg nach Süden folgt. Zwei Stationen erschließen „Calgary Stampede", das traditionelle Fest- und Messegelände der Stadt. Zwischen diesen beiden Stationen wurde 2021 ein östliches Aufstellgleis gebaut, wobei die Brücke über den Elbow River um ein drittes Tragwerk erweitert wurde; dieses Gleis ersetzte ein ehemaliges drittes Gleis am

which it follows on its way south. Two stations serve Calgary Stampede, the city's traditional festival and fair grounds. Between these two stations, an eastern siding was built in 2021 by adding a third span to the Elbow River crossing; this siding replaced a former third track at Victoria Park / Stampede station, which was rebuilt in 2023 and now has a direct street-level access at its southern end (17th Avenue). The trains then enter another 700 m tunnel built to avoid a surface alignment through Union Cemetery. Back on the surface, the route runs along Burnsland Road through an industrial area down to 39th Avenue station before joining the corridor of the CP branch line to Lethbridge via a short tunnel under 42nd Avenue. All three tunnels on this route were excavated by cut-and-cover. To avoid at-grade intersections, major roads like Glenmore Trail, MacLeod

Somerset/Bridlewood – SD-160 # 2220

Erlton/Stampede – U2 #2018

![Bridgeland/Memorial – S200 #2451](Bridgeland/Memorial – S200 #2451)

Bridgeland/Memorial – S200 #2451

Bahnhof Victoria Park/Stampede, der 2023 umgebaut wurde und nun an seinem südlichen Ende (17th Ave) über einen direkten Zugang auf Straßenniveau verfügt. Anschließend fahren die Züge durch einen weiteren 700 m langen Tunnel, der gebaut wurde, um eine oberirdische Trassierung durch einen Friedhof zu umgehen. Zurück an der Oberfläche verläuft die Strecke entlang der Burnsland Road durch ein Industriegebiet bis zur Station 39th Avenue, bevor sie über einen kurzen Tunnel unter der 42nd Avenue den Korridor der CP-Nebenstrecke nach Lethbridge erreicht. Alle drei Tunnel dieser Strecke wurden in offener Bauweise hergestellt. Um niveaugleiche Kreuzungen zu vermeiden, wurden für Hauptstraßen wie den Glenmore Trail, den MacLeod Trail (in der Nähe des Heritage Drive) und den Southland Drive Brücken über die Bahntrasse errichtet. Alle Stationen hatten anfangs

Trail (near Heritage Drive) and Southland Drive were rebuilt with bridges over the railway. The stations were initially all built with 80 m long platforms, but they have all since been extended to 105 m. At some stations, passengers cross the tracks to reach the platform. The original 12.5 km line was later extended in two stages to its current terminus at Somerset-Bridlewood (6.2 km); another 3.8 km extension to 210th Avenue S is planned.

*The **Northeast Line** was opened in 1984, only three years after the South Line. At the same time, the Downtown Transit Mall was extended west by one station, creating a new terminus at 10th Street SW. At the other end, an inbound platform was built between 3rd and 4th Streets SE, which disappeared in 2011 when it was combined with the original Olympic Plaza platform to create the new City Hall westbound platform. The*

Rundle – SD-160 #2315

Saddletowne

Marlborough – S200 #2423

80 m lange Bahnsteige, die später auf 105 m verlängert wurden. An einigen Stationen müssen die Fahrgäste die Gleise überqueren, um zum Bahnsteig zu gelangen. Die ursprünglich 12,5 km lange Strecke wurde später in zwei Etappen bis zu ihrem heutigen Endpunkt Somerset-Bridlewood (6,2 km) verlängert. Eine weitere 3,8 km lange Verlängerung zur 210th Avenue S ist geplant.

Die **Nordostlinie** wurde 1984, nur drei Jahre nach der Südlinie, eröffnet. Gleichzeitig wurde die Transit Mall im Stadtzentrum um eine Station nach Westen erweitert, wodurch eine neue Endstation an der 10th Street SW entstand. Am anderen Ende wurde zwischen der 3rd und 4th Street SE stadteinwärts ein Bahnsteig errichtet, der 2011 verschwand, als er mit dem früheren Bahnsteig Olympic Plaza zum neuen Bahnsteig Richtung Westen der Haltestelle City Hall zusammengelegt wurde. Die Nordostlinie, jetzt Teil der Blue Line, zeichnet sich durch ihre Trassierung im Mittelstreifen von Hauptstraßen aus. Sie verlässt das Stadtzentrum auf einer für die Stadtbahn errichteten, 500 m langen, gebogenen Brücke über den Bow River, die sie direkt auf den Mittelstreifen des Memorial Drive bringt. An der 36th Street NE schwenkt die Blue Line in einem 250 m langen Tunnel nach Norden in Richtung der ursprünglichen Endstation Whitehorn. Alle Stationen dieses Abschnitts sind nur über Fußgängerbrücken oder, im Fall von Zoo und Barlow/Max Bell, über eine Unterführung erreichbar. Lediglich Whitehorn verfügt sowohl über eine Fußgängerbrücke als auch einen ebenerdigen Zugang über das Gleis in Richtung Norden am südlichen Ende der Haltestelle. Auf dem Abschnitt entlang des Memorial Drive gibt es nur zwei, auf dem Abschnitt entlang der 36th Street jedoch zahlreiche Bahnübergänge, die alle durch automatische Schranken, Glocken und Warnlichter gesichert sind.

northeastern leg is characterised by its alignment in the median of major roads. It is now part of the Blue Line, which leaves the city centre on a 500 m purpose-built curved bridge over the Bow River which takes it directly onto the median of Memorial Drive. At 36th Street NE, a 250 m tunnel allows the CTrain to turn north towards the original terminus Whitehorn. All the stations on this section are only accessible via footbridges, or in the case of Zoo and Barlow/Max Bell via an underpass. Only Whitehorn has a footbridge as well as an access across the northbound track at its southern end. There are only two level crossings on the Memorial Drive section, but numerous on the 36th Street section, all protected by automatic barriers, bells and flashing lights.

22 years later in 2007, the Blue Line was extended to McKnight-Westwinds, where a second LRT maintenance facility was built, before reaching its current terminus Saddletowne in 2012. The extension continues in the median of 36th Street NE, but near the depot the tracks pass onto the eastern side of Metis Trail up to Martindale. The last section runs through a residential area protected by noise barriers. The last three stations have less of a metro-style design, with passengers crossing tracks, and offset side platforms at Martindale. A further extension is planned north to Stonegate, an area under development.

*The **Northwest Line**, now part of the Red Line, was built later than initially planned due to local opposition to its rather urban alignment. The line diverges from the downtown trunk route at 9th Street SW, where it heads north and crosses the Bow River and Memorial Drive on a purpose-built bridge with a pedestrian and bicycle path on the lower deck. After stopping at Sunnyside, it starts a steep climb up to the Southern Alberta Institute*

Crowfoot – S200 #2443+2453+2435

22 Jahre später, im Jahr 2007, wurde die Blue Line bis McKnight-Westwinds, wo ein zweiter LRT-Betriebshof errichtet wurde, verlängert, bevor sie 2012 ihre derzeitige Endstation Saddletowne erreichte. Die Strecke führt erst im Mittelstreifen der 36th Street NE weiter, schwenkt in der Nähe des Betriebshofs dann auf die Ostseite des Metis Trail und folgt diesem bis Martindale. Auf dem letzten Abschnitt trennen Lärmschutzwände die Trasse von den angrenzenden Wohngebieten. Die letzten drei Stationen sind weniger aufwändig als einfache Stadtbahnhaltestellen gestaltet, an denen die Fahrgäste die Gleise überqueren; Martindale erhielt sogar versetzte Seitenbahnsteige. Eine weitere Verlängerung nach Norden ins Entwicklungsgebiet Stonegate ist geplant.

Die **Nordwestlinie**, heute Teil der Red Line, wurde infolge des Widerstands der Anrainer gegen ihre eher urbane Trassierung später als ursprünglich geplant umgesetzt. Die Strecke zweigt an der 9th Street SW von

of Technology (SAIT), crossing 10th Street NW on a curved viaduct. After serving the North Hill Shopping Centre at Lions Park, it enters a 250 m tunnel to get to the northern side of 16th Avenue NW. After Banff Trail station, another 400 m tunnel brings the Red Line onto the median of Crowchild Trail, which it follows in metro style without any level crossings for 10.5 km all the way to its current terminus at Tuscany. So while the stations from Sunnyside to Banff Trail are accessed at grade (SAIT also has a footbridge), the outer stations are all reached via footbridges from either side of the expressway.

Only opened in 2012, the **West Line** is the newest leg of the system and features a mix of alignments, mostly grade-separated. For this extension, the old rudimentary terminus at 10th Street SW was replaced by a new station a block further west called Downtown West-Kerby, which has facing side platforms. Just after crossing 11th Street NW, the Blue Line ascends

Dalhousie – SD-160 #2313

Sunnyside <> 8th Street – Bow River Bridge

SAIT/AUArts/Jubilee <> Sunnyside – SD-160 #2269+2253

der Innenstadttrasse ab, führt nach Norden und überquert den Bow River und den Memorial Drive auf einer eigens für sie gebauten Brücke mit einem Fuß- und Radweg auf dem Unterdeck. Nach einem Halt in Sunnyside beginnt ein steiler Aufstieg zum Southern Alberta Institute of Technology (SAIT), wobei die Bahn die 10th Street NW auf einem gebogenen Viadukt überquert. Nach Halt an der Station Lions Park beim North Hill Shopping Centre fährt die Red Line durch einen 250 m langen Tunnel, um zur Nordseite der 16th Avenue NW zu gelangen. Nach der Station Banff Trail folgt ein weiterer 400 m langer Tunnel, der die Red Line schließlich auf den Mittelstreifen des Crowchild Trail bringt, auf dem sie 10,5 km lang ganz im Stil einer Metro ohne Bahnübergänge bis zu ihrem aktuellen Endpunkt Tuscany bleibt. Während also die Stationen von Sunnyside bis Banff Trail ebenerdig zugänglich sind (SAIT verfügt auch über eine Fußgängerbrücke), sind die äußeren Stationen nur über Fußgängerbrücken von beiden Seiten der Stadtautobahn aus erreichbar.

Die erst 2012 eröffnete **Westlinie** ist der neueste Ast des Stadtbahnnetzes. Auf diesem Ast findet man eine Mischung aus Trassierungen, die größtenteils kreuzungsfrei geplant wurden. Für diese Netzerweiterung wurde die alte einfache Endhaltestelle an der 10th Street SW durch eine neue Station Downtown West-Kerby mit gegenüberliegenden Seitenbahnsteigen einen Block weiter westlich ersetzt. Kurz nachdem sie die 11th Street NW überquert hat, erklimmt die Blue Line ein 1,4 km langes Viadukt, das sich über die 9th Avenue und die 14th Street SW sowie die CN-Bahngleise erstreckt, bevor die Stadtbahn Calgarys einzigen Hochbahnhof Sunalta erreicht. Das Viadukt führt entlang der Bahngleise und über die nach Osten führenden Fahrspuren des Bow Trail weiter. Die Blue Line verläuft dann im Mittelstreifen dieser zweispurigen Straße

a 1.4 km viaduct, which spans across 9th Avenue and 14th Street SW as well as the CN railroad tracks before arriving at Sunalta, Calgary's only elevated station. The viaduct continues alongside the rail tracks and across the eastbound lanes of Bow Trail. The Blue Line then runs in the median of this dual-carriageway before stopping at the at-grade Shaganappi Point station, whose side platforms can be directly accessed from street level. The trains then enter a 1 km tunnel containing Westbrook, Calgary's only underground station, which was supposedly built in provision of a proposed branch to Mount Royal University. The line surfaces on the north side of 17th Avenue SW, but remains below street level in an open trench up to 45th Street station. It continues west alongside 17th Avenue, but eventually dives under it to reach the terminus at 69th Street, which is again located in an open trench.

Sunalta > Shaganappi Point – S200 #2406

Westbrook – bislang der einzige unterirdische Bahnhof in Calgary | *so far Calgary's only underground station*

und hält an der ebenerdigen Station Shaganappi Point, deren Seitenbahnsteige direkt vom Straßenniveau aus zugänglich sind. Die Züge fahren dann in einen 1 km langen Tunnel, in dessen Verlauf Calgarys einziger U-Bahnhof Westbrook liegt und der angeblich im Hinblick auf einen geplanten Abzweig zur Mount Royal University gebaut wurde. Die Linie verläuft anschließend auf der Nordseite der 17th Avenue SW, bleibt aber bis zur Station 45th Street in einem offenen Einschnitt. Sie führt weiter nach Westen entlang der 17th Avenue, taucht dann aber unter dieser hindurch und erreicht die Endstation an der 69th Street, die wiederum in einem offenen Einschnitt liegt.

Sunalta – SD-160 #2323

Sirocco – S200 #2431

69th Street

CTrain-Fahrzeuge

Calgary bestellte im Juli 1977 27 Fahrzeuge des Frankfurter Typs **U2** bei Duewag/Siemens, also ein Jahr bevor der gleiche Triebwagen in Edmonton den regulären Betrieb aufnahm. Alle Fahrzeuge (Nr. 2001-2027) wurden im Jahr 1980 ausgeliefert, die Endmontage erfolgte in den Anderson Shops in Calgary. Eine zweite Serie mit 56 identischen Wagen (Nr. 2028-2083) folgte 1983/84. Im Jahr 1988 wurden zu Testzwecken zwei Fahrzeuge (Nr. 2101, 2102) mit Drehstromantrieb in den Fuhrpark aufgenommen. Tw. 2090 wurde aus zwei beschädigten Fahrzeugen zusammengebaut. Die U2-Wagen sind 23 m lang (24,3 m über Kupplung) und 2,65 m breit. Es handelt sich um Gelenkfahrzeuge mit zwei angetriebenen Drehgestellen und einem nicht angetriebenen Drehgestell unter dem Gelenk. Sie werden mit 600 V Gleichstrom betrieben, der über eine Oberleitung zugeführt wird. Bei einer Fußbodenhöhe von 978 mm über Schienenoberkante ist ein stufenloser Einstieg an allen Stationen möglich. Die Höchstgeschwindigkeit beträgt 80 km/h. Seit 2016 wurde etwa die Hälfte der U2-Fahrzeuge ausgemustert und durch neue Wagen ersetzt; die übrigen sind in der Hauptverkehrszeit als Verstärker vor allem auf der Red Line zu sehen.

Zur Erweiterung des Netzes wurden bei Siemens insgesamt 72 Wagen (Nr. 2201-2272) des Typs **SD-160** bestellt, die im kalifornischen Sacramento gebaut und zwischen 2001 und 2007 ausgeliefert wurden. Die Wagen sind mit einem Drehstromantrieb ausgestattet und wurden zwischen 2009 und 2011 mit einer Klimaanlage nachgerüstet. Eine zweite Serie von 38 Wagen (Nr. 2301-2338) wurde zwischen 2010 und 2012 mit einer leicht veränderten Stirnseite geliefert.

Sowohl für den weiteren Netzausbau als auch als Ersatz für die über 40 Jahre alten U2-Wagen bestellte Calgary Transit 2013 das Nachfolgemodell von Siemens, den Typ **S200**. Die anfängliche Bestellung von 63 Wagen wurde später auf 69 (Nr. 2401-2469) erhöht, die allesamt zwischen 2016 und 2019 geliefert wurden. Mit einer Länge über Kupplung von 25,8 m haben sie ähnliche Maße wie die älteren Typen. Die Fußbodenhöhe beträgt 982 mm über Schienenoberkante. Um die Kapazität zu erhöhen, verfügen sie überwiegend über Längssitze. Ihre Höchstgeschwindigkeit beträgt ebenfalls 80 km/h.

Ursprünglich hatten die CTrain-Haltestellen nur Bahnsteige für 3-Wagen-Züge, doch bis 2015 wurden alle verlängert, wodurch der Einsatz von 100 m langen 4-Wagen-Zügen möglich wurde.

CTrain Rolling Stock

Calgary ordered 27 cars of Frankfurt's **U2** model from Duewag/Siemens in July 1977, i.e. a year before the same type of train started regular service in Edmonton. They were all (nos. 2001-2027) delivered in 1980, with the final assembly being carried out in Calgary's Anderson Shops. A second batch of 56 identical cars (nos. 2028-2083) came in 1983/84. In 1988, two vehicles (nos. 2101, 2102) equipped with an AC drive were added to the fleet for trial purposes. Car no. 2090 was assembled from two damaged vehicles. The U2 cars are 23 m long (24.3 m over couplers) and 2.65 m wide; they are articulated with two powered bogies, plus one unpowered bogie under the articulation. They run on 600 V DC taken from an overhead power line. With a floor height of 978 mm above the top of the rail, they allow stepfree boarding at all stations. Their maximum speed is 80 km/h. Since 2016, about half of the U2 vehicles have been retired and replaced by new rolling stock; the remaining U2 cars can primarily be seen on the Red Line during rush-hour service.

For the system's expansion, an order was placed with Siemens for a total of 72 cars (nos. 2201-2272) of the **SD-160** model; they were built in Sacramento, California, and delivered between 2001 and 2007. The cars are equipped with an AC drive, and between 2009 and 2011, were retrofitted with an air-conditioning system. A second batch of 38 cars (nos. 2301-2338) with a slightly modified front came between 2010 and 2012.

To cater for the new extensions, but also to replace the over 40-year-old U2s, Calgary Transit ordered Siemens's successor model, the **S200**, in 2013. The initial order of 63 cars was later increased to 69 (nos. 2401-2469), all of which were delivered between 2016 and 2019. With a length over couplers of 25.8 m, they have similar dimensions to the older types used in Calgary. The floor height is 982 mm above the top of the rail. To increase capacity, they have mostly longitudinal seating. Their maximum speed is also 80 km/h.

Initially, the CTrain stations were only equipped with platforms long enough for 3-car trains, but by 2015, they had all been lengthened to allow the use of 100 m long 4-car trains.

U2

S200

![Station rendering](© calgary.ca)

CTrain – Green Line

Das bedeutendste Stadtbahnprojekt in Calgary ist der Bau der Green Line, die eine völlig neue Verbindung zwischen den nördlichen und südöstlichen Vororten (46 km) schaffen wird. Wie bei der Valley Line in Edmonton ist für die Green Line der Einsatz von Niederflurfahrzeugen geplant, aber im Gegensatz zur neuen Linie in Edmonton wird sie das Stadtzentrum in einem Tunnel durchqueren und entlang ihres ersten Abschnitts in Richtung Südosten auch mehrere Hochbahnabschnitte aufweisen. Die erste Ausbaustufe ist 20 km lang und verläuft von der 16th Avenue N bis Shepard im Südosten. Im Jahr 2023 wurde mit der Verlegung von Versorgungsleitungen im Stadtzentrum begonnen. Von der Centre Street N/16th Avenue kommend wird die Green Line den Bow River auf einer Brücke überqueren und dann nördlich des Eau Claire Market sofort in den 3 km langen Innenstadttunnel einfahren. Der Tunnel wird unter der 2nd Street SW gebaut, ein Übergang zu den bestehenden Linien wird an der 7th Avenue geschaffen (Richtung Westen umsteigende Fahrgäste müssen einen Block nach Osten laufen). Nach Unterquerung des Eisenbahnkorridors biegt die Green Line an der 11th Avenue nach Osten ab und durchfährt das als „Beltline" bekannte Viertel, wobei sie an der Centre Street und an der 4th Street SE unterirdisch hält. Die Züge erreichen dann die Oberfläche und überqueren parallel zu den CP-Gleisen den Elbow River. Die Stationen Ramsay/Inglewood und 26th Avenue SE liegen in Hochlage, die übrigen dann ebenerdig.

Bereits 2021 bestellte Calgary Transit beim spanischen Hersteller CAF 28 Niederflurstraßenbahnen des bewährten Typs URBOS 100, mit einer Option auf weitere 24 Fahrzeuge – die siebenteiligen Bahnen sind 42 m lang und voraussichtlich ab 2027 im Einsatz.

The most significant of all the Calgary light rail projects is the Green Line, which will add a completely new cross-city link between the northern and southeastern suburbs (46 km). Like the Valley Line in Edmonton, the Green Line will use low-floor vehicles, but unlike Edmonton's line, it will cross the city centre in tunnel and also feature several viaducts along its initial segment towards the southeast. Stage 1 is 20 km long and runs from 16th Avenue N to Shepard in the southeast. Utilities relocation was launched in the city centre in 2023. Coming from Centre Street N/16th Avenue, the Green Line will cross the Bow River on a bridge and then immediately enter the 3 km downtown tunnel north of the Eau Claire Market. The tunnel will be built under 2nd Street SW, providing interchange with the existing lines at 7th Avenue (westbound passengers will have to walk one block east to continue their journey). After passing the railway corridor, the tunnel will turn east under 11th Avenue through the area known as the Beltline, with underground stations at Centre Street and 4th Street SE, after which the trains will emerge and cross the Elbow River alongside the CP railroad tracks, before serving the elevated Ramsay/Inglewood and 26th Avenue SE stations. The remaining stations will be at ground level.

Already in 2021, Calgary Transit ordered 28 low-floor trams of the well-known URBOS 100 model from CAF of Spain, with an option for a further 24 vehicles — the seven-section trams will be 42 m long and are expected to start service in 2027.

 **Green Line Project** - www.calgary.ca/green-line.html

Urbos 100 (© CAF)

Nelson Electric Tramway Society

In der kleinen Stadt Nelson, BC, ungefähr auf halber Strecke zwischen Vancouver und Calgary (662 km bzw. 616 km auf der Straße), betreibt die *Nelson Electric Tramway Society* eine Museumsstraßenbahn auf einer 2 km langen Strecke entlang des Westarms des Kootenay Lake. Von Mitte Mai bis Mitte Oktober verkehren täglich alle 30 Minuten (11:00–16:30 Uhr) der restaurierte Triebwagen Nr. 23 (1906 für die Forest City Railway in Cleveland gebaut; im Linienverkehr in Nelson von 1924 bis 1949) und/oder der Wagen Nr. 400 (ein Birney-Zweirichtungswagen, Baujahr 1921) aus Victoria, der Hauptstadt von British Columbia. Wagenschuppen und Werkstatt sind das ganze Jahr dienstags und donnerstags vormittags geöffnet.

About halfway between Vancouver and Calgary (662 km and 616 km on the road, respectively), in the small town of Nelson, BC, the Nelson Electric Tramway Society operates a heritage streetcar line on a 2 km route along the West Arm of Kootenay Lake. Either the restored streetcar #23 (built in 1906 for the Forest City Railway in Cleveland; in regular service in Nelson from 1924 to 1949) or the ex-Victoria car #400 (a double-ended Birney Car, built in 1921) are in daily service every 30 minutes mid-May to mid-October (11:00-16:30); carbarn & workshops are open Tuesday & Thursday mornings all year.

For more information: www.nelsonstreetcar.org

2023 © Michael Dill

Edmonds – 2x SkyTrain Mark III

VANCOUVER, BC

Die Stadt Vancouver hat 665.000 Einwohner auf einer Fläche von nur 115 km². Sie grenzt im Norden an den Burrard Inlet und den Hafen, im Süden an den Nordarm des Fraser River, der sie von der Stadt Richmond (230.000 Einw.) trennt, und im Osten an die Stadt Burnaby (250.000 Einw.). Weiter östlich jenseits des Fraser River liegt die Stadt Surrey, mit rund 570.000 Einwohnern die zweitgrößte Stadt in der Provinz British Columbia. Das als „Metro Vancouver Regional District" bekannte Gebiet umfasst den gesamten Ballungsraum, aber auch weitläufige bergige bzw. dünn besiedelte Gebiete mit fast 2,7 Millionen Einwohnern auf einer Fläche von 2.878 km². Die Hauptstadt der Provinz British Columbia ist nicht Vancouver, sondern Victoria auf Vancouver Island.

Die Pacific Central Station von Vancouver kann aus zwei Richtungen erreicht werden: „The Canadian" der kanadischen *VIA Rail* verkehrt zweimal pro Woche zwischen Vancouver und Toronto über Winnipeg und Edmonton (4.466 km, 92-97 Stunden). Mit zwei Zügen täglich fährt Amtrak auf der „Cascades"-Linie von/nach Seattle im US-Bundesstaat Washington (~230 km, 4h25) etwas häufiger, einmal pro Tag sogar weiter von/ bis Portland, Oregon (8h20). Ausgehend von Vancouver veranstaltet *Rocky Mountaineer* exklusive Zugreisen für Touristen nicht nur auf der Hauptstrecke nach Jasper, sondern auch über Whistler und Quesnel.

The City of Vancouver has a population of 665,000 in an area of just 115 km², and is bordered by the Burrard Inlet and harbour in the north, the North Arm of the Fraser River and the City of Richmond (pop. 230,000) in the south, and the City of Burnaby (pop. 250,000) in the east. Further east across the Fraser River lies the City of Surrey, with some 570,000 inhabitants the second-largest by population in British Columbia. The area known as the 'Metro Vancouver Regional District' covers the entire conurbation but also large mountainous and sparsely populated areas, with a total of almost 2.7 million inhabitants in an area of 2,878 km². Vancouver is by far the largest urban area in British Columbia, but the province's capital is Victoria, on Vancouver Island.

Vancouver's Pacific Central Station can be reached from two directions: 'The Canadian', operated by VIA Rail, runs twice a week between Vancouver and Toronto via Winnipeg and Edmonton (4,466 km, 92-97 hours). A more frequent service is provided by Amtrak, with two daily 'Cascades' round trips to Seattle in the U.S. state of Washington (~230 km, 4h 25min), with one train continuing south to Portland, Oregon (8h 20min). Starting from Vancouver, the 'Rocky Mountaineer' offers exclusive train journeys for tourists not only on the main route to Jasper, but also via Whistler and Quesnel.

TransLink - www.translink.ca
VIA Rail - www.viarail.ca

Amtrak Cascades - amtrakcascades.com
Rocky Mountaineer - www.rockymountaineer.com

● **Coquitlam Central** – SkyTrain Mark II

● **Templeton** – Canada Line Flughafenast | *airport branch*

Für den gesamten öffentlichen Nahverkehr im Raum Vancouver ist TransLink verantwortlich. Vancouvers Metro-Netz, bekannt als „SkyTrain", wird von der *British Columbia Rapid Transit Company* (Expo & Millennium Line) und *ProTrans BC* (Canada Line) betrieben. Die *Coast Mountain Bus Company* betreibt neben herkömmlichen Bussen auch ein umfangreiches Netz von Obuslinien. Für Einzelfahrten (SkyTrain, SeaBus und Busse) ist das TransLink-Gebiet in drei Tarifzonen unterteilt. Die Fahrpreise liegen zwischen 3,15 $ und 6,20 $. Abends und am Wochenende gilt jedoch auf dem gesamten Netz der Tarif für nur eine Zone. Tageskarten kosten 11,25 $ und sind in allen Zonen gültig; sie sind als Compass-Tickets an Fahrkartenautomaten an SkyTrain-Stationen erhältlich, können aber auch auf eine Compass Card aufgeladen werden (erstattbare 6 $ für die Karte). Bis 2013 wurden alle SkyTrain-Stationen mit Zugangssperren nachgerüstet. Für Fahrten, die abends am Flughafen beginnen, ist ein Aufpreis von 5 $ zu zahlen! Für die Regionalbahn West Coast Express gilt ein eigener Tarif.

All public transport in the Vancouver area is managed by TransLink. Vancouver's metro system, known as the 'SkyTrain', is operated by the 'British Columbia Rapid Transit Company' (Expo and Millennium Lines) and 'ProTrans BC' (Canada Line). The 'Coast Mountain Bus Company' operates not only buses, but also an extensive network of trolleybus routes. For single journeys (SkyTrain, SeaBus and buses), the TransLink area is divided into 3 fare zones, with fares ranging from $3.15 to $6.20, but only a 1-zone fare is charged in the evenings and at weekends; day passes cost $11.25 and are valid in all zones. Day passes are available as single-use Compass Tickets from ticket vending machines at SkyTrain stations, but can also be loaded onto a stored-value Compass Card ($6 refundable deposit for the card). By 2013, all SkyTrain stations had been retrofitted with fare gates. A $5 add-on fare is payable for trips starting at the airport in the evenings! Special fares apply on the West Coast Express commuter train.

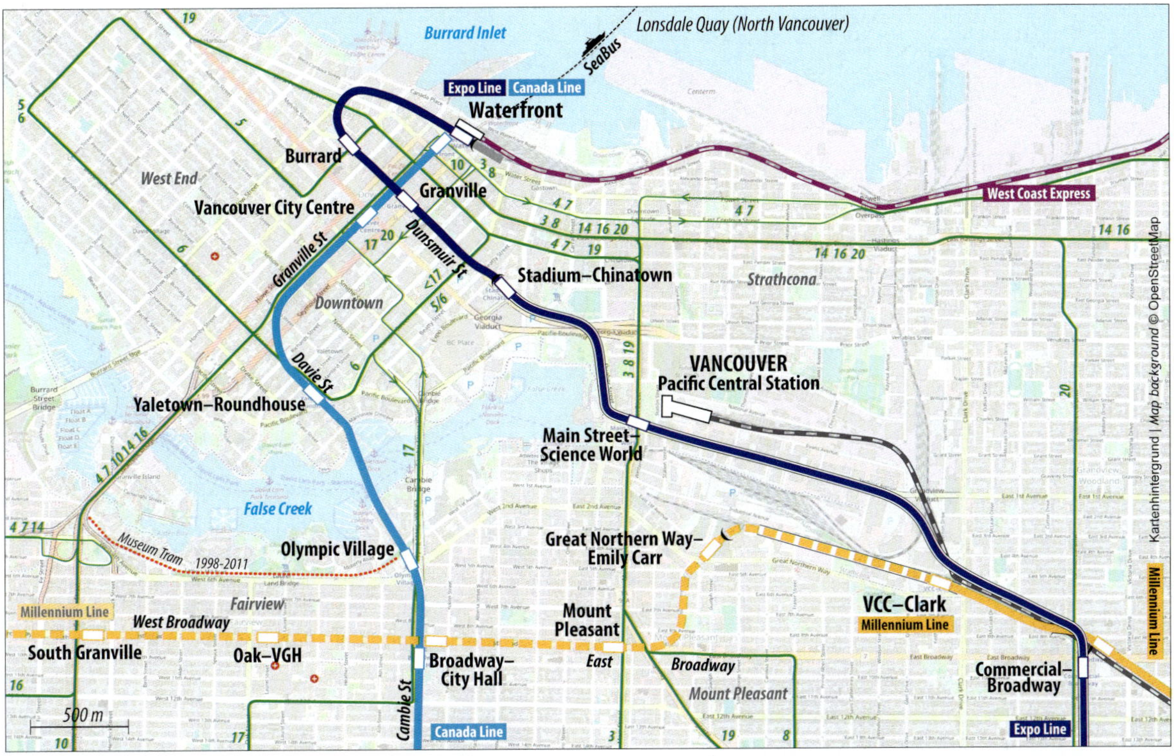

VANCOUVER

Whistler
Quesnel

WEST VANCOUVER

NORTH VANCOUVER

North Vancouver

Lonsdale Quay

Burrard Inlet

19

137

Expo Line **Canada Line**

Waterfront

English Bay

Burrard

Vancouver City Centre

Granville

Stadium–Chinatown

VANCOUVER

4

14

Yaletown–Roundhouse

Main St–
Science World

1)

Brentwood
Town Centre

Holdom

Sperling–
Burnaby
Lake

4

14

Olympic Village

4)   3)

Commercial–
Broadway

Rupert

Gilmore

**VCC–
Clark**

Arbutus

Broadway–
City Hall

2)

Millennium Line

Renfrew

Renfrew

14

University of
British Columbia

1) Great Northern Way – Emily Carr
2) Mount Pleasant
3) Oak – VGH
4) South Granville

King Edward

7

Nanaimo

7

16

7

29th Avenue

Joyce–Collingwood

16

Oakridge–
41st Avenue

8

Patterson

Metrotown

19

Langara–
49th Avenue

Royal Oak

16

Cambie St

Edmonds

BURNABY

VANCOUVER

10
17

3

Marine Drive

8

20

Fraser River (North Arm)

D

Canada Line

**YVR–
Airport**

Templeton

Bridgeport

Sea Island
Centre

Capstan

Aberdeen

No. 3 Road

Lansdowne

Canada Line

**Richmond–
Brighouse**

Strait of Georgia

RICHMOND

Fraser River (South Arm)

SKYTRAIN

Fahrerlose Metro | *Driverless Metro*

im Bau | *under construction*

geplant | *planned*

ⓓ Betriebshof | *Depot & Workshop*

Obus | *Trolleybus*

Pendlerbahn | *Commuter Railway*

Fernbahn | *Long-distance train route*

Güterbahn | *Freight Line ***

Autobahnen u. Hauptstraßen
*Freeways & Main Roads ***

*** vereinfachte Auswahl | *simplified selection*

5 km

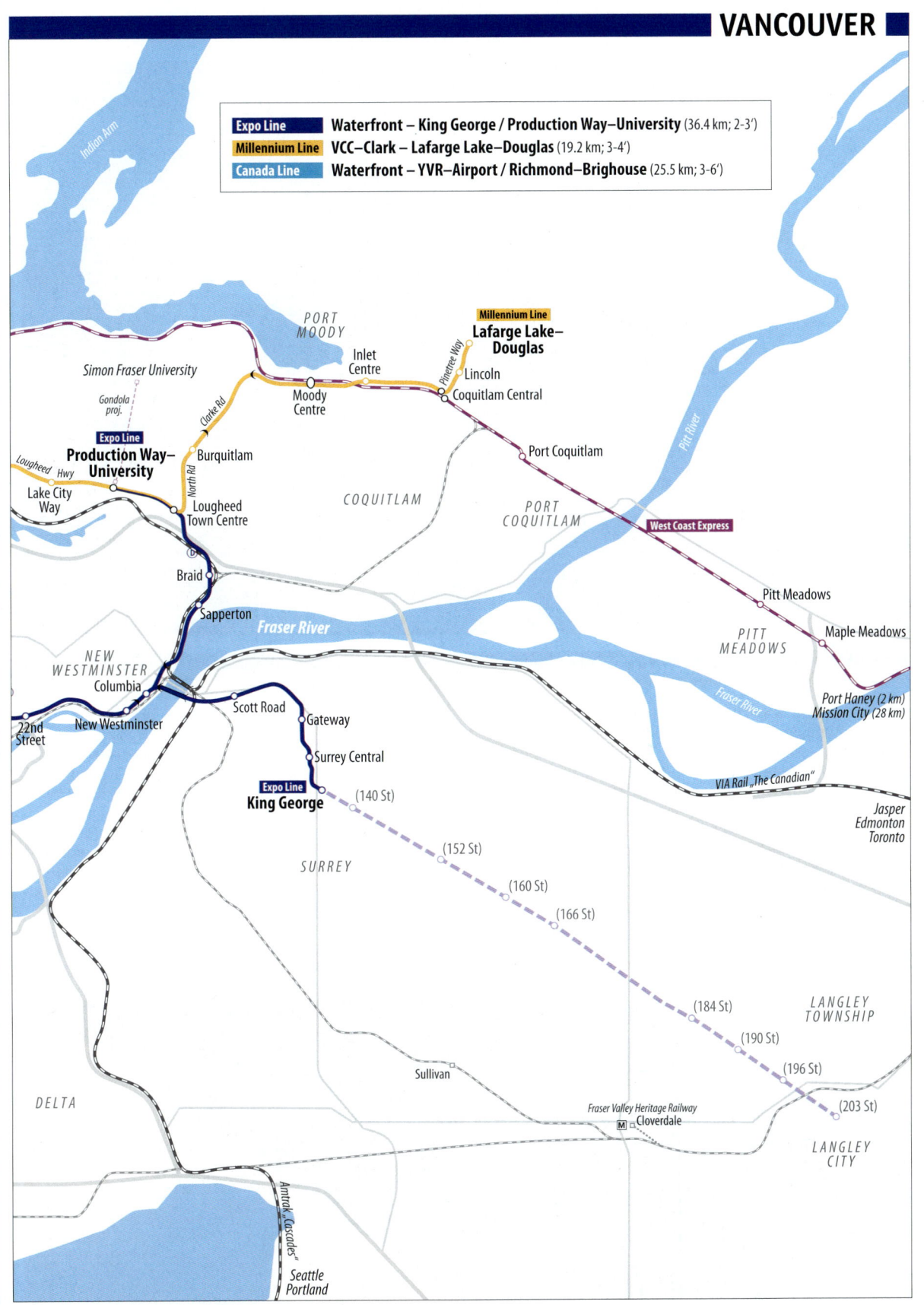

Expo Line Waterfront – King George / Production Way–University (36.4 km; 2-3')
Millennium Line VCC–Clark – Lafarge Lake–Douglas (19.2 km; 3-4')
Canada Line Waterfront – YVR–Airport / Richmond–Brighouse (25.5 km; 3-6')

Indian Arm

PORT MOODY

Inlet Centre

Millennium Line
Lafarge Lake–Douglas

Pinetree Way

Lincoln

Moody Centre

Coquitlam Central

Simon Fraser University

Gondola proj.

Clarke Rd

Expo Line
Production Way–University

Burquitlam

Port Coquitlam

North Rd

Lougheed Hwy

Lake City Way

Lougheed Town Centre

COQUITLAM

PORT COQUITLAM

Pitt River

West Coast Express

Braid

Sapperton

Fraser River

PITT MEADOWS

Pitt Meadows

NEW WESTMINSTER

Columbia

Maple Meadows

Fraser River

Scott Road

Gateway

22nd Street

New Westminster

Surrey Central

Port Haney (2 km)
Mission City (28 km)

Expo Line
King George

(140 St)

VIA Rail „The Canadian"

SURREY

(152 St)

(160 St)

Jasper
Edmonton
Toronto

(166 St)

(184 St)

LANGLEY TOWNSHIP

(190 St)

(196 St)

Sullivan

Fraser Valley Heritage Railway
Cloverdale

(203 St)

DELTA

LANGLEY CITY

Amtrak „Cascades"

Seattle Portland

● **Burrard** – Mark II (2. Serie | *second batch*)

Expo Line & Millennium Line

Vancouvers ursprüngliches SkyTrain-Netz besteht aus der Expo Line und der Millennium Line, die miteinander verflochten sind – wie der Name andeutet, wurden die ersten Abschnitte des fahrerlosen Metro-Systems vorwiegend auf Viadukten errrichtet. Die beiden Linien teilen sich einen 1,8 km langen Abschnitt zwischen Lougheed Town Centre und Production Way-University, um die Anbindung an die Simon Fraser University zu verbessern, vor allem aber um die Umsteigemöglichkeiten zwischen den beiden Linien an einem gemeinsamen Mittelbahnsteig zu erlauben (der anfängliche Linksverkehr am dreigleisigen Bahnhof Lougheed Town Centre verursachte zu viele Verspätungen). Die Züge der Expo Line fahren leer 650 m weiter, bevor sie auf das andere Gleis wechseln können.

The interlaced Expo & Millennium lines are Vancouver's original SkyTrain routes — as the name suggests, the early sections of the driverless metro system were built primarily on viaducts. The two lines share a 1.8 km section between Lougheed Town Centre and Production Way-University not only to improve access to Simon Fraser University, but also to improve the transfer options between the two lines on a single island platform (the initial left-hand operation at the 3-track Lougheed Town Centre station caused too many delays). Expo Line trains continue empty for 650 m before they can switch to the other track for their return journey.

In Vancouver, the first electric streetcars ran in as early as 1890, and just a year later, the Vancouver &

● **Burrard**

Expo Line & Millennium Line
- 60.2 km (Ⓤ 5.4 km) - 37 Stations (Ⓤ 4)
Expo Line: 36.4 km, 22 Stations
Millennium Line: 25.5 km, 17 Stations

03-01-1986: Waterfront – New Westminster (21.4 km)
14-02-1989: New Westminster – Columbia (0.6 km)
16-03-1990: Columbia – Scott Road (2.5 km)
28-03-1994: Scott Road – King George (4 km)
05-01-2002: Columbia – Braid (3.8 km)
31-08-2002: Braid – Commercial-Broadway (15.4 km)
21-11-2003: + Lake City Way
06-01-2006: Commercial-Broadway – VCC-Clark (0.8 km)
02-12-2016: Lougheed Town Centre – Lafarge Lake-Douglas
              (10.9 km)
~ 2026: VCC-Clark – Arbutus (5.7 km)

Waterfront – Abgang zur Canada Line geradeaus, zur Expo Line und zum West Coast Express rechts – *access to the Canada Line straight ahead, to the Expo Line and the West Coast Express to the right*

Bereits 1890 fuhren in Vancouver die ersten elektrischen Straßenbahnen und nur ein Jahr später startete auch die *Vancouver & Westminster Tramway Company* mit Straßenbahnlinien in New Westminster sowie einer Überlandlinie zwischen Vancouver und New Westminster über Central Park in Burnaby. Drei unabhängige Straßenbahnbetriebe wurden 1897 zur *British Columbia Electric Railway* (BCER) vereint, einem Vorläufer der heutigen TransLink. BCER betrieb einst mehrere andere Überlandstrecken in der Region, die jedoch bis 1958 alle eingestellt wurden. In Surrey betreibt die *Fraser Valley Historical Railway Society* gelegentlich Fahrten mit restaurierten BC Electric-Wagen zwischen den Stationen Cloverdale und Sullivan (siehe fvhrs.org).

● **Expo Line**:
In der zweiten Hälfte der 1960er Jahre, als Edmonton und Calgary die Wiedereinführung eines städtischen Schienenverkehrsmittels untersuchten, tat Vancouver dasselbe. Auch hier schien anfangs eine Stadtbahn die bevorzugte Wahl zu sein, doch angesichts der Tatsache, dass Vancouver weitgehend auf den Bau von Stadtautobahnen verzichtet hatte, befürchtete man, dass durch zu viele Bahnübergänge die Verkehrsprobleme noch zunehmen würden. Ermutigt durch die in Vancouver stattfindende Expo 86 mit Schwerpunkt Verkehr und Kommunikation fiel die endgültige Entscheidung 1981 zugunsten eines innovativen vollautomatischen Metro-Systems, des ALRT (Automated Light Rapid Transit), das von der UTDC (später Teil von Bombardier) entwickelt worden war. Im Jahr 1982 wurden zu Demonstrations- und Testzwecken der Hochbahnhof Main Street sowie ein 1100 m langer Gleisabschnitt errichtet. Der neue SkyTrain sollte die

Westminster Tramway Company started a streetcar service in New Westminster as well as an interurban line between Vancouver and New Westminster via Central Park in Burnaby. Three independent streetcar companies were merged in 1897 to become the British Columbia Electric Railway (BCER), a predecessor of today's TransLink. BCER operated several other interurban routes in the region, but by 1958 all services had ended. In Surrey, the Fraser Valley Historical Railway Society occasionally operates heritage rides between the original Cloverdale and Sullivan stations (see fvhrs.org).

● *Expo Line:*
Around the time when Edmonton and Calgary were studying the reintroduction of urban rail services in the second half of the 1960s, Vancouver started doing the same. Light rail seemed to be the preferred choice there too, but given the fact that Vancouver had renounced building significant portions of grade-separated freeways within its city limits, a ground-level light rail system would have implied an excessive number of level crossings, thus causing even more traffic

Main Street–Science World – Mark I (in neuem Anstrich | *in new livery*)

wichtigsten Expo-Standorte an der Waterfront und rund um den False Creek verbinden. Mit dem Baubeginn im Jahr 1983 wurde der erste Abschnitt der SkyTrain-Linie Anfang 1986 in Betrieb genommen, also wenige Monate vor Eröffnung der Expo 86.

Die Linie beginnt unterirdisch an der Station Waterfront, die parallel zum seit 1995 vom West Coast Express genutzten Bahnsteig gebaut wurde. Dieser gehört zum beeindruckenden Bahnhof von 1914, einst Endpunkt der *Canadian Pacific Railway* und von *VIA Rail* bis 1979 genutzt. Die SkyTrain-Fahrzeuge wenden im Freien hinter dem Bahnhof, fahren dann jedoch auf ihrem Weg durch die Innenstadt durch einen 1,3 km langen Tunnel. Anstatt einen komplett neuen Tunnel zu bauen, wurde der Dunsmuir-Tunnel, ein Verbindungstunnel von 1930, umgebaut, indem die Tunnelsohle abgesenkt wurde, so dass eine doppelstöckige Trassierung für den SkyTrain möglich wurde. An den U-Bahnhöfen Burrard und Granville wurde infolgedessen der stadteinwärtige Bahnsteig über dem stadtauswärtigen angeordnet. Der Rest der Strecke wurde vorwiegend als Hochbahn errichtet, wobei von Broadway/Commercial bis nach New Westminster die 1955 aufgegebene Trasse der Überlandlinie der *BC Electric* genutzt werden konnte. Einige kurze Abschnitte sind ebenerdig oder im Einschnitt, darunter die Station 29th Avenue, aber auch die Station Edmonds, an die sich ein kurzer abgedeckter Abschnitt mit einem über dem SkyTrain angelegten Park anschließt. Der Betriebshof des SkyTrain befindet sich zwischen den Stationen Edmonds und 22nd Street. Mit der Gestaltung der Bahnhöfe wurde die „Architektengruppe U-Bahn" aus Wien und Allen Parker & Associates aus Vancouver beauftragt. Das Ergebnis

problems. Encouraged by Expo 86, which was to be held in Vancouver with a focus on transportation and communication, in 1981 the final choice was made for an innovative fully automated metro system, the ALRT (Automated Light Rapid Transit) developed by UTDC (later part of Bombardier). In 1982, Main Street station plus a 1,100 m section of track was built for demonstration and testing purposes. The new SkyTrain was to link the Expo's major sites near Waterfront and around False Creek. With construction starting in 1983, the original SkyTrain line was launched at the beginning of 1986, a few months before Expo 86 opened.

The line starts at Waterfront, an underground station built parallel to the platform used by the West Coast Express since 1995. The impressive railway station was opened in 1914 as the Canadian Pacific Railway's Vancouver terminal, but VIA Rail stopped using the station in 1979. While SkyTrain vehicles reverse in the open air beyond the station, they enter a 1.3 km tunnel on their way through the city centre. Instead of building a completely new tunnel, the Dunsmuir Tunnel, originally opened in 1930 to link two rail yards, was rebuilt by excavating the bottom of the tunnel to allow a two-deck alignment for the SkyTrain. At Burrard and Granville stations, this resulted in the inbound platform being placed above the outbound. The rest of the line was primarily built as an elevated structure, taking advantage from Broadway/Commercial all the way to New Westminster of the former alignment of the BC Electric interurban line, which had been abandoned in 1955. Some short sections are at or below grade, including 29th Avenue station as well as Edmonds station,

Main Street–Science World > Stadium–Chinatown

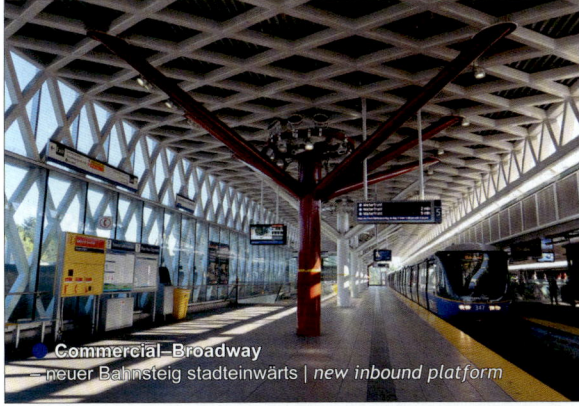

Commercial–Broadway
– neuer Bahnsteig stadteinwärts | *new inbound platform*

29th Avenue

Patterson

Patterson

SkyBridge (Columbia > Scott Road)

waren Gestaltungselemente, die denen des Wiener U-Bahn-Netzes ähneln.

Die erste Erweiterung des SkyTrain-Netzes umfasste einen kurzen Tunnel in New Westminster mit der teilweise nach oben offenen Station Columbia sowie die eigens für den SkyTrain errichtete 616 m lange Schrägseilbrücke (SkyBridge) über den Fraser River ins benachbarte Surrey. Von der Brücke bis zur heutigen Endstation King George, die 1994 erreicht wurde, verkehren die Züge durchgehend in Hochlage. Jetzt, 30 Jahre später, könnte bald mit dem Bau einer Hochbahnverlängerung bis nach Langley City (16 km) begonnen werden. Zwischen 2014 und 2016 wurde der Hochbahnhof Main Street-Science World umgebaut; er erhielt dabei einen östlichen Zugang sowie auf gesamter Länge eine seitliche Verglasung. Im Jahr 2019 wurde auf der Ostseite des Bahnhofs Commercial-Broadway ein zusätzlicher Seitenbahnsteig eröffnet, um den bestehenden Mittelbahnsteig zu entlasten; die Türen der stadteinwärts fahrenden Züge werden nun auf beiden Seiten geöffnet.

which is followed by a short covered section with a park laid out above the line. The SkyTrain's Operations and Maintenance Centre is located between Edmonds and 22nd Street stations. The design of the stations was awarded to 'Architektengruppe U-Bahn' of Vienna and Allen Parker & Associates of Vancouver, resulting in design elements similar to those found on Vienna's U-Bahn network.

The first extension of the SkyTrain system included a short tunnel in New Westminster with the partly uncovered subsurface station Columbia, and most noteworthy, the dedicated 616 m cable-stayed SkyBridge across the Fraser River, which takes the SkyTrain to Surrey. From the bridge to the current terminus King George, which was reached in 1994, trains run on a viaduct. Now 30 years later, the construction of an elevated extension all the way to Langley City (16 km) may soon be starting. Between 2014 and 2016, Main Street-Science World station was rebuilt with an eastern access and glassed wind shields along the full length of the elevated platform. In 2019, an additional side platform was opened on the eastern side of Commercial-Broadway station to relieve the existing island platform; the doors on the inbound trains now open on both sides.

King George

Scott Road

Gateway

Burquitlam

● **Millennium Line**:

Nachdem der SkyTrain eine Gesamtlänge von 28,5 km erreicht hatte, wurde der Ausbau einige Jahre später mit einem Abzweig von New Westminster über Lougheed und Burnaby zurück nach Vancouver fortgesetzt, woraus schließlich die Millennium Line enstand, während die bestehende Strecke fortan als Expo Line bezeichnet wurde (bis 2016 verkehrten beide Linien gemeinsam auf dem Abschnitt zwischen Waterfront und Columbia). Um auf den 2002 eröffneten neuen Ast zu gelangen, zweigen die Züge nördlich des Bahnhofs Columbia kreuzungsfrei ab und fahren dann zwecks Unterquerung der Zufahrtsstraßen zur Patullo-Brücke durch einen 600 m langen Tunnel, bevor sie die Hauptbahnstrecke überqueren, auf der „The Canadian" sowie Amtraks „Cascades" von der New Westminster-Eisenbahnbrücke nach Vancouver fahren. Der SkyTrain fährt aufgeständert größtenteils entlang der Eisenbahn weiter und erreicht den jetzt dreigleisigen Hochbahnhof Lougheed Town Centre. Die darauffolgenden 8,6 km wurden als Viadukt neben oder mittig über dem Lougheed Highway bis zur Station Gilmore errichtet, von wo aus die Strecke der Eisenbahntrasse folgt, zunächst aufgeständert, ab der Nanaimo Street jedoch im Einschnitt bis zur Station Commercial-Broadway, wo die ursprüngliche SkyTrain-Strecke gekreuzt wird. Anstatt eine große Schleife zu schaffen, ermöglichte die gewählte Trasse im Einschnitt eine Westverlängerung der Millennium Line – eine kurze Erweiterung bis VCC-Clark wurde 2006 fertiggestellt, doch mit dem Bau einer weiteren 5,7 km langen Verlängerung entlang des Broadway, die nun größtenteils unterirdisch verläuft, wurde erst 2021 begonnen, die Fertigstellung ist für 2026 geplant. Der Bau der Streckentunnel

● *Millennium Line:*

With the SkyTrain having reached a total length of 28.5 km, expansion continued a few years later with a branch from New Westminster via Lougheed and Burnaby back to Vancouver, which would become the Millennium Line, while the existing line was named the Expo Line (until 2016 both lines shared the section between Waterfront and Columbia). To serve the new branch opened in 2002, trains diverge in a grade-separated junction just north of Columbia station and run through a 600 m tunnel to dive below the approach roads to Patullo Bridge, before crossing the mainline track that carries 'The Canadian' and Amtrak's 'Cascades' from the New Westminster Rail Bridge into Vancouver. The Skytrain carriages continue on an elevated structure mostly alongside the mainline railway before reaching the now 3-track station at Lougheed Town Centre. The following 8.6 km was built as a viaduct alongside or in the median of Lougheed Highway up to Gilmore station, from where the line follows the railway corridor, first elevated but from Nanaimo Street below grade to Commercial-Broadway station, where it intersects with the original SkyTrain route. Instead of creating a loop, the alignment chosen allowed for a western extension of the Millennium Line — a short extension to VCC-Clark was completed in 2006, but the construction of a further 5.7 km extension along Broadway, now mostly underground, only started in 2021 for completion in 2026. The running tunnels are being excavated using tunnel boring machines, while the stations are being built by cut-and-cover.

Production Way–University

erfolgt mit Tunnelbohrmaschinen, während die Stationen in offener Bauweise errichtet werden.

In der Zwischenzeit wurde jedoch die „Evergreen Line" gebaut, der 10,9 km lange Abzweig von Lougheed nach Port Moody und Coquitlam. Dazu gehörten ein drittes Gleis und ein Seitenbahnsteig sowie eine niveaugleiche Verzweigung an der Station Lougheed Town Centre und ein 2,1 km langer Tunnel entlang der Clarke Road ohne Bahnhof. In Port Moody wurde die SkyTrain-Station günstig neben dem bestehenden Bahnsteig des West Coast Express platziert, während an der Station Coquitlam Central beim Umsteigen ein kurzer Fußweg erforderlich ist. Auf einem ebenerdigen Abschnitt zwischen Inlet Centre und Coquitlam Central wurde ein kleine Wartungsanlage errichtet, um die ursprüngliche Anlage in Edmonds zu

In the meantime, however, the 'Evergreen Line' was built, i.e. the 10.9 km branch from Lougheed to Port Moody and Coquitlam. This project included a third track, an additional side platform and a flat junction at Lougheed Town Centre as well as a 2.1 km tunnel along Clarke Road without any stations. At Port Moody, the SkyTrain station was conveniently placed adjacent to the existing West Coast Express platform, while at Coquitlam Central a short walk is required to transfer. On an at-grade section between Inlet Centre and Coquitlam Central, a small maintenance centre was established to relieve the original facility at Edmonds. At Coquitlam Central, a somewhat awkward junction was built in preparation for a possible branch to Port Coquitlam. To improve access to the Coquitlam town centre, Lincoln

Commercial–Broadway > VCC–Clark

Inlet Centre – Mark II (1. Serie | first batch)

Rupert – Fernbahngleise | *mainline tracks* (> Seattle & Edmonton)

entlasten. Bei Coquitlam Central wurde bereits eine etwas kuriose Ausfädelung für einen möglichen Abzweig nach Port Coquitlam mitgebaut. Um den Zugang zum Stadtzentrum von Coquitlam zu verbessern, wurde 2012, als mit dem Bau der Strecke bereits begonnen worden war, der Hochbahnhof Lincoln in das Projekt aufgenommen. Dieser Ast wurde im Dezember 2016 eröffnet, womit die Millennium Line zu einer weitgehend eigenständigen Linie wurde, die nun von VCC-Clark bis Lafarge Lake-Douglas verkehrt, während der Abschnitt Columbia – Lougheed Town Centre nun als Ast der Expo Line betrieben wird.

station was added to the project in 2012 when the construction of the line had already started. The branch was opened in December 2016, when the Millennium Line became a largely independent line running from VCC-Clark to Lafarge Lake-Douglas, leaving the Columbia – Lougheed Town Centre section as a branch off the Expo Line.

Coquitlam Central > Lincoln

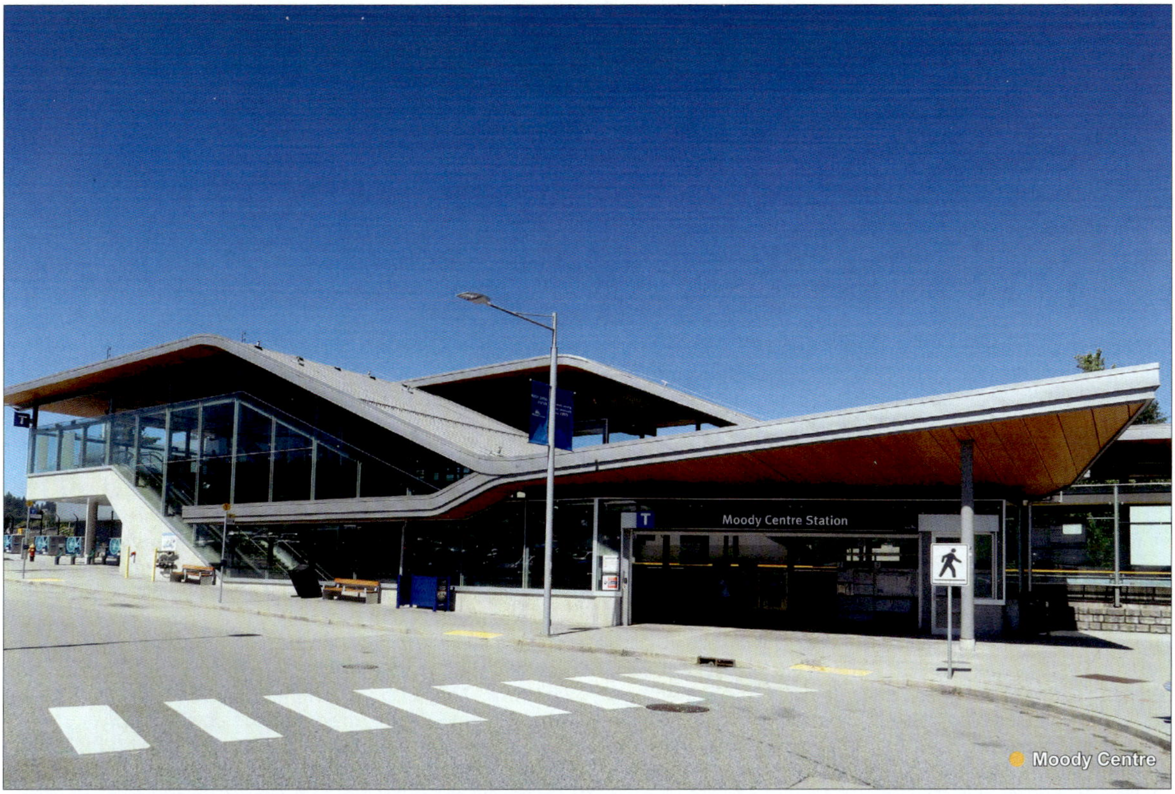

Moody Centre

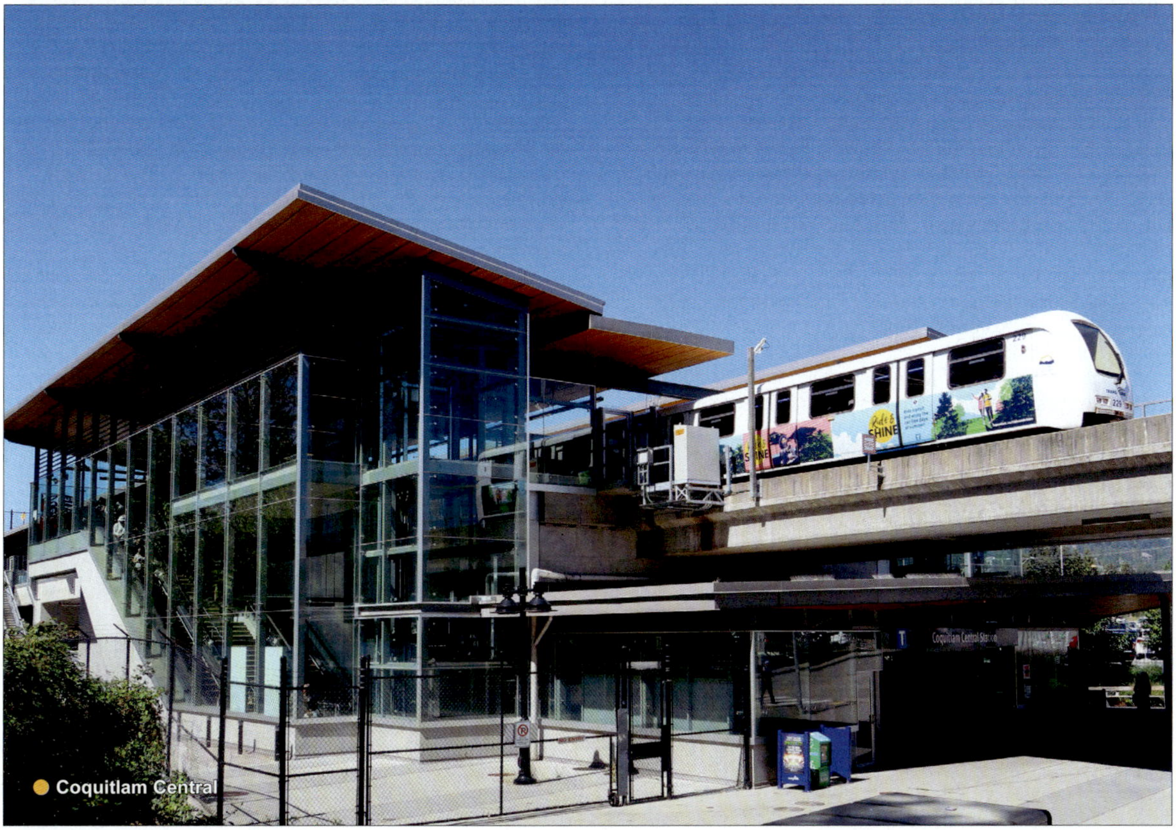

Coquitlam Central

Mark I (im originalen Anstrich | *in original livery*)

Mark I (in Mark II-Anstrich | *in Mark II livery*)

- SkyTrain-Fahrzeuge:

Die auf den ersten beiden SkyTrain-Linien eingesetzten Fahrzeuge verfügen über lenkbare Achsdrehgestelle zur Bewältigung enger Kurven und zur Reduzierung von Lärmemissionen sowie über lineare Induktionsmotoren (LIM) mit einer durchgehenden magnetischen Reaktionsschiene, die zwischen den beiden Fahrschienen angeordnet ist. Das automatische Zugsteuerungssystem mit beweglichen Blöcken basiert auf dem in Deutschland entwickelten SelTrac-System, das von SEL Canada Ltd. (später Teil von Alcatel, heute Thales) geliefert wurde. Die LIMs ziehen 650 V DC von einer seitlichen Stromschiene, was an Bord in Drehstrom umgewandelt wird. Sie übernehmen auch den Großteil der Bremsvorgänge, wobei Energie in das Stromnetz zurückgespeist wird.

Die heutige Flotte besteht aus drei Generationen: Insgesamt 150 **Mark I**-Einheiten, d.h. Doppeltriebwagen (2 x 12,7 m lang, 2,4 m breit), die als Einzel-, Doppel- oder Dreifacheinheiten (76,2 m) eingesetzt werden. Sie ähneln den Fahrzeugen, die beim People Mover in der Innenstadt von Detroit sowie bis 2023 auf der Scarborough RT in Toronto im Einsatz sind bzw. waren. Sie wurden von der UTDC (*Urban Transportation Development Corporation Ltd.*; 1992 von Bombardier übernommen) hergestellt und in vier Serien geliefert: 56 (Nr. 001-056; 1984), 58 (Nr. 061-118; 1985), 16 (Nr. 121-136; 1991) und 20 (Nr. 137-156; 1995). Sie sind heute in verschiedenen Lackierungen im Einsatz, vom Original bis zur Neulackierung im Mark II- und Mark III-Stil.

Für die Eröffnung der Millennium Line im Jahr 2002 wurden insgesamt 60 **Mark II**-Einheiten (Nr. 201-260)

- SkyTrain Rolling Stock:

The rolling stock used on the two original SkyTrain lines features steerable axle bogies to manage tight curves and reduce noise emissions, and linear induction motors (LIM) with a continuous magnetic reaction rail placed between the two running rails. The moving-block automatic train control system is based on the SelTrac system developed in Germany and supplied by SEL Canada Ltd. (later part of Alcatel, now Thales). The LIMs use 650 V DC from a third rail, which is converted to AC onboard. They also perform most of the braking, with energy being recuperated into the power supply system.

*The present fleet consists of three generations. First were a total of 150 **Mark I** units, i.e. married pairs (2x12.7 m long, 2.4 m wide) operating as single, double or triple (76.2 m) units. They are similar to the rolling stock used on the Scarborough RT in Toronto until 2023, and still in service on the people mover in downtown Detroit. They were manufactured by UTDC (Urban Transportation Development Corporation Ltd.; acquired by Bombardier in 1992) and came in four batches: 56 (nos. 001-056; 1984), 58 (nos. 061-118; 1985), 16 (nos. 121-136; 1991) and 20 (nos. 137-156; 1995). They can be seen in different liveries, from the original to the Mark II and Mark III-style repaint.*

*For the Millennium Line opening in 2002, a total of 60 **Mark II** units (nos. 201-260) were ordered; they are also married pairs (2x16.7 m long, 2.4 m wide), but with a gangway between the two coupled cars. The first 20 Mk II units were manufactured by Bombardier in Kingston, Ontario, and the other 40 locally in Burnaby, BC. To*

Mark II (erste Serie | *first batch*)

Mark II (erste Serie | *first batch*)

Mark V (© Alstom/TransLink)

bestellt; es handelt sich ebenfalls um Doppeltriebwagen (2x16,7 m lang, 2,4 m breit), allerdings mit einem Übergang zwischen zwei gekuppelten Wagen. Die ersten 20 Mark II-Einheiten wurden von Bombardier in Kingston, Ontario, hergestellt, die anderen 40 vor Ort in Burnaby, BC. Um den Betrieb während der Olympischen Winterspiele 2010 zu bewältigen, wurde die Flotte um eine zweite Serie von 48 Mark II-Einheiten (Nr. 301-348) aufgestockt. Ähnliche Züge verkehren auf der Kelana Jaya (ex-Putra)-Linie in Kuala Lumpur oder beim AirTrain am New Yorker Flughafen JFK.

Für die Verlängerung der Millennium Line nach Coquitlam im Jahr 2016 wurde der Bestand mit der dritten Generation von SkyTrain-Wagen, den **Mark III**-Einheiten, erweitert, die zur INNOVIA Metro 300-Familie von Bombardier gehören. Diese Triebzüge bestehen aus vier mit Übergängen verbundenen Wagen. Eine erste Serie von 7 Einheiten/28 Wagen (Nr. 401-428) wurde 2016 in Dienst gestellt, gefolgt von weiteren 14 Einheiten/56 Wagen (Nr. 429-484) von 2018 bis 2020.

Für die im Bau befindlichen Erweiterungen, aber auch als Ersatz für die ältesten Mark I-Fahrzeuge bestellte TransLink im Jahr 2020 bei Bombardier, kurz bevor das Unternehmen von Alstom übernommen wurde, insgesamt 205 neue **Mark V**-Wagen. Dies entspricht insgesamt 41 Fünf-Wagen-Zügen, die die gesamte Länge eines 85 m langen Bahnsteigs einnehmen werden. Die Bestellung wurde im Jahr 2021 um 6 Züge (30 Wagen) aufgestockt, die Auslieferung soll zwischen Ende 2023 und 2028 erfolgen.

increase service during the 2010 Winter Olympics, the fleet was expanded with a second batch of 48 Mk II units (nos. 301-348). Similar trains can be found on the Kelana Jaya (ex-Putra) Line in Kuala Lumpur and on New York's JFK AirTrain system.

*For the Millennium Line extension to Coquitlam in 2016, the fleet was enhanced with the third generation of SkyTrain cars, the **Mark III** units, which belong to Bombardier's INNOVIA Metro 300 family. These trainsets are made up of four cars with gangways between them. A first batch of 7 units/28 cars (nos. 401-428) entered service in 2016, followed by another 14 units/56 cars (nos. 429-484) delivered from 2018 to 2020.*

*For the extensions under construction, but also to replace the oldest Mk I vehicles, TransLink ordered a total of 205 new **Mark V** cars from Bombardier in 2020, just before the company was taken over by Alstom. This will result in 41 five-car trains, which will occupy the full length of an 85 m platform. The order was increased by 6 trains (30 cars) in 2021, with delivery expected between late 2023 and 2028.*

Mark III

● Bridgeport

Canada Line

Auch wenn mittlerweile für alle drei Metro-Linien der Begriff „SkyTrain" verwendet wird, wurde die Canada Line bewusst unabhängig von den anderen Linien konzipiert und die Wahl der Technologie den Konsortien überlassen, die sich für den Bau einer Schnellbahn bewarben, die von der Innenstadt Vancouvers bis Richmond verlaufen und einen Abzweig zum Flughafen bekommen sollte. Mitte 2005 wurden Verträge mit dem *InTransitBC*-Konsortium unter Führung des kanadischen Unternehmens SNC-Lavalin unterzeichnet. Für die Fahrzeuge war die Firma Hyundai Rotem aus Südkorea zuständig, die Züge mit konventionellen Elektromotoren lieferte; mit 3 m sind diese viel breiter als die SkyTrain-Fahrzeuge, können aber nur als 2-Wagen-Züge betrieben werden, da die Bahnsteige nur 40-50 m lang gebaut wurden. Wie auf den älteren Linien gibt es trotz fahrerlosem Betrieb keine Bahnsteigtüren.

Die Eröffnung der neuen Linie war für die XXI. Olympischen Winterspiele im Februar 2010 in Vancouver geplant; analog zu den bestehenden Linien wurde der Name „Olympic Line" vorgeschlagen, die kanadische Bundesregierung bestand jedoch darauf, sie „Canada Line" zu nennen, um den nationalen finanziellen Beitrag zu diesem Projekt zu würdigen.

Die Canada Line beginnt an der Station Waterfront, wo der zweigleisige Endbahnhof senkrecht zur Station der Expo Line liegt; der Umsteigeweg führt über die Haupthalle des alten Fernbahnhofs. Die Strecke verläuft Richtung Südwesten unterhalb der Granville Street, Haupteinkaufsstraße der Stadt und wichtiger Trolleybus-Korridor. Der U-Bahnhof Vancouver City Centre liegt an der Kreuzung

Although the term 'SkyTrain' is now used for all three rapid transit lines, the Canada Line was conceived as a non-SkyTrain line, leaving the choice of technology to the consortia bidding to build a metro line from downtown Vancouver to the City of Richmond with a branch to the airport. In mid-2005, contracts were signed with the InTransitBC consortium, led by the Canadian company SNC-Lavalin. The rolling stock came from Hyundai Rotem of South Korea, which supplied trains with conventional electric motors; at 3 m they are much wider than the SkyTrain vehicles, but they can only operate as 2-car sets as the platforms were only built 40-50 m long. Like on the older lines there are no platform screen doors despite the choice of driverless operation.

The new line was scheduled to open in time for the XXI Olympic Winter Games held in Vancouver in February 2010; analogously to the existing lines, the name 'Olympic Line' was suggested, but the Canadian federal government insisted on calling it the 'Canada Line' to honour the national financial contribution to the project.

The Canada Line starts at Waterfront, where the two-track terminus lies perpendicular to the Expo Line station; the interchange between the two lines leads

Canada Line
- 19.2 km (Ⓤ 9 km) - 17 Stations (Ⓤ 8)

17-08-2009: Waterfront – YVR Airport / Richmond-Brighouse
       2024: + Capstan

Waterfront

mit der West Georgia Street, einen Block vom U-Bahnhof Granville der Expo Line entfernt. Es gibt jedoch keinen direkten Übergang zwischen den beiden U-Bahnhöfen. Die Strecke führt noch drei Blocks weiter und schwenkt dann nach Südosten in die Davie Street. Yaletown-Roundhouse ist die letzte Station auf der Innenstadthalbinsel, bevor die Canada Line unter dem False Creek hindurchfährt, um die Station Olympic Village zu erreichen. Die Streckentunnel unter dem Stadtzentrum und der Bucht wurden mit Tunnel-bohrmaschinen aufgefahren, während die Bahnhöfe sowie der restliche unterirdische Abschnitt, von Olympic Village unterhalb der Cambie Street nach Süden bis zum Portal nördlich der Station Marine Drive, in offener Bauweise errichtet wurden; im U-Bahnhof King Edward liegen die Bahnsteige übereinander. Südlich der Station Marine Drive überquert die Canada Line den Fraser River auf der eigens für sie errichteten 550 m langen Schrägseilbrücke North Arm Bridge, die von zwei Türmen getragen wird und über einen Fuß- und Fahrradweg auf dem Unterdeck verfügt. Am Südufer verläuft die Strecke weiter auf einem Viadukt, wobei sich der Betriebshof der Linie unter der aufgestän-derten Trasse erstreckt. Die zweigleisige Verzweigungssta-tion Bridgeport verfügt über einen Mittelbahnsteig, so dass auch das Umsteigen ums Eck einfach ist. Die Verzweigung selbst ist kreuzungsfrei ausgelegt. Der Ast nach Richmond führt weiter nach Süden über der No. 3 Road; einen Block südlich des Hochbahnhofs Lansdowne wird die Strecke eingleisig, an der Endstation Richmond-Brighouse steht nur eine Bahnsteigkante zur Verfügung. Zwischen 2021 und 2024 wurde beiderseits des Viadukts die neue Station

through the main concourse of the old railway station. It runs southwest below Granville Street, the city's main shopping street and an important trolleybus corridor. Vancouver City Centre station lies at the intersection with West Georgia Street, one block from Granville station on the Expo Line; there is no direct transfer between the two stations, though. The route continues for another three blocks before turning southeast and getting aligned with Davie Street. Yaletown-Roundhouse is the last station on the downtown peninsula, before the Canada Line passes below False Creek to reach Olympic Village station. The running tunnels beneath the city centre and the inlet were excavated using tunnel boring machines, while the stations and the remaining underground section, from Olympic Village south under Cambie Street to a portal north of Marine Drive station, were built by the cut-and-cover method; King Edward station has stacked platforms. South of Marine Drive, the Canada Line crosses the Fraser River on the purpose-built 550 m long cable-stayed North Arm Bridge, supported by two towers and with a pedestrian and bicycle path on the lower deck. On the south bank, the line continues on a viaduct, with the line's depot extending beneath the elevated tracks. Bridgeport is a simple two-track station with an island platform, thus allowing easy transfer in the opposite direction. The two southern branches then diverge in a grade-separated junction. The Richmond branch continues south above No.3 Road; one block south of Lansdowne station, the line becomes single-track, with a single platform edge at the Richmond-Brighouse

● **Waterfront**
— **Eingang** | *Entrance* Granville Street

Capstan angebaut. Eine südliche Verlängerung ist derzeit nicht geplant. Der Ast zum Flughafen überquert den Moray-Kanal und eine Zufahrtsstraße zum Flughafen auf der Middle Arm Bridge, verläuft dann aber ebenerdig mit zwei Stationen auf Sea Island. Die letzten 1000 m sind wieder aufgeständert und die allerletzten 600 m, einschließlich der Endstation am Flughafen YVR, sind eingleisig.

Zur Inbetriebnahme im Jahr 2009 lieferte Hyundai Rotem 20 fahrerlose Doppeltriebwagen (Nr. 101/102-120/220) mit Übergang zwischen den beiden Wagen. Sie sind 41 m lang und 3 m breit. Um die Zugfolge zu verkürzen, kamen 2019/2020 weitere 12 Fahrzeuge desselben Typs hinzu (Nr. 121/221-132/232). Ähnlich wie die anderen SkyTrain-Linien wird die Canada Line mit dem SelTrac CBTC-System von Thales betrieben. Aufgrund der begrenzten Bahnsteiglänge kann sie jedoch nur mit Zwei-Wagen-Einheiten betrieben werden.

terminus. Between 2021 and 2024, the new Capstan station was erected around the viaduct. A southern extension is currently not planned. The airport branch crosses the Moray Channel on the Middle Arm Bridge before continuing at grade, serving two intermediate stations on Sea Island. The last 1000 m is elevated, and the very last 600 m including the YVR Airport terminus is single-track.

For the start of service in 2009, Hyundai Rotem supplied 20 driverless two-car sets (nos. 101/102-120/220) connected by a gangway. They are 41 m long and 3 m wide. To shorten headways, another 12 two-car sets of the same type were added in 2019/2020 (nos. 121/221-132/232). Similar to the other SkyTrain lines, the Canada Line is operated using the Thales SelTrac CBTC system. Restricted by the limited platform length, it can only run with two-car sets.

● **Bridgeport**

●

Way out

CANADA LINE
Yaletown Station

Last Trains

Waterfront 1:19
Richmond 1:18
YVR Airport 1:08

Yaletown–Roundhouse

Way out

EXIT

YVR Airport
Richmond-Brighouse
YVR Airport

FIRE DOOR
KEEP CLOSED

Oakridge–41st Avenue

Marine Drive – *tunnel portal*

Aberdeen

Granville Street/Helmcken Street

◼ Trolleybus

Heute ist Vancouver die einzige Stadt Kanadas mit Obussen. In den frühen 1950er Jahren, der Blütezeit dieses städtischen Verkehrsmittels, gab es im ganzen Land insgesamt 16 Trolleybusbetriebe. Als letzte verschwanden die Obusse in Hamilton (1992), Toronto (1993) und schließlich in Edmonton (2009).

Im Auftrag von TransLink betreibt die *Coast Mountain Bus Company* 13 Linien, allesamt gänzlich innerhalb der Stadt Vancouver, mit Ausnahme der Linie 19, die Mitte der 1980er Jahre nach Metrotown in Burnaby verlängert wurde, als auch andere Linien im Zuge der Inbetriebnahme des SkyTrain erweitert oder geändert wurden.

Der Obusbetrieb wurde am 13. August 1948 aufgenommen, wobei die meisten Linien frühere Straßenbahnlinien ersetzten, zuletzt die Linie 14 in der Hastings Street im Jahr 1955. Die jüngste Erweiterung des Trolleybus-Netzes war eine kurze Strecke zur University of British Columbia im Jahr 1988.

Die Obusflotte besteht derzeit aus 262 New Flyer-Niederflur-Trolleybussen, die zwischen 2005 und 2009 ausgeliefert wurden: 188 Solobusse des Typs E40LFR (12 m) und 74 Gelenkfahrzeuge des Typs E60LFR (18 m).

Straßenbahnen verkehrten in Vancouver zuletzt zwischen 1998 und 2011, und zwar auf einer Museumsbahn von Granville Island bis Olympic Village. Rund um die Olympischen Winterspiele 2010 wurden zwei Flexity-Fahrzeuge aus Brüssel eingesetzt.

Today, Vancouver is the only city in Canada to operate trolleybuses. In the early 1950s, the heyday of this type of urban electric transport, the country boasted a total of 16 trolleybus cities. The last to close were Hamilton (1992), Toronto (1993) and finally Edmonton (2009).

On behalf of TransLink, Coast Mountain Bus Company operates 13 routes, all lying entirely within the City of Vancouver, except for route 19 which was extended to Metrotown in Burnaby in the mid-1980s when other routes were also extended or modified to serve the newly opened SkyTrain stations.

Trolleybus service was launched on 13 August 1948 with most routes replacing former streetcar lines, the last of which (route 14 on Hastings Street) was closed in 1955. The most recent extension to the trolleybus network was a short route to the University of British Columbia in 1988.

Vancouver now operates a fleet of 262 New Flyer low-floor trolleybuses, delivered between 2005 and 2009: 188 E40LFR (12 m) and 74 articulated E60LFR (18 m) vehicles.

Trams last ran in Vancouver between 1998 and 2011, on a heritage tramway route from Granville Island to Olympic Village. Around the 2010 Winter Olympics, the service was provided with two Flexity vehicles from Brussels.

Granville St/Smithe St

Waterfront

■ West Coast Express

Am 1. November 1995 startete TransLink den West Coast Express (WCE) – eine typisch nordamerikanische Pendlerbahn mit lediglich fünf Zügen, die morgens von Mission (05:25-07:25) über Port Haney, Coquitlam und Moody bis Waterfront in der Innenstadt von Vancouver verkehren, von wo sie am späten Nachmittag (15:50-18:20) zurückkehren. Die Fahrt auf der gesamten Strecke dauert 1 Stunde und 17 Minuten. Der WCE ist nur von Montag bis Freitag in Betrieb, mit gelegentlichen Fahrten an Feiertagen zu Großveranstaltungen. Es gilt ein Entfernungstarif (7,85-13,10 $ für eine einfache Fahrt). Kombitickets für den WCE und andere TransLink-Verkehrsmittel sind verfügbar.

Auf dem WCE sind Wendezüge mit dieselelektrischen Lokomotiven (am östlichen Zugende) und vier bis zehn Doppelstockwagen im Einsatz. Diese gehören TransLink, verkehren jedoch auf Gleisen der *Canadian Pacific Railway* (CP).

On 1 November 1995, TransLink introduced the West Coast Express (WCE), a typical North American commuter rail service, with five trains running in the morning from Mission (05:25-07:25) via Port Haney, Coquitlam and Moody to Waterfront station in downtown Vancouver, from where they return in the late afternoon (15:50-18:20). A ride along the entire route takes one hour and 17 minutes. The WCE operates only Monday to Friday, with occasional trips on holidays for major events. Special fares apply ($7.85-$13.10 one way), with combined tickets for the WCE and other TransLink services available.

The WCE uses push-pull trains made up of diesel-electric locomotives (at the eastern end of the train) and four to ten double-deck carriages. These are the property of TransLink, but they run on tracks owned by the Canadian Pacific Railway (CP).

Waterfront

Waterfront – links Kehranlage der Expo Line
– on the left, Expo Line reversing tracks

Waterfront > Lonsdale Quay

■ SeaBus

Der SeaBus wurde 1977 von TransLink eingeführt, um eine schnelle und häufige Verbindung zwischen Vancouver (Waterfront) und North Vancouver (Lonsdale Quay), die durch den Burrard Inlet (3,24 km) getrennt sind, anzubieten. Der SeaBus verfügt über eine Flotte von vier Doppelendfähren, von denen zwei im Normalbetrieb im Einsatz sind (tagsüber alle 15 Minuten, spätabends alle 30 Minuten). Die Fahrt über die Bucht dauert 10-12 Minuten und ist vollständig in das TransLink-Tarifsystem integriert (2-Zonen-Ticket erforderlich).

Auf dem False Creek verkehren hingegen je nach Bedarf kleine Fähren der Privatfirmen Aquabus und False Creek Ferries, die jedoch nicht in den Tarifverbund integriert sind, auch wenn sie quasi das einzige öffentliche Verkehrsmittel zum beliebten Markt auf Granville Island sind.

The SeaBus service was launched by TransLink in 1977 to provide a fast and frequent service between Vancouver (Waterfront) and North Vancouver (Lonsdale Quay), which are separated by the Burrard Inlet (3.24 km). SeaBus has a fleet of four double-ended ferries, with two in service during normal operation (every 15 minutes daytime, 30 minutes late evenings). The trip across the inlet takes 10-12 minutes and is fully integrated into the TransLink fare system (2-zone ticket required).

On False Creek, small ferries operated by the private companies Aquabus and False Creek Ferries provide a frequent service depending on demand, but they are not integrated into the TransLink fare system, even though they are virtually the only public means of transport to access the popular market on Granville Island.

Lonsdale Quay

False Creek

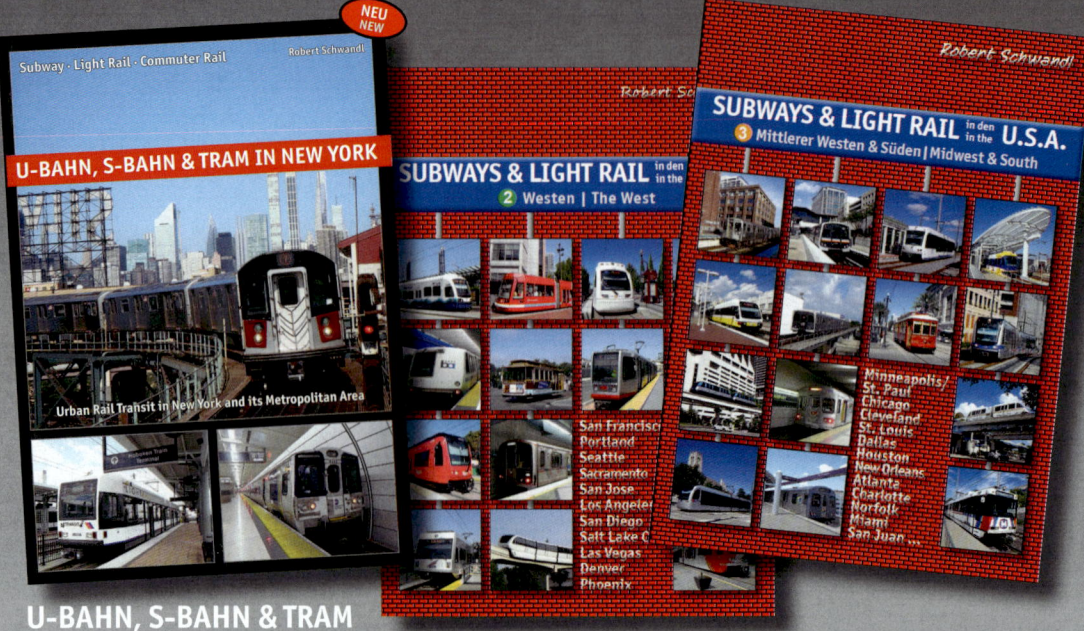
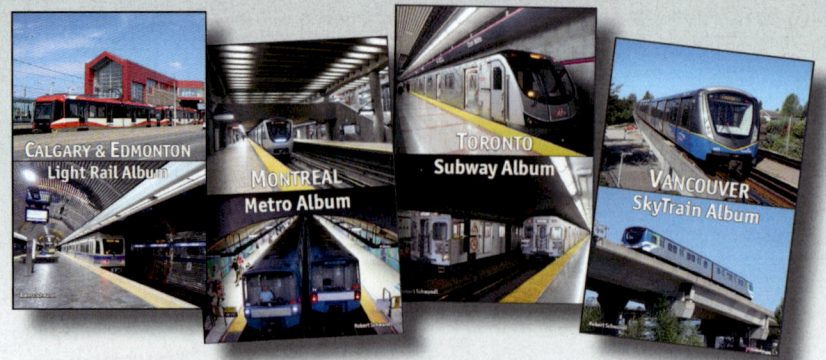